Beginning theory

'Barry provides a clear step-by-step guide to everything from stylistics to deconstruction. He also encourages his readers to question some of the assumptions of theory thereby rendering it less intimidating. Students will find the book extremely useful.'

Times Higher Education Supplement

For students encountering literary and cultural theory for the first time, there is a bewildering variety of approaches, theorists and technical language to cope with. *Beginning theory* will help those students to do just that.

Unlike many books which assume certain positions about the theories and the critics which they present, Peter Barry's lucid introduction allows students to develop their own ideas once first principles have been grasped. The emphasis is very much on 'theory in practice', with exercises and questions to help the student understand the methodology and practice of literary theory.

Peter Barry is Senior Lecturer in English at the University of Wales, Aberystwyth.

Beginning theory

An introduction to
literary and cultural theory

Peter Barry

Manchester University Press
Manchester and New York

Distributed exclusively in the USA and Canada by St Martin's Press

Copyright © Peter Barry 1995

Published by Manchester University Press
Oxford Road, Manchester M13 9NR, UK
and Room 400, 175 Fifth Avenue, New York, NY 10010, USA

Distributed exclusively in the USA and Canada
by St Martin's Press, Inc., 175 Fifth Avenue, New York, NY 10010, USA

British Library Cataloguing-in-Publication Data
A catalogue record for this book is available from the British Library

Library of Congress Cataloging-in-Publication Data
Barry, Peter
    Beginning theory: an introduction to literary and cultural theory
  / Peter Barry.
        p. cm.
    Includes bibliographical references.
    ISBN 0–7190–4325–5. — ISBN 0–7190–4326–3 (pbk.)
    1. Criticism. I. Title.
PN81.B367   1995
801′.95—dc20   94–43136
                                                                                    CIP

ISBN 0 7190 4325 5 *hardback*
       0 7190 4326 3 *paperback*

First published 1995

99 98 97   10 9 8 7 6 5

Typeset in Great Britain
by Northern Phototypesetting Co Ltd, Bolton

Printed in Great Britain
by Clays Ltd, St. Ives Plc.

Contents

Acknowledgements

> You'd better not look down,
> If you want to keep flying

So says the great B. B. King. It is excellent advice, and trying to stick to it helped me to complete this book. I was also greatly helped by the advice and expertise of Anita Roy, Humanities Editor at Manchester University Press. Annie Eagleton was a meticulous and helpful copy-editor, and Alison Abel provided valuable help at the proof-reading stage.

Many of the chapters are based on material I used on the 'Introduction to Literature' and 'Concepts of Criticism' courses at LSU. The former is taught by a 'team-ministry' of various colleagues, whose comments and advice I have been most grateful for over the past few years. In particular, I must thank Gillian Skinner for reading sections of the manuscript and making a number of extremely useful suggestions, all of which I have acted upon. Nicola King supplied the 'What feminist critics Do' checklist, and I have adopted this idea for all the chapters. Of course, all the faults which remain in the book are entirely my own responsibility.

Steve Dorney rescued me when my technical expertise proved unequal to the task of producing hard copy from my (as I thought) cunningly adapted disks. Marian and Tom enabled me to write the book by giving me frequent periods of study leave from Sainsbury's and 'Playdays'. The book is for my mother and in memory of my father, Francis Barry.

I will be most interested to hear from any users of this book who might wish to write to me (either via Manchester

University Press, or directly to English Department, UCW, Aberystwyth, Dyfed SY23 3DY, Wales, UK. If anything in the book seems unclear, or unnecessary, or misrepresented, or wrongly omitted, or fails to acknowledge a source, I will endeavour to improve or rectify matters in any subsequent edition.

Sections of Chapter 3 have previously appeared (in a slightly different form) in *The Use of English* and *The English Review*.

Peter Barry
LSU
April 1995

Introduction

About this book

The 1980s probably saw the high-water mark of literary theory. That decade was the 'moment' of theory, when the topic was fashionable and controversial. In the 1990s there has been a steady flow of books and articles with titles like *After Theory* (Thomas Docherty, 1990) or 'Post-Theory' (Nicolas Tredell, in *The Critical Decade*, 1993). As such titles suggest, the 'moment of theory' has probably passed. So why another 'primer' of theory so late in the day?

The simple answer is that after the moment of theory there comes, inevitably, the 'hour' of theory, when it ceases to be the exclusive concern of a dedicated minority and enters the intellectual bloodstream as a taken-for-granted aspect of the curriculum. At this stage the glamour fades, the charisma is 'routinised', and it becomes the day-to-day business of quite a large number of people to learn or teach (or both) this material. There are evident dangers of over-simplifying things and so offering a false reassurance to students facing the difficulties of this topic for the first time. All the same, the main responsibility of anyone attempting a book like this one is to meet the demand for clear explanation and demonstration. If the task were impossible, and the mountain of theory could be climbed only by experts, then the whole enterprise of establishing it on undergraduate courses would have been a mistake.

The emphasis on practice means that this is a 'work-book', not just a 'text-book'. As you read you will find suggested activities, headed 'STOP and THINK', which are designed to give you some 'hands-on' experience of literary theory and its problems. You will not just be reading about it, reducing theory to a kind of spectator sport played only by superstars, but starting to do it for yourself. Becoming a participant in this way will help you to make *some* personal sense of theory, and will, I hope, increase your confidence, even if you suspect that your practical efforts remain fairly rudimentary. It is also hoped that the 'STOP and THINK' activities will provide the basis for initiating seminar discussion if this book is being used in connection with a taught course on critical theory.

All the critical approaches described in this book are a reaction against something which went before, and a prior knowledge of these things cannot be assumed. Hence, I start with an account of the 'liberal humanism' against which all these newer critical approaches, broadly speaking, define themselves. Likewise, the currently successful versions of Marxist, feminist, psychoanalytic, and linguistic criticism all define themselves against earlier versions of each of these, and therefore I try in each case to explain the earlier versions first. I think that many of the current difficulties students have with theory arise from trying to miss out this stage. My approach amounts to throwing you in at the shallow end. Potentially this is more painful than being thrown in at the deep end – the technique used in most other student introductions to literary theory – but it does reduce the risk of drowning.

It should, perhaps, be stressed that the other general introductions to theory that are now available represent a stage on from this one. They offer an even and comprehensive coverage of the entire field, but with relatively little in the way of practical discussion of applications. I find them very useful, but they seem to me to be recapitulations of literary theory, often from a viewpoint more philosophical than literary, rather than introductions to it. The evenness of the coverage means that the pace never varies, so that there is no opportunity to stop and dwell upon an example in a reflective way. By contrast, I haven't tried to be comprehensive, and I do try to provide variation in pace by selecting questions, or examples, or key essays for closer treatment. Generally, the available introductions don't grapple with the problems of teaching or learning theory: the only two that try to do so are Durant and Fabb's *Literary Studies in Action* and Lynn's *Texts and Contexts* (see Further reading section). Both these are interesting but eccentric books whose rather fragmented format prevents any real flow of discussion or explanation.

At undergraduate level the main problem is to decide how much theory can reasonably be handled by beginners. Time is not unlimited, and there is a need to think about a realistic syllabus rather than an ideal one. Theorists, like novelists, are dauntingly plentiful, and the subject of theory cannot succeed in lecture rooms and seminars unless we fashion it into a student-centred syllabus. We are rightly dismissive these days of the notion of teaching a 'Great Tradition' of key novelists, as advocated by the critic F. R. Leavis. But Leavis's Great Tradition was essentially a syllabus, manageable within a year-long undergraduate course on the novel. It is possible to read and adequately discuss a novel or two by Austen, Eliot, James, Conrad, and Lawrence within that time. We need to make sure that what is presented as theory today likewise makes teaching sense.

When we are about to move into something new it is sensible to first take stock of what we already have, if only so that the distance travelled can later be measured. So in the first chapter of this book I invite you to look back critically and reflectively on your previous training in literary studies. We then go on to look at the assumptions behind traditional literary criticism, or 'liberal humanism' as theorists usually call it.

The term 'liberal humanism' became current in the 1970s, as a shorthand (and mainly hostile) way of referring to the kind of criticism which held sway before theory. The word 'liberal' in this formulation roughly means not politically radical, and hence generally evasive and non-committal on political issues. 'Humanism' implies something similar; it suggests a range of negative attributes, such as 'non-Marxist' and 'non-feminist', and 'non-theoretical'. There is also the implication that liberal humanists believe in 'human nature' as something fixed and constant which great literature expresses. Liberal humanists did not (and do not, as a rule) use this name of themselves, but, says an influential school

of thought, if you practise literary criticism and do not call yourself a Marxist critic, or a structuralist, or a stylistician, or some
such, then you are probably a liberal humanist, whether or not
you admit or recognise this.

In the course of explaining some of the major critical ideas now
current, this book provides summaries or descriptions of a
number of important theoretical essays. But I want to stress at the
outset that it is important, too, that you read some of the major
theorists at first hand. Yet as soon as you begin to turn the pages
of Barthes, Lacan, Foucault, or Derrida you will encounter writing which looks dauntingly difficult and off-putting. How, then,
to cope?

I suggest that it is much better to read *intensely* in theory than
to read *widely*. By this I mean that you will gain little from reading chapter after chapter of a book that is making little sense to
you. You will gain much more by using the same amount of reading time to read one crucial and frequently mentioned chapter or
article several times for yourself. Having a detailed knowledge of
what is actually said in the pages of a well-known argument, being
aware of how the argument unfolds and how it is qualified or contextualised, will be far more useful to you than a superficial overall impression gained from commentaries or from desperate
skim-reading. However daunting the material, you have to make
your reading meditative, reflective, and personal. Try to become
a slow reader. Further, some intensive reading of this kind will
enable you to quote lines other than the handful that are cited in
all the commentaries. And most importantly, your view of things
will be your own, perhaps quirky and incomplete, but at least not
just the echo and residue of some published commentator's pre-
packed version. In a nut-shell, intensive reading is often more
useful than extensive reading. 'English studies' is founded on the
notion of close reading, and while there was a period in the late
1970s and early 1980s when this idea was frequently disparaged,
it is undoubtedly true that nothing of any interest can happen in
this subject without close reading.

I suggest, therefore, that you try out for yourself a useful form
of intensive reading, the technique known as 'SQ3R'. This breaks
down the reading of a difficult chapter or article into five stages,

as designated by the letters 'SQRRR', or 'SQ3R', as is it usually given. The five stages are:

S   – That is, *Survey* the whole chapter or section fairly rapidly, skimming though it to get a rough sense of the scope and nature of the argument. Remember that information is not evenly spread throughout a text. It tends to be concentrated in the opening and closing paragraphs (where you often get useful summaries of the whole), and the 'hinge points' of the argument are often indicated in the opening and closing sentences of paragraphs.

Q   – Having skimmed the whole, set yourself some *Questions*, some things you hope to find out from what you are reading. This makes you an 'active' reader rather than a passive one, and gives your reading a purpose.

R1 – Now *Read* the whole piece. Use a pencil if the copy is your own to underline key points, query difficulties, circle phrases worth remembering, and so on. Don't just sit in front of the pages. If the book is not your own jot *something* down on paper as you read, however minimal.

R2 – Now, close the book and *Recall* what you have read. Jot down some summary points. Ask whether your starting questions have been answered, or at least clarified. Spell out some of the difficulties that remain. In this way, you record some concrete outcomes to your reading, so that your time doesn't simply evaporate uselessly once the book is closed.

R3 – This final stage is the *Review*. It happens after an interval has elapsed since the reading. You can experiment, but initially try doing it the following day. Without opening the book again, or referring back to your notes, review what you have gained from the reading; remind yourself of the question you set yourself, the points you jotted down at the *Recall* stage, and any important phrases from the essay. If this produces very little, then refer back to your notes. If they make little sense, then repeat the *Survey* stage, and do an accelerated *Read*, by reading the first and last paragraphs

of the essay, and skim-reading the main body assisted by
your pencilled markings.

You may well have evolved a study technique something like
this already. It is really just common sense. But it will help to
ensure that you gain *something* from a theoretical text, no matter
how intially forbidding it might be.

Finally, it will, I hope, go without saying that no comprehen-
siveness is possible in a format such as this. Clearly, also, this
book does not contain all you need to know about theory, and it
does not in itself (without the reading it refers you to) constitute
a 'course' in literary theory. It leaves out a good deal, and it deals
fairly briskly with many topics. It is a starter-pack, intended to
give you a sense of what theory is all about, and suggest how it
might affect your literary studies. Above all, it aims to *interest* you
in theory.

Approaching theory

If you are coming to literary theory soon after taking courses in
such subjects as media studies, communications studies, or socio-
linguistics, then the general 'feel' of the new theoretical
approaches to literature may well seem familiar. You will already
be 'tuned in' to the emphasis on ideas which is one of their characteristics; you will be undaunted by their use of technical terminology, and unsurprised by their strong social and political
interests. If, on the other hand, you took a 'straight' 'A' Level literature or 'Access' course with the major emphasis on set books,
then much of what is contained in this book will probably be new
to you. Initially, you will have the problem of getting on the
wave-length of these different ways of looking at literature. As
you would expect in studying at degree level, you will encounter
problems which do not have generally agreed solutions, and it is
inevitable that your understanding of the matters discussed here
will remain partial, in both senses of that word, as everybody's
does.

But whichever of these two categories you fall into, I want to
assure you at the outset that the doubts and uncertainties you will

have about this material are probably *not* due to:

1. any supposed mental incapacity of your own, for example, to your not having 'a philosophical mind', or not possessing the kind of X-ray intellect which can penetrate jargon and see the sense beneath, or
2. the fact that your schooling did not include intensive tuition in, say, linguistics or philosophy, or
3. the innate and irreducible difficulty of the material itself (a point we will come back to).

Rather, nearly all the difficulties you will have will be the direct result of the way theory is written, and the way it is written about. For literary theory, it must be emphasised, is not innately difficult. There are very few inherently complex ideas in existence in literary theory. On the contrary, the whole body of work known collectively as 'theory' is based upon some dozen or so ideas, none of which are in themselves difficult. (Some of them are listed on page 34). What *is* difficult, however, is the language of theory. Many of the major writers on theory are French, so that much of what we read is in translation, sometimes of a rather clumsy kind. Being a Romance language, French takes most of its words directly from Latin, and it lacks the reassuring Anglo-Saxon layer of vocabulary which provides us with so many of our brief, familiar, everyday terms. Hence, a close English translation of a French academic text will contain a large number of longer Latinate words, always perceived as a source of difficulty by English-speaking readers. Writing with a high proportion of these characteristics can be off-putting and wearying, and it *is* easy to lose patience.

But the frame of mind I would recommend at the outset is threefold. *Firstly*, we must have some *initial* patience with the difficult surface of the writing. We must avoid the too-ready conclusion that literary theory is just meaningless, pretentious jargon (that is, that the theory is at fault). *Secondly*, on the other hand, we must, for obvious reasons, resist the view that we ourselves are intellectually incapable of coping with it (that is, that we are at fault). *Thirdly*, and crucially, we must not assume that the difficulty of theoretical writing is *always* the dress of profound ideas – only that it *might* sometimes be, which leaves the onus of discrimination on us. To sum up this attitude: we are looking, in literary theory, for something we can use, not something which will use us. We ought not to issue theory with a blank cheque to spend our time for us. (If we do, it will certainly spend more than we can afford.) Do not, then, be *endlessly* patient with theory. Require it to be clear, and expect it, in the longer term, to deliver something solid. Don't be content, as many seem to be, just to see it as 'challenging' conventional practice or 'putting it in question' in some never quite specified way. Challenges are fine, but they have to amount to something in the end.

STOP and THINK – *Reviewing your study of literature to date*

Before we go on, into what may well be a new stage in your involvement with literature, it would be sensible to 'take stock' and reflect a little on the nature of our literary education to date. The purpose of doing this is to begin the process of making visible, and hence open to scrutiny, the methods and procedures which have become so familar to you (probably going back to the time when you began secondary school) that they are no longer visible at all as a distinct intellectual practice. But stock-taking is not part of our normal intellectual routine, unfortunately, and it is a difficult and demanding thing to do. Yet please do not skip this section, since theory will never make any sense to you until you feel the need for it yourself. What I would like you to do is to try to become conscious of the nature of your own previous work in English, by recalling:

1. what first made you decide to study English, what you hoped to gain from doing so, and whether that hope was realised;
2. which books and authors were chosen for study and what they had in common;
3. which books and authors now seem conspicuously absent;
4. what, in general terms, your previous study taught you

(about 'life', say, or conduct, or about literature itself).

Doing this will help you to begin to obtain a perspective on your experience of literature to date. Spend an hour or so doing it. I carried out a similar exercise myself as part of the process of working on this book, and some of the result is given below. It is intended more as a prompt than a model, and I have not responded in any systematic way to the four questions above. Reproducing it will perhaps help to 'personalise' the voice behind this book, but I leave you to decide whether you want to look at this before or after doing your own.

My own *stock-taking*

Since literary theory is the topic of this book I will concentrate on detailing the course of my acquaintanceship with it. In fact, I heard nothing at all about literary theory as an undergraduate at London University in the late 1960s. I took a straightforward 'Wulf-to-Woolf' English course (*Beowulf* to Virgina Woolf) with compulsory Old and Middle English papers. Essentially, I now realise, the English course I followed in the late 1960s retained the shape and the outlook of the pioneer English degree courses established at London University more than a century before.

The one innovation in English teaching at London was to recognise the existence of something called American literature and to appoint a lecturer* to teach it. As a result of taking this American course I became an enthusiast for a range of American poets who were part of the 'alternative culture' of the time. At the same time, and for several years afterwards, I was also trying to write poetry of more or less this kind. It quickly became apparent that conventional criticism could make very little of poetry like this. So by the early 1970s I was beginning to look at newer critical approaches than those I had encountered at university. But I wasn't at that time an advocate of literary theory, since 'theory' as such was then a non–existent category in literary studies.

---

* The lecturer was Eric Mottram, who died in January 1995.

The change of emphasis seems to have happened in my own case around 1973, when the words 'structuralism' and 'semiotics' begin to feature in notes about what I was reading and in the titles of the books and articles I was interested in. Structuralism, we were then learning, was a new kind of literary theory which had recently become prominent in France, and semiotics ('the science of signs') was one of its sub-branches. I was loosely connected with the London Graduate Seminar started by Frank Kermode after he became Professor of English at University College, London. The group debated the work of the structuralist Roland Barthes and caught Kermode's enthusiasm for it. I bought and read everything by Barthes then in print in England, no great undertaking since all that was available was *Writing Degree Zero* and *Elements of Semiology*, probably his least interesting and least accessible books. His much more engaging collection *Mythologies* appeared in English in 1973 in the Paladin imprint. 1973 was also the year when *The Times Literary Supplement* devoted the major part of two issues (5 and 12 October) to a 'Survey of Semiotics', with articles by Umberto Eco, Tzvetan Todorov, and Julia Kristeva, major names in these new kinds of critical theory and encountered then (in my case) for the first time. This interest in theory was consolidated in 1981 when I was asked to devise a course on literary theory as part of the BA programme at my previous college, and, in turn, a decade or so of teaching that course has led to this book.

1

Theory before 'theory' – liberal humanism

The history of English studies

It is difficult to understand liberal humanism (that is, the traditional approach to English studies, see the Introduction, pp. 3–4) without knowing something about how English developed as an academic subject. So this is the topic of the next few pages.

STOP and THINK

The multiple choice questions below indicate the scope of what is touched upon in this section. Underline what you think are the right answers before reading further, and then correct your answers, if necessary, as you read on:

1. When do you think English was first taught as a degree subject in England?: was it 1428, 1528, 1628, 1728, 1828, or 1928?
2. At which institution was English first taught as a degree subject in England?: was it Oxford University, Cambridge University, London University, Southampton University, or none of these?
3. Until the nineteenth century you had to be a member of the Anglican (Episcopalian) Church and male to take a degree in England. True or false?

4. Until the nineteenth century lecturers on degree courses
    in England had to be unmarried Church of England clergy.
    True or false?
5. Until the nineteenth century women were not allowed to
    take degrees in England. True or false?
6. In the early twentieth century women could take degree
    courses in England, but were not allowed to receive
    degrees. True or false?

To explain the rise of English studies we need to indicate
briefly what higher education was like in England until the first
quarter of the nineteenth century. The short answer is that it was
a Church of England monopoly. There were only two universities, Oxford and Cambridge. These were divided into small individual colleges which were run like monastic institutions. Only
men could attend them, of course, and students had to be Anglican communicants and attend the college chapel. The teachers
were ordained ministers, who had to be unmarried, so that they
could live in the college. The subjects available were the classics
(ancient Greek and Latin literature), divinity (which was taken by
those seeking ordination) and mathematics. Anyone who was
Catholic, Jewish, or Methodist, or atheist was barred from entry,
and hence, in effect, barred from the professions and the Civil
Service. As far as higher education was concerned, then, you
could say that right up to the 1820s, the organisation of higher
education had not changed since the Middle Ages.

Many attempts were made to reform the situation, expand
higher education, and introduce practical subjects into the curriculum, but they all came up against entrenched conservative
forces. The breakthough came in 1826 when a University College
was founded in London with a charter to award degrees, to men
and women of all religions or none. From 1828 English was
offered as a subject for study, and they appointed the first English Professor of English in 1829. However, it was not really English as we know it. It was mainly the study of English language,
merely using literature as a source of linguistic examples. English
literature as such was first taught at King's College, London

(another college of what later became London University) beginning in 1831.

In 1840 F. D. Maurice was appointed Professor at King's. He
introduced the study of set books, and his inaugural lecture lays
down some of the principles of liberal humanism; the study of
English literature would serve 'to emancipate us ... from the
notions and habits which are peculiar to our own age', connect-
ing us instead with 'what is fixed and enduring'. Maurice
regarded literature as the peculiar property of the middle class
and the expression of their values. For him the middle class represents the essence of Englishness (the aristocracy are part of an
international elite, and the poor need to give all their attention to
ensuring mere survival) so middle-class education should be
peculiarly English, and therefore should centre on English literature. Maurice was well aware of the political dimension of all this.
People so-educated would feel that they belonged to England,
that they had a country. 'Political agitators' may ask what this can
mean 'when his neighbour rides in a carriage and he walks on
foot', but 'he will feel his nationality to be a reality, in spite of
what they say'. In short, learning English will give people a stake
in maintaining the political *status quo* without any redistribution
of wealth.

You can see from this that the study of English literature is
being seen as a kind of substitute for religion. It was well known
that attendance at church below middle-class level was very
patchy. The worry was that the lower classes would feel that they
had no stake in the country and, having no religion to teach them
morality and restraint, they would rebel and something like the
French revolution would take place. The Chartist agitation of the
1830s was thought to be the start of this, and the first English
courses are put in place at exactly the same time.

The conventional reading of the origins of the subject of English is that this kind of thinking begins with Matthew Arnold in
the 1850s and reaches its height with the publication of the Newbolt Report on the Teaching of English in England in 1921. It is
evident from material like Maurice's inaugural lecture that this
was happening much earlier. However, I do not accept the simplistic view that the founders of English were motiviated merely

by a desire for ideological control. This was undoubtedly one of
their motives, but the reality was much more complicated. There
was, behind the teaching of early English, a distinctly Victorian
mixture of class guilt about social inequalities, a genuine desire to
improve things for everybody, a kind of missionary zeal to spread
culture and enlightenment, and a self-interested desire to maintain social stability.

London University degrees were taught by external licence at
university colleges in major industrial cities – Liverpool, Birmingham, Manchester, Sheffield, Leeds, and so on, all these places
eventually becoming major universities in their own right. Hence
the spread of the subject at degree level throughout the country.
However, Oxford and Cambridge were suspicious of the new subject of English and held out against it, Oxford until 1894 and
Cambridge until 1911.

In the last quarter of the nineteenth century there was vigorous discussion and campaigning to establish a Chair in English at
Oxford. In 1887 the first attempt was defeated largely because of
a speech in the Convocation by the Professor of History, Edward
Freeman. Freeman's speech is another key document: it touches
upon several problems in English which are still unresolved. He
said:

> We are told that the study of literature 'cultivates the taste, edu-
> cates the sympathies and enlarges the mind'. These are all excel-
> lent things, only we cannot examine tastes and sympathies.
> Examiners must have technical and positive information to exam-
> ine.

This is a problem which has never been entirely solved in English. What, exactly, is its knowledge component? As a way of
attaching specific and technical information to the study of English, early supporters had advocated the systematic study of language, but early advocates of English wanted to separate literature
and language study, so that the one could be done without the
other. Freeman's famous response was: 'what is meant by distinguishing literature from language if by literature is meant the
study of great books, and not mere chatter about Shelley?'

Freeman won the argument. Literature had to be studied along with language, otherwise it would not be an academic subject at all. So when the English course was finally set up at Oxford in 1894 it contained a very heavy element of historical language study – Anglo-Saxon, Gothic, Letto-Slavonic, Middle English, etc., from which it has still not managed to free itself.

A greater sense of direction was given to English in the Cambridge English school in the 1920s. Because Cambridge English was the most recently founded, dating only from 1911, it had the least weight of tradition to fight against, so change was relatively easy. The engineers of this change were a group of people who began teaching at Cambridge in the 1920s. They were: I. A. Richards, William Empson, and F. R. Leavis.

I. A. Richards was the founder of a method of studying English which is still the norm today. Firstly, it made a decisive break between language and literature. Richards pioneered the technique called Practical Criticism (the title of his book in 1929). This made a close study of literature possible by isolating the text from history and context. Instead of having to study, say, the Renaissance period as a distinct historical moment, with its characteristic outlook, social formations, and so on, students could learn the techniques of practical criticism and simply analyse 'the words on the page'. The gain from this was that it was no longer possible to offer a vague, flowery, metaphorical effusion and call it criticism. Richards argued that there should be much more close attention to the precise details of the text.

A second Cambridge pioneer was a pupil of Richards, William Empson, who presented his tutor with the manuscript of the book which was published in 1930 with the title *Seven Types of Ambiguity*. This book took the Richards method of close verbal analysis to what many felt to be an extreme. Empson identified seven different types of verbal difficulty in poetry (which is what he meant by ambiguity) and gave examples of them, with worked analyses. Another Cambridge critic, F. R. Leavis, said in a review that it is a highly disturbing book because it uses intelligence on poetry as seriously as if it were mathematics. Not everybody liked this ultra-close form of reading. T. S. Eliot called it the lemon-squeezer school of criticism, and his own critical writing is always on a much more generalised level.

The last of these Cambridge pioneers was F. R. Leavis, probably the most influential figure in twentieth-century British criticism. In 1929 he met and married Q. D. Roth, subsequently known as Q. D. Leavis. He had written his doctoral thesis on the relationship between journalism and literature. She had written hers on popular fiction. These were revolutionary topics, and a certain excitement and glamour attached to this couple in the 1930s. In 1932 they founded an important journal called *Scrutiny* and produced it together for twenty-one years. As the title implies, it extended the 'close-reading' method beyond poetry to novels and other material.

Leavis's faults as a critic are that his close readings often turn out to contain lengthy quotations on which there is surprisingly little comment. The assumption is that the competent reader will see there what Leavis sees. As has been said of him, he often gives the impression that he is analysing the text when he is really just paraphrasing it. Secondly, his approach to literature is overwhelmingly moral; its purpose is to teach us about life, to transmit humane values. His critical terms are never properly defined. He famously refused the invitation offered by the critic René Wellek in the 1930s that he should 'spell out the principles on which he operated in a more explicit way than hitherto'. The result was one more degree of isolation for literary studies. In the period of its growth just surveyed, it claimed independence from language studies, from historical considerations, and from philosophical questions. The consensus which held the subject together from the 1930s to the 1960s rested upon the acceptance of these demarcations. The 'project' of 'theory' from the 1960s onwards is in essence to re-establish connections between literary study and these three academic fields from which it had so resolutely separated itself.

Ten tenets of liberal humanism

The personal account on pp. 9–10 mainly responds to the second and third of the four questions given earlier. I'm now going to expand on the implications of the fourth question, which asked what it is, exactly, that we learn when we 'do' English in the traditional way. Of course, we learn things about specific books and authors, but I mean here the more general values and attitudes which we absorb from English, and which remain as a kind of distilled essence of the subject when all these specific details have been forgotten. These are not usually formulated and stated, but they are, in a sense, all the more real for that, being simultaneously both pervasive and invisible. They can only be brought to the surface by a conscious effort of will, of the kind we are now trying to make. So what follows is a list of some of the elements which seem to constitute this 'distilled essence' of the subject, that is, the corpus of attitudes, assumptions, and ideas which we pick up, probably unawares, as we do it. These seem to have been what we were learning when we studied English – these are the values and beliefs which formed the subject's half-hidden curriculum:

1. The first thing, naturally, is an attitude to literature itself; good literature is of timeless significance; it somehow transcends the limitations and peculiarities of the age it was written in, and thereby speaks to what is constant in human nature. Such writing is 'not for an age, but for all time' (as Ben Jonson said of Shakespeare): it is 'news which stays news' (Ezra Pound's definition of literature).

2. The second point is the logical consequence of the first. The literary text contains its own meaning within itself. It doesn't require any elaborate process of placing it within a context, whether this be:

   (a) *Socio-political* – the context of a particular social 'background' or political situation, or
   (b) *Literary-historical* – whereby the work could be seen as the product of the literary influences of other writers, or as shaped by the conventions of particular genres, or
   (c) *Autobiographical* – that is, as determined by the personal details of the author's life and thought.

Of course, as scholars, most academics would assert the value of studying these contexts, but as critics their adherence to the approach which insists upon the primacy and self-sufficiency of the 'words on the page' commits them to the process which has been called 'on-sight close reading'. Essentially, this removes the text from all these contexts and presents it 'unseen' for unaided explication by the trained mind.

3. To understand the text well it must be detached from these contexts and studied in isolation. What is needed is the close verbal analysis of the text without prior ideological assumptions, or political pre-conditions, or, indeed, specific expectations of any kind, since all these are likely to interfere fatally with what the nineteenth-century critic Matthew Arnold said was the true business of criticism, 'to see the object as in itself it really is'.

4. Human nature is essentially unchanging. The same passions, emotions, and even situations are seen again and again throughout human history. It follows that continuity in literature is more important and significant than innovation. Thus, a well-known eighteenth-century definition of poetry maintains that it is 'what oft was thought but ne'er so well expressed'. Likewise, Samuel Johnson famously denigrated Sterne's novel *Tristram Shandy* on the grounds of its novelty, that is, its originality.

5. Individuality is something securely possessed within each of us as our unique 'essence'. This transcends our environmental influences, and though individuality can change and develop (as do characters in novels), it can't be transformed – hence our uneasiness with those scenes (quite common, for instance, in Dickens) which involve a 'change of heart' in a character, so that the whole personality is shifted into a new dimension by force of circumstance – the miser is transformed and changes his ways, or the good man or woman becomes corrupted by wealth. Such scenes imply a malleability in the essence of character which is at odds with this underlying assumption of English studies. The discipline as a whole believed in what is now called the 'transcendent subject', which is the belief that the individual ('the subject') is antecedent to, or transcends, the forces of society, experience,

and language.

6. The purpose of literature is essentially the enhancement of life and the propagation of humane values; but not in a programmatic way: if literature, and criticism, become overtly and directly political they necessarily tend towards propaganda. And as Keats said, 'we distrust literature which has a palpable design upon us', that is, literature which too obviously wants to convert us or influence our views.

7. Form and content in literature must be fused in an organic way, so that the one grows inevitably from the other. Literary form should not be like a decoration which is applied externally to a completed structure. Imagery, for instance, or any other poetic form which is detachable from the substance of the work in this way, rather than being integrated with it, is merely 'fanciful' and not truly 'imaginative' (the distinction made by Coleridge in the *Biographia Literaria*).

8. This point about organic form applies above all to 'sincerity'. Sincerity (comprising truth-to-experience, honesty towards the self, and the capacity for human empathy and compassion) is a quality which resides *within* the language of literature. It isn't a fact or an intention *behind* the work, which could be gleaned by comparing, say, a poet's view of an event with other more 'factual' versions, or from discovering independent, external information about an author's history or conduct. Rather, sincerity is to be discovered within the text in such matters as the avoidance of cliché, or of over-inflated forms of expression; it shows in the use of first hand, individualistic description, in the understated expression of feeling, whereby (preferably) the emotion is allowed to emerge implicitly from the presentation of an event. Moreover, when the language achieves these qualities, then the truly sincere poet can transcend the sense of distance between language and material, and can make the language seem to 'enact' what it depicts, thus apparently abolishing the necessary distance between words and things.

9. Again, the next idea follows from the previous one. What is valued in literature is the 'silent' showing and demonstrating of something, rather than the explaining, or saying, of it.

Hence, ideas as such are worthless in literature until given the concrete embodiment of 'enactment'. Thus, several of the explicit comments and formulations often cited in literary history contain specific denigrations of ideas as such and have a distinct anti-intellectual flavour to them. Here we see the elevation of the characteristic 'Eng Lit' idea of *tactile enactment*, of sensuous immediacy, of the concrete representation of thought, and so on. According to this idea (which is, of course, itself an idea, in spite of the fact that the idea in question is a professed distrust of ideas) words should mime, or demonstrate, or act out, or sound out what they signify, rather than just representing it in an abstract way. This idea is stated with special fervency in the work of F. R. Leavis. (For a critique of the 'enactment' idea see 'The Enactment Fallacy', by the present author, in *Essays in Criticism*, July 1980. For a general discussion see James Gribble's *Literary Education: a Revaluation*, Cambridge University Press, 1983, Chapter 2).

10. The job of criticism is to interpret the text, to mediate between it and the reader. A theoretical account of the nature of reading, or of literature in general, isn't useful in criticism, and will simply, if attempted, encumber critics with 'preconceived ideas' which will get between them and the text. Perhaps in this phrase 'preconceived ideas' we get another glimpse into the nature of this pervasive distrust of ideas within liberal humanism, for there seems to be the notion that somehow *all* ideas are 'preconceived', in the sense that they will come between the reader and text if given half a chance. There is, in fact, the clear mark here of what is called 'English empiricism', which can be defined as a determination to trust only what is made evident to the senses or experienced directly. Ultimately this attitude goes back at least to the philosophy of John Locke (1632–1704), which gives a philosophical expression to it. His book *Essay Concerning Human Understanding* (1690) puts forward the view that ideas are formed when direct sense impressions from the world are imprinted on the mind. The mind then assembles these, so giving rise to the process of thinking. Locke rejected introspective speculation as a source of valid knowledge and

insisted on the need for direct experience and evidence of things. Traditional English studies, we might say, has always been Lockean in this sense.

The above list contains a series of propositions which I think many traditional critics would, on the whole, subscribe to, if they were in the habit of making their assumptions explicit. Together, ideas like these, and the literary practice which went with them, are now often referred to as 'liberal humanism'.

Literary theorising from Aristotle to Leavis – some key moments

So far I have perhaps given the impression that theoretical positions about literature were never explicitly formulated by liberal humanists, at least in Britain, and that everything remained implicit. Yet a widely current body of theoretical work existed from the start within English studies, and references were often made to it in books and essays. The average student or teacher of 'Eng Lit' up to the 1970s would probably have had a fairly limited direct contact with this body of work, since the whole thrust of the subject was away from this kind of generalised position-taking.

What, then, constituted the body of theory about literature that has existed for many centuries as an available under-pinning for the study of literature, even if literary students seldom had any extensive first hand acquaintance with it? Well, the material goes back to Greek and Latin originals. Critical theory, in fact, long pre-dates the literary criticism of individual works. The earliest work of theory was Aristotle's *Poetics*, which, in spite of its title, is about the nature of literature itself: Aristotle offers famous definitions of tragedy, insists that literature is about character, and that character is revealed through action, and he tries to identify the required stages in the progress of a plot. Aristotle was also the first critic to develop a 'reader-centred' approach to literature, since his consideration of drama tried to describe how it affected the audience. Tragedy, he said, should stimulate the emotions of pity and fear, these being, roughly, sympathy for and empathy with the plight of the protagonist. By the combination of these emotions came about the effect Aristotle called 'catharsis', whereby these emotions are exercised, rather than exorcised, as the audience identifies with the plight of the central character.

The first prestigious name in English writing about literature is that of Sir Philip Sidney, who wrote his 'Apology for Poetry' in about 1580. Sidney was intent on expanding the implications of the ancient definition of literature first formulated by the Latin poet Ovid, who had said that its mission is '*docere delictendo*' – to teach by delighting (meaning, approximately, by entertaining). Sidney also quotes Horace, to the effect that a poem is 'a speaking picture, with this end, to teach and delight'. Thus, the giving of pleasure is here allowed a central position in the reading of literature, unlike, say, philosophy, which is implicitly stigmatised as worthy and uplifting, but not much fun. The notion of literature giving pleasure will now seem an unremarkable sentiment, but Sidney's aim was the revolutionary one of distinguishing literature from other forms of writing, on the grounds that, uniquely, literature has as its primary aim the giving of pleasure to the reader, and any moral or didactic element is necessarily either subordinate to that, or at least, unlikely to succeed without it. In a religious age, deeply suspicious of all forms of fiction, poetry, and representation, and always likely to denounce them as the work of the devil, this was a very great step to take. In English too, then, critical theory came before practical criticism, as Sidney is writing about literature in general, not about individual works or writers.

Literary theory after Sidney was significantly advanced by Samuel Johnson in the eighteenth century. Johnson's *Lives of the Poets* and *Prefaces to Shakespeare* can be seen both as another major step forward in critical theory, and as the start of the English tradition of practical criticism, since he is the first to offer detailed commentary on the work of a single author. Prior to Johnson, the only text which had ever been subjected to this intensive scrutiny was the Bible, and the equivalent sacred books of other religions. The extension of this practice to works other than those thought to be the direct product of divine inspiration marks a significant moment of progress in the development of secular humanism.

After Johnson came a major burgeoning of critical theory in the work of the Romantic poets: Wordsworth, Coleridge, Keats, and Shelley. One of the main texts is Wordsworth's *Preface to Lyrical Ballads*. What Wordsworth wrote in this preface was the product of collaborative discussions between himself and Coleridge. The introduction was added to the second edition of the ballads, published in 1800, after the first, of 1798, had been met with puzzlement. The book blends high literature and popular literature, since it contains literary ballads constructed on the model of the popular oral ballads of ordinary country people. The original readers of *Lyrical Ballads* also disliked the abandonment of the conventions of verbal decorum. These conventions had imposed a high degree of artificiality on poetic language, making it as different as possible from the language of ordinary everyday speech. Thus, a specialised poetic vocabulary had tended to enjoin the avoidance of simple everyday terms for things, and an elaborate system of rhyme and a highly compressed form of grammar had produced a verbal texture of much greater density than that of ordinary language. Suddenly, two ambitious young poets were trying to make their poetic language as much like prose as possible, avoiding the conventions of diction and verbal structure which had held sway for so long. Thus, this book is one of a number of significant critical works in literary theory whose immediate aim is to provide a rationale for the critic's own poetic work, and to educate the audience for it. It also anticipates issues of great interest to contemporary critical theory, such as the relationship between poetic language and 'ordinary' language, and that between 'literature' and other kinds of writing.

A second significant work from the Romantic era was Coleridge's misleadingly titled *Biographia Literaria*. The title might lead us to expect a work like Johnson's *Lives of the Poets*, but in fact much of it directly addresses the ideas contained in Wordsworth's *Preface*, showing by a close consideration of aspects of his work that Wordsworth writes his best poetry when he is furthest away from adherence to his own theories of what poetry should be. Indeed, in the years during which he and Coleridge had drifted apart as friends, they had also taken radically different views about the nature of poetry. Coleridge came to disagree completely with the view that the language of poetry must strive to become more like the language of prose. He saw this as an impoverishment of the poetic effect which must ultimately prove suicidal. The argument dovetails neatly with the works already cited: if literature and other works differ in their aims and effects, as Aristotle and Sidney had maintained, and if poetry, unlike other kinds of writing, aims to teach by entertaining, then the major way in which the entertaining is done must be through the language in which it is written. The language entertains by its 'fictive' qualities – this is the source of the aesthetic effect. Something like this is also connoted in Shelley's *A Defence of Poetry* (1821) which sees poetry as essentially engaged in what a group of twentieth-century Russian critics later called 'defamiliarisation'. Shelley anticipates this term, since for him poetry 'strips the veil of familiarity from the world ... it purges from our inward sight the film of familiarity ... It compels us to feel that which we perceive, and to imagine that which we know'. This remarkable critical document also anticipates T. S. Eliot's notion of impersonality (put forward in his 1919 essay 'Tradition and the Individual Talent') whereby there is a distinction between (as we might call it) the author (who is the person behind the work) and the writer (who is, so to speak, the 'person' *in* the work). In Eliot's view, the greater the separation between the two the better, since 'the more perfect the artist, the more completely separate in him will be the man who suffers and the mind which creates', so that poetry is not simply the conscious rendering of personal experience into words. Shelley registers all this a hundred years earlier in his characteristically magisterial prose:

> the mind in creation is as a fading coal, which some invisible influence, like an inconstant wind, awakens to transitory brightness; this power arises from within, like the colour of a flower which fades and changes as it is developed, *and the conscious portions of our natures are unprophetic either of its approach or of its departure.*
>
> (*A Defence*, lines 999–1003, my italics)

There is also an anticipation here of the Freudian notion of the mind as made up of conscious and unconscious elements. Indeed, the idea of the unconscious is an essential one in Romanticism, and implicit in everything written about poetry by another major Romanticist, John Keats. Keats did not write formal literary theory in the way Wordsworth, Coleridge, and Shelley did, but he did reflect on poetry in a sustained way in his letters. He too formulates a notion of the workings of the unconscious, for instance in a letter to Bailey of 22 November 1817 when he speaks of how 'the simple imaginative Mind may have its rewards in the repetition of its own silent Working coming continually on the Spirit with a fine suddenness'. The 'silent working' of the mind is the unconscious and the 'spirit' into which it erupts is the conscious. Keats's idea of 'negative capability' also amounts to this same privileging of the unconscious, this same desire to allow it scope to work, negative capability being 'when a man is capable of being in uncertainties, mysteries, doubts without any irritable reaching after fact and reason' (letter to his brothers, 21 December 1817). In the critical writings of the Romantics, then, there are many anticipations of the concerns of critical theory today.

After the Romantics the main developments in critical theory were the work of mid and late Victorians, George Eliot, Matthew Arnold, and Henry James. George Eliot's critical work ranges widely over classical and continental writers, and philosophical issues, as did Coleridge's. It is worth emphasising this, since there are two distinct 'tracks' in the development of English criticism. One track leads through Samuel Johnson and Matthew Arnold to T. S. Eliot and F. R. Leavis. This might be called the 'practical criticism' track. It tends to centre upon the close analysis of the work of particular writers, and gives us our familiar tradition of 'close reading'. The other track lies through Sidney, Wordsworth, Coleridge, George Eliot, and Henry James. This track is very much 'ideas-led' rather than 'text-led': it tends to tackle big general issues concerned with literature – How are literary works structured? How do they affect readers or audiences? What is the nature of literary language? How does literature relate to the contemporary and to matters of politics and gender? What can be said about literature from a philosophical point of view? What is the nature of the act of literary composition? These 'track two' preoccupations are very similar to the concerns of the critical theorists who became prominent from the 1960s onwards, and it is important to realise that these concerns are not an exotic imposition upon 'native' Anglo-American approaches to literature but, rather, have been part of it from the beginning.

The insistence upon 'close reading' in the 1920s sprang partly from the work of Matthew Arnold in the previous century. Arnold has remained a key canonical figure in the history of English criticism, partly because F. R. Leavis adopted and adapted several of his ideas and attitudes and gave them twentieth-century currency. Arnold feared that the decline of religion would leave an increasingly divided society with no common system of beliefs, values, and images, with potentially disastrous consequences. He saw literature as a possible replacement for religion in this regard, but believed that the middle classes, on whom the burden and responsibility of democracy largely fell, had been progressively debased by materialism and philistinism. The critic would help such people to recognise 'the best that has been known and thought in the world' and thus enable them to give individual assent to the canon of great works which had emerged through the collective wisdom of the ages.

Arnold's most significant thinking is contained in the essays 'The Function of Criticism at the Present Time' and 'The Study of Poetry'. He stresses the importance for literature of remaining 'disinterested', by which he means politically detached and uncommitted to any specific programme of action. The goal of literary criticism is that of attaining pure, disinterested knowledge, that is, to use another of his favourite phrases, of simply appreciating 'the object as in itself it really is' without wanting to press the insight gained into the service of a specific line of action. Arnold's key literary-critical device is the notion of the Touchstone, which avoids any definitions of desirable literary qualities, and merely suggests using aspects of the literature of the past as a means of measuring and assessing the literature of today. The way the Touchstone works is concisely explained in J. A. Cuddon's *Dictionary of Literary Terms and Literary Theory* (3rd edition, Blackwell, 1991):

A touchstone is ... so-called because gold is tried by it. Matthew

> Arnold used the word in his essay *The Study of Poetry* (1880) in
> connection with literary criteria and standards:

Arnold advises that we should 'have always in mind lines and
expressions of the great masters, and apply them as a Touchstone
to other poetry'. He suggests that his Touchstone method should
provide the basis for a 'real' rather than an 'historic' or 'personal'
estimate of poetry. (See Cuddon, p. 980)

In the first half of the twentieth century, the key critical names
in Britain were F. R. Leavis, T. S. Eliot, William Empson, and
I. A. Richards. All except Eliot were at Cambridge in the 1920s
and 1930s, involved in the pioneering English School there which
had a powerful influence on the teaching of English worldwide
up to the 1970s. Eliot's contribution to the canon of received critical ideas was the greatest, his major critical ideas being:

- the notion of the 'dissociation of sensibility', developed in the
  course of his review article on Herbert Grierson's edition of
  The Metaphysical Poets,
- the notion of poetic 'impersonality', developed in the course
  of his two-part essay 'Tradition and the Individual Talent',
  and
- the notion of the 'objective correlative', developed in his essay
  on *Hamlet*.

All these ideas have become controversial: the idea that a 'dissociation of sensibility' occurred in the seventeenth century, radically separating thought from feeling, is one for which historical
evidence has never been found. Later in his career Eliot denied
that he thought the dissociation had been caused by the English
Civil War, though he added rather cryptically that he thought it
might have been caused by the same factors as those which
brought about the Civil War – a nice distinction. The best use of
the idea is simply as a way of describing the special qualities of
mind and sensibility which we detect in the Metaphysical poets:
as a historical generalisation it seems quite without support. The
best critique of the idea can be found in Frank Kermode's book
Romantic Image .

The idea of impersonality was partly Eliot's way of deflecting current thinking about poetry away from ideas of originality and self-expression which derived from Romanticism. Eliot's own personality, and the education he had received at Harvard, made this emphasis on the individual highly distasteful. It was much more congenial to him to see poetry not as a pouring out of personal emotion and personal experience, but as a transcending of the individual by a sense of tradition which spoke through, and is transmitted by, the individual poet. The best parts of a poet's work, he says, are not those which are most original, but those in which the voice of his predecessors can be most clearly heard speaking though him. Hence, there is a large distinction to be drawn between the mind of the individual, experiencing human being, and the voice which speaks in the poetry. This was not an original thought – Shelley, as we saw, had something very like it in his *Defence of Poesy* – but Eliot was the first to make it the cornerstone of a whole poetic aesthetic.

The objective correlative, finally, is really another encapsulation of English empiricist attitudes: it holds that the best way of expressing an emotion in art is to find some vehicle for it in gesture, action, or concrete symbolism, rather than approaching it directly or descriptively. This is undoubtedly true: little is gained in fiction or poetry by having characters (or narrators) say what they feel: it has to be *shown* in some way in words or actions. This is perhaps little more than the ancient distinction (first made by Plato) between *mimesis* and *diegesis*. The former is a *showing* of something, in the character's own words, or in actions which we actually see on the stage, if it is a play, while the latter is *telling* the audience or reader about things they don't see for themselves or experience in the direct speech of the characters. All Eliot's major critical ideas are thus flawed and unsatisfactory, and perhaps their long-standing currency is indicative of the theoretical vacuum into which they were launched.

The most influential British critic prior to the theory movement was F. R. Leavis. Leavis, like Arnold in the previous century, assumed that the study and appreciation of literature is a pre-condition to the health of society. He too distrusted abstract thought and looked for a system of literary appreciation (like Arnold's Touchstones) which by-passed fixed criteria, arguing instead for an openness to the qualities of the text. Like Arnold, finally, he rejected any attempt to politicise either literature or criticism directly.

The two differ, however, in a few notable regards: Arnold, for example, takes the pantheon of past great writers more or less for granted: he does not question the excellence of Dante, for instance, which is why Dante can become a Touchstone. By contrast, Leavis sometimes wrote essays attacking the reputations of major established figures, and, indeed, it was the essence of his method to argue that some reputations would *not* stand up to the kind of close textual scrutiny he constantly recommended. Arnold, in his critical ideas, seems essentially to license and encourage the amateur. You may not have read *everything*, he implies (how could you, since you don't have the unlimited time of the professional critic?), but if you have read the best, and can identify its qualities, then you can be confident in looking at new writing and reaching a true judgement on it. This 'protestant' aesthetic encourages a direct relationship between the individual reader and the literary greats.

F. R. Leavis began as an admirer of Eliot's critical work as well as of his poetry, but later greatly modified his views. He avoided the coining of critical vocabulary, and instead used as critical terms words and phrases which already had established lay senses: 'life', for instance, is used by Leavis almost as a critical term, as is the notion of 'felt experience'. For Leavis the crucial test is whether the work is conducive to 'life' and vitality. Leavis's extreme popularity was partly due to the fact that he was essentially a kind of combined avatar of Johnson and Arnold, offering again the former's moralism and the latter's social vision and anti-theoretical critical practice. Leavis is still so pervasive an influence that little more need be said about him here.

William Empson and I. A. Richards can perhaps be taken as a pair, though the latter was the tutor of the former in the late 1920s. Empson's book *Seven Types of Ambiguity* (1930) was itself somewhat ambiguous in its effects. On the one hand, its ultra-close readings of texts demonstrated the kind of text-led extreme which might be seen as the logical development of the 'track one' tradition of British criticism described above. The word 'ambiguity' in the book's title can be translated as 'verbal difficulty', and Empson unravels his examples by meticulous textual surgery, rather than references out to a wider context. On the other hand, though, Empson's basic attitude towards language is that it is really a very slippery medium indeed: when we handle language we need to be aware that the whole thing is likely to explode into meanings we hadn't suspected of being there at all. As we go from ambiguity type one to type seven we seem to be approaching the frontiers of language, where the territory eventually becomes un-mappable, and we seem to end up looking into a void of linguis-tic indeterminacy. This can be seen as an anticipation from within the British tradition of post-structuralist views about the unreli-ability of language as a medium (see p. 64). But the placing of language within *any* context naturally tends to reduce or elimi-nate ambiguity. (For instance, the word 'pain', when you hear it spoken in isolation, is ambiguous, since it sounds the same as 'pane', but encounter it in the context of any actual situation of usage and the ambiguity disappears). Hence the later Empson drew back from the linguistic void by stressing, in particular, the autobiographical context in which literary works, in his view, are grounded.

I. A. Richards, finally, is the pioneer of the decontextualised approach to literature which became the norm in Britain from the 1930s to the 1970s as 'practical criticism' and in America during roughly the same period as the 'New Criticism'. Richards's exper-iments in the 1920s of presenting students and tutors with unan-notated, anonymous poems for commentary and analysis gave rise to the ideal of removing the props of received opinion and knowl-edge and fostering a 'true judgement' based on first hand opin-ion. It is easy to see the connection between this and Arnold's 'Touchstones'. What is certain is that this decisive 'Ricardian' moment established the 'track one' 'practical' tradition of criti-cism so completely for so long that a selective amnesia descended on the discipline and it came to be widely regarded as the *only* tradition that had ever existed.

The subsequent conflict between liberal humanism and 'theory' is a pretty fundamental one, but it is worth reminding ourselves that it is actually much older than the 1970s when it broke out with such force in Britain, America, and elsewhere. Similar debates and arguments took place in the 1930s, for instance between F. R. Leavis, whom we might regard as the archetypal British liberal humanist, and the critical theorist René Wellek. Leavis and Wellek debated the relationship between literary criticism and philosophy in the pages of Leavis's journal *Scrutiny*. Wellek's point against Leavis was simply that practical criticism was *not* enough – he ought to spell out the theoretical assumptions on which his readings, and his procedures generally, were based. In Wellek's view a series of 'close readings' of Romantic poets in Leavis's book *Revaluations* is offered to the reader in a theoretical vacuum. As he politely put it, 'I could wish that you had stated your assumptions more explicitly and defended them systematically' (*Scrutiny*, March 1937, p. 376). This refusal to accept the liberal humanist method as simply the 'natural' and taken-for-granted way of 'doing' literature is the crux of theory's general response to it. Though less politely than Wellek, theorists make the same demand as he did – spell out what you do, and why, when you read and criticise literature, so that your methods can be evaluated along with others. Implicit in this demand is the view that if these things are made explicit (as we tried to do in the previous section) then the weaknesses of liberal humanist assumptions and procedures will become apparent, and other approaches will have a chance of replacing them.

The work of all the figures discussed in this section can be found in the collection *English Critical Texts*, ed. D. J. Enright and Ernst de Chickera (Oxford University Press, 1962).

Liberal humanism in practice

It is perhaps unnecessary to supply a full-scale example of liberal humanist practice, since that practice will surely be familiar to anyone reading this book. However, I will sketch out, mainly for comparative purposes, what I would consider to be a characteristic liberal humanist reading of Edgar Allan Poe's tale 'The Oval Portrait' (see Appendix 1) since the tale will be used later to illustrate structuralism in practice.

A liberal humanist approach to this tale (or, to be more specific, a Leavisite approach) might focus on the evident conflict of values in the story between 'art' and 'life'. The central point of commentary and interpretation might be the moralist argument that true value lies in the 'lived life' of the unique individual, and that it is disastrous for the artist to fail to recognise a necessary subservience of art to a communal reality. Further, when artists begin to see themselves as Faustian super-heroes, able to cross all boundaries of taste, taboo, and conduct, and even to assume the god-like role of creating and sacrificing life itself, then a hubristic act is committed which ultimately dries up the sources of the life of art itself. Hence, the artist in this tale in his isolated turret, feeding vampire-like on the vital energies of his sitter, is an emblem of a debased and degenerate form of art whose values are of the purely aesthetic 'art for art's sake' kind and have no reference to any wider notion of personal and psychic health.

Two things stand out in this approach: firstly, this kind of reading is driven (ultimately) by its moral convictions (laudable in themselves, of course) rather than by any model of what constitutes a systematic approach to literary criticism. The robust championing of 'life' in the above sketch makes the term 'Leavisite' seem an appropriate one to apply to it. The second notable aspect of it is that it seems to by-pass matters of form, structure, genre, and so on, and launches straight into the discussion of matters of content. If the sketch were filled out, there would doubtless be comments on such characteristics as structure, symbol, and design, but they would probably be *secondary* in nature, intended as concrete support for the *primary* focus of the reading, which is the moral position taken. I am not, of course, dismissing such an approach as worthless: my intention is simply to characterise it and distinguish it from other approaches.

The transition to theory

The growth of critical theory in the post-war period seems to comprise a series of 'waves', each associated with a specific decade, and all aimed against the liberal humanist consensus just illustrated, which had been established between the 1930s and the 1950s. In the 1960s, firstly, there were two older, but still unassimilated, rival new approaches, these being *Marxist criticism*, which had been pioneered in the 1930s and then reborn in the 1960s, and *psychoanalytic criticism*, which was of the same vintage and was similarly renewing itself in the 1960s. At the same time two new approaches were mounting vigorous direct assaults on liberal humanist orthodoxies, namely *linguistic criticism*, which came into being in the early 1960s, and early forms of *feminist criticism*, which started to become a significant factor at the end of the decade.

Then, in the 1970s news spread in literary-critical circles in Britain and the United States of controversial new critical approaches, in particular *structuralism* and *post-structuralism*, both of which originated in France. The effect of these two was so powerful as to produce, by the late 1970s and early 1980s, a situation which was frequently referred to as a 'crisis' or 'civil war' in the discipline of English. The questions these two approaches centred upon concerned matters of language and philosophy, rather than history or context. In the 1980s a shift occurred which is sometimes called the 'turn to history', whereby history, politics, and context were reinstated at the centre of the literary-critical agenda. Thus, in the early 1980s two new forms of political/historical criticism emerged, *new historicism* from the United States and *cultural materialism* from Britain. Both these take what might be called a 'holistic' approach to literature, aiming to integrate literary and historical study while at the same time maintaining some of the insights of the structuralists and post-structuralists of the previous decade.

Finally, in the 1990s a general flight from overarching grand explanations seems to be taking place, and there is what looks like a decisive drift towards dispersal, eclecticism, and 'special-interest' forms of criticism and theory. Thus, the approach known as *postcolonialism* rejects the idea of a universally applicable Marxist explanation of things and emphasises the separateness or otherness of post-imperial nations and peoples. Likewise, *postmodernism* stresses the uniquely fragmented nature of much contemporary experience. Feminism, too, shows signs of dissolving into a loose federation known as gender studies, with gay and lesbian texts emerging as distinct fields of literature, and hence implying and generating appropriate and distinct critical approaches: also part of this 1990s federation is black feminist (or 'womanist') criticism. The necessary limits on a book like the present one make it impossible to include everything, and for the time being it does not venture beyond postcolonialism and postmodernism.

Some recurrent ideas in critical theory

These different approaches each have their separate traditions and histories, but several ideas are recurrent in critical theory and seem to form what might be regarded as its common bedrock. Hence, it makes some sense to speak of 'theory' as if it were a single entity with a set of underlying beliefs, as long as we are aware that doing so is a simplification. Some of these recurrent underlying ideas of theory are listed below.

1. Many of the notions which we would usually regard as the basic 'givens' of our existence (including our gender identity, our individual selfhood, and the notion of literature itself) are actually fluid and unstable things, rather than fixed and reliable essences. Instead of being solidly 'there' in the real world of fact and experience, they are 'socially constructed', that is, dependent on social and political forces and on shifting ways of seeing and thinking. In philosophical terms, all these are *contingent* categories (denoting a status which is temporary, provisional, 'circumstance-dependent') rather than *absolute* ones (that is, fixed, immutable, etc.). Hence, no overarching fixed 'truths' can ever be established. The results of all forms of intellectual enquiry are provisional only. There is no such thing as a fixed and reliable truth (except for the statement that this is so, presumably). The position on these matters which theory attacks is often referred to, in a kind of shorthand, as *essentialism*, while many of the theories discussed in this book would describe themselves as *anti-essentialist*.

2. Theorists generally believe that all thinking and investigation is necessarily affected and largely determined by prior ideological commitment. The notion of disinterested enquiry is

therefore untenable: none of us, they would argue, is capable of standing back from the scales and weighing things up dispassionately: rather, all investigators have a thumb on one side or other of the scales. Every practical procedure (for instance, in literary criticism) presupposes a theoretical perspective of some kind. To deny this is simply to try to place our own theoretical position beyond scrutiny as something which is 'commonsense' or 'simply given'. This contention is problematical, of course, and is usually only made explicit as a counter to specific arguments put forward by opponents. The problem with this view is that it tends to discredit one's own project along with all the rest, introducing a *relativism* which disables argument and cuts the ground from under any kind of commitment.

3. Language itself conditions, limits, and predetermines what we see. Thus, all reality is constructed through language, so that nothing is simply 'there' in an unproblematical way – everything is a linguistic/textual construct. Language doesn't *record* reality, it shapes and creates it, so that the whole of our universe is textual. Further, for the theorist, meaning is jointly constructed by reader and writer. It isn't just 'there' and waiting before we get to the text but requires the reader's contribution to bring it into being.

4. Hence, any claim to offer a definitive reading would be futile. The meanings within a literary work are never fixed and reliable, but always shifting, multi-faceted and ambiguous. In literature, as in all writing, there is never the possibility of establishing fixed and definite meanings: rather, it is characteristic of language to generate infinite webs of meaning, so that all texts are necessarily self-contradictory, as the process of deconstruction will reveal. There is no final court of appeal in these matters, since literary texts, once they exist, are viewed by the theorist as independent linguistic structures whose authors are always 'dead' or 'absent'.

5. Theorists distrust all 'totalising' notions. For instance, the notion of 'great' books as an absolute and self-sustaining category is to be distrusted, as books always arise out of a particular socio-political situation, and this situation should not

be suppressed, as tends to happen when they are promoted to 'greatness'. Likewise, the concept of a 'human nature', as a generalised norm which transcends the idea of a particular race, gender, or class, is to be distrusted too, since it is usually in practice *Eurocentric* (that is, based on white European norms) and *androcentric* (that is, based on masculine norms and attitudes). Thus, the appeal to the idea of a generalised, supposedly inclusive, human nature is likely in practice to marginalise, or denigrate, or even deny the humanity of women, or disadvantaged groups.

To sum up these five points: for theory:

Politics is pervasive,
Language is constitutive,
Truth is provisional,
Meaning is contingent,
Human nature is a myth.

If, at later points in this book, or later in your study of theory, you begin to find that your grasp of things is slipping it would be worthwhile coming back to this list to remind yourself of the basic frame of mind which theory embodies. It is very likely that a concept with which you are having difficulty will turn out to be a version of one of these positions.

Selected reading

Books representing the liberal humanist position

Alter, Robert, *The pleasures of reading in an Ideogical Age* (Simon and Schuster, 1989).

Polemical anti-theoretical introduction, 'The disappearance of reading', and final chapter, 'Multiple readings and the bog of indeterminacy'; the chapters in between are on traditional literary critical concepts such as 'Character', 'Style' and 'Perspective'.

Gardner, Helen, *In Defence of the Literary Imagination* (Oxford University Press, 1982).

Based on a course of lectures responding to a book by Frank Kermode (then a champion of theory). A vigorous defence of traditional human-

ist scholarship and criticism against what she saw as the malign influence of theory.

Gribble, James, *Literary Education: A Re-evaluation* (Cambridge University Press, 1983).

One of several books from the early 1980s which mounted a defence
of traditional literary scholarship against theory. See chapter one, 'Literature and Truth': chapter four, 'The Subjection of Criticism to
Theory': chapter five 'Literature and the Education of the Emotions'.

Steiner, George, *Real Presences: Is There Anything in What We Say?*
(Faber, 1989).

Steiner is a polyglot, polymath humanist whose work has never been
anti-theoretical. In the two long essays in this book he grapples with
the problem of relating theoretical accounts to the actual experience of
responding to literature and the other arts.

Watson, George, *The Certainty of Literature: Essays in Polemic* (Harvester, 1989).

Watson's opposition to contemporary theory is absolute and
unqualified, as the title of this book implies.

Books about the rise of English as an academic subject

Baldick, Chris, *The Social Mission of English Studies 1848-1932* (Oxford
University Press, 1983).

A clearly argued history of literary criticism in England from Matthew
Arnold. Detailed, and with a clear introduction.

Doyle, Brian, 'The hidden history of English Studies' in *Re-Reading
English* ed. Peter Widdowson (Methuen, 1982), pp. 17–31.

Asks 'why and how did English become a major subject in higher education?' An influential account, though the emphasis is slightly different from the one I have offered here.

Eagleton, Terry, 'The Rise of English', chapter one in his *Literary
Theory: An Introduction* (Blackwell, 1983).

A polemical and very readable account of the growth of 'English',
broadly in line with Doyle's.

Graff, Gerald, *Professing Literature: An Institutional History* (Chicago,
University of Chicago Press, 1987).

A detailed account of the growth of English studies in the United
States.

Kearney, Anthony, *The Louse on the Locks of Literature: John Churton*

Collins (Scottish Academic Press, 1986).

Collins was a nineteenth-century pioneer of English studies. This enjoyable book includes an account (on which I have drawn in the relevant part of this chapter) of debates in the press and Parliament on the proposed new academic subject of 'English'.

Mulhern, Francis, *The Moment of Scrutiny* (New Left Books, 1979).

Scrutiny was the journal founded by F. R. Leavis in 1932, so this widely respected book continues the story of 'English' from where Baldick (above) leaves off.

Palmer, D. J., *The Rise of English Studies* (Oxford University Press, 1965).

A readable account.

Potter, Stephen, *The Muse in Chains: A Study in Education* (Cape, 1937, rpt. Folcroft, 1973).

An early account of early English. The specimen examination papers from the nineteenth century (included in the appendices) are very revealing.

Tillyard, E. M. W., *The Muse Unchained: an Intimate Account of the Revolution in English Studies at Cambridge* (London, Bowes & Bowes, 1958).

Continues the story of English from where Potter (above) leaves off, describing Cambridge in the 1920s and 1930s and the early careers of Richards, Empson, and Leavis. Palmer, Potter, and Tillyard together provide what might be called liberal humanism's own account of its development, distinctly different from that offered by Baldick, Doyle, Eagleton, and Mulhern.

Structuralism

Structuralist chickens and liberal humanist eggs

Structuralism is an intellectual movement which began in France in the 1950s and is first seen in the work of the anthropologist Claude Lévi-Strauss (1908–) and the literary critic Roland Barthes (1915–1980). It is difficult to boil structuralism down to a single 'bottom-line' proposition, but if forced to do so I would say that its essence is the belief that things cannot be understood in isolation – they have to be seen in the context of the larger structures they are part of (hence the term 'structuralism'). Structuralism was imported into Britain mainly in the 1970s and attained widespread influence, and even notoriety, throughout the 1980s.

The structures in question here are those imposed by our way of perceiving the world and organising experience, rather than objective entities already existing in the external world. It follows from this that meaning or significance isn't a kind of core or essence *inside* things: rather, meaning is always *outside*. Meaning is always an attribute of things, in the literal sense that meanings are *attributed* to the things by the human mind, not contained within them. But let's try to be specific about what it might mean to think primarily in terms of structures when considering literature. Imagine that we are confronted with a poem, Donne's 'Good Morrow', let's say. Our immediate reaction as structuralists would probably be to insist that it can only be understood if we first have a clear notion of the genre which it parodies and subverts. Any single poem is an example of a particular genre, and the genre and the example relate to each other rather as a phrase spoken in English relates to the English language as a structure with all its rules, its conventions, and so on. In the case of Donne's poem the relevant genre is the *alba* or 'dawn song', a poetic form dating from the twelfth century in which lovers lament the approach of daybreak because it means that they must part.

But the *alba*, in turn, can hardly be understood without some notion of the concept of courtly love, and, further, the *alba*, being a poem, presupposes a knowledge of what is entailed in the conventionalised form as utterance known as poetry. These are just some of the cultural structures which Donne's poem is part of. You will see that your structuralist 'approach' to it is actually taking you further and further away from the text, and into large and comparatively abstract questions of genre, history, and philosophy, rather than closer and closer to it, as the Anglo-American tradition demands. Now if we use the crude analogy of chickens and eggs, we can regard the containing structures (the *alba*, courtly love, poetry itself as a cultural practice) as the chicken, and the individual example (Donne's poem in this case) as the egg. For structuralists, determining the precise nature of the chicken is the most important activity, while for the liberal humanists the close analysis of the egg is paramount.

Thus, in the structuralist approach to literature there is a constant movement away from the interpretation of the individual literary work and a parallel drive towards understanding the larger, abstract structures which contain them. These structures, as I suggested at the start of this section, are usually abstract such as the notion of the literary or the poetic, or the nature of narrative itself, rather than 'mere' concrete specifics like the history of the *alba* or of courtly love, both of which, after all, we could quite easily find out about from conventional literary history. The arrival of structuralism in Britain and the USA in the 1970s caused a great deal of controversy, precisely because literary studies in these countries had traditionally had very little interest in large abstract issues of the kind structuralists wanted to raise. The so-called 'Cambridge revolution' in English studies in the 1920s had promulgated *the opposite* to all this: it enjoined close study of the text in isolation from all wider structures and contexts: it was relentlessly 'text-based' and tended to exclude wider questions, abstract issues, and ideas. Structuralism in that sense turned English studies on its head, and devalued all that it had held dear for around half a century, asking long-repressed questions such as: what do we mean by 'literary'? 'How do narratives work?' 'What *is* a poetic structure?' Traditional critics, in a word, did not welcome the suggestion that they ought to switch their attention from eggs to chickens.

Signs of the fathers – Saussure

Though structuralism proper began, as we said, in the 1950s and 1960s, it has its roots in the thinking of the Swiss linguist Ferdinand de Saussure (1857–1913). Saussure was a key figure in the development of modern approaches to language study. In the nineteenth century linguistic scholars had mainly been interested in historical aspects of language (such as working out the historical development of languages and the connections between them, and speculating about the origins of language itself). Saussure concentrated instead on the patterns and functions of language in use today, with the emphasis on how meanings are maintained and established and on the functions of grammatical structures.

But what exactly did Saussure say about linguistic structures which the structuralists later found so interesting? This can be summarised as three pronouncements in particular. Firstly, he emphasised that the meanings we give to words are purely *arbitrary*, and that these meanings are maintained by convention only. Words, that is to say, are 'unmotivated signs', meaning that there is no inherent connection between a word and what it designates. The word 'hut', for instance, is not in any way 'appropriate' to its meaning, and all linguistic signs are arbitrary like this. (There is the minor exception of a small number of onomatopoeic words like 'cuckoo' and 'hiss', but even these vary between languages.) Insisting that linguistic signs are arbitrary is a fairly obvious point to make, perhaps, and it is not a new thing to say (Plato said it in Ancient Greek times), but it is a new concept to *emphasise* (which is always much more important), and the structuralists were interested in the implication that if language as a sign system is based on arbitrariness of this kind then it follows that language isn't a reflection of the world and of experience, but a system which stands quite separate from it. This point will be further developed later.

Secondly, Saussure emphasised that the meanings of words are (what we might call) *relational*. That is to say, no word can be defined in isolation from other words. The definition of any given word depends upon its relation with other 'adjoining' words. For example, that word 'hut' depends for its precise meaning on its position in a 'syntagmatic chain', that is, a chain of words related in function and meaning each of which could be substituted for any of the others in a given sentence. The syntagmatic chain in this case might include the following:

hovel shed hut house mansion palace

The meaning of any one of these words would be altered if any one of the others were removed from the chain. Thus, 'hut' and 'shed' are both small and basic structures, but they are not quite the same thing: one is primarily for shelter (a night-watchman's hut, for instance), while the other is primarily for storage: without the other, each would have to encompass *both* these meanings, and hence would be a different word. Likewise, a mansion can be defined as a dwelling which is bigger and grander than a mere house, but not as big and grand as a palace. Thus, we define 'mansion' by explaining how its meaning relates to that of the two words on either side of it. If we have paired opposites then this mutually defining aspect of words is even more apparent: the terms 'male' and 'female', for example, mainly have meaning in relation to each other: each designates the absence of the characteristics included in the other, so that 'male' can be seen as mainly meaning 'not female', and vice versa. Similarly, we could have no concept of 'day' without the linked concept of 'night', no notion of 'good' without a 'bad' to define it against. This 'relational' aspect of language gave rise to a famous remark of Saussure's: 'In a language there are only differences, without fixed terms'. All words, then, exist in 'differencing networks', like these 'dyads', or paired opposites, and like the syntagmatic chain of 'dwelling place' words given earlier.

Saussure used a famous example to explain what he meant by saying that there are no intrinsic fixed meanings in language – the example of the 8.25 Geneva to Paris express train (see the *Course*, pp. 108-9, and Jonathan Culler's discussion of this example in *Structuralist Poetics*, p. 11). What is it that gives this train its identity? It isn't anything material, since each day it will have a different engine and carriages, different drivers and passengers, and so on. If it is late, it won't even leave at 8.25. Does it even have to be a train? I once asked at Southampton station for the Brighton train, and the ticket collector pointed to a bus standing outside the station and said, 'That's it'. It was a Sunday, and because of engineering works on the line a bus service was being used to ferry passengers beyond the sections being worked upon. Sometimes, then, a 'train' *doesn't* have to be a train. Saussure's conclusion is that the only thing which gives this train its identity is its position in a structure of differences: it comes *between* the 7.25 and the 9.25, that is, its identity is purely relational.

Thirdly, for Saussure, language *constitutes* our world, it doesn't just record it or label it. Meaning is always *attributed* to the object or idea by the human mind, and constructed by and expressed through language: it is not already contained within the thing. Well-known examples of this process would be the choice between paired alternatives like 'terrorist' or 'freedom fighter'. There is no neutral or objective way of designating such a person, merely a choice of two terms which 'construct' that person in certain ways. Another example of the same concept is seen in the two ways of referring to the domestic tax imposed in Britain by the Thatcher government: opponents of this tax called it the poll tax, evoking images of the Middle Ages and the Peasants' Revolt. The government itself called the tax the community charge, avoiding the negative word 'tax' and making use of the favoured term 'community'. The term for this tax used by a given individual immediately indicated a political position, and, again, no neutral or 'objective' alternative was available. It has been said that there are three versions of every story, your version, my version, and the truth, but the case here is more complicated than that, since *all* the available terms are purely linguistic – there is no truth about these matters which exists securely outside language.

Wherever we look, we see language constituting the world in this way, not just reflecting it. For instance, the words for colours *make* a reality, they don't just name things which are 'there': the spectrum isn't divided into seven primary colours; all the colours merge into one another. So we might have had fourteen names rather than seven. Another example is the terms we give to the seasons of the year. We have four distinct names ('spring', 'summer', etc.), but actually the year runs continuously without any breaks or decisive changes. It isn't, in reality, divided into four. Why not have six seasons, or eight? Since change is continuous throughout the year the divisions could be made anywhere at all. The seasons, then, are a *way of seeing* the year, not an objective fact of nature. So Saussure's thinking stressed the way language is arbitrary, relational, and constitutive, and this way of thinking about language greatly influenced the structuralists, because it gave them a model of a system which is self-contained, in which individual items relate to other items and thus create larger structures.

One other distinction made by Saussure gave structuralists a way of thinking about the larger structures which were relevant to literature. He used the terms *langue* and *parole* to signify, respectively, language as a system or structure on the one hand, and any given utterance in that language on the other. A particular remark in French (a sample of *parole*) only makes sense to you if you are already in possession of the whole body of rules and conventions governing verbal behaviour which we call 'French' (that is, the *langue*). The individual remark, then, is a discrete item which only makes sense when seen in relation to a wider containing structure, in the classic structuralist manner. Now, structuralists make use of the *langue/parole* distinction by seeing the individual literary work (the novel *Middlemarch*, let's say) as an example of a literary *parole*. It too only makes sense in the context of some wider containing structure. So the *langue* which relates to the *parole Middlemarch* is the notion of the novel as a genre, as a body of literary practice.

STOP and THINK

Consider some of the points made so far in this section about language.

Firstly, can you think of other examples of language constituting reality, rather than merely naming something which is already there? Your examples may be of a similar type to those mentioned above ('freedom fighter', 'poll tax', the seasons). You may also like to consider the significance in this context of those 'speech acts' which are known as 'performatives', that is, the kind of utterance which *is* the reality it designates, such as making a promise ('I promise to tell him') or formally opening some new facility ('I now declare this bridge opened').

Secondly, can you see any flaws in the line of argument about language and reality put forward by Saussure? For instance, does it make sense to posit a category of pure difference? Do you see any force in the counter-view once put forward by the critic Christopher Ricks, that you can't just have difference, you have to have difference *between* things? (See his article 'In Theory' in *London Review of Books*, April 1981, pp. 3–6.) If you accepted Ricks's argument, and agreed that you can only have difference between things, what implications would this have for the Saussurean argument that languages have only differences, without fixed terms?

Thirdly, are you convinced by that train? Is its position in the timetable really the *only* thing which gives it its identity? Saussure supplements the example with another one:

> Why can a street be completely rebuilt and still be the same? Because it does not constitute a purely material entity; it is based on certain conditions that are distinct from the materials that fit the conditions, e.g. its location with respect to other streets'
>
> (*Course*, pp. 108–9).

A counter-argument might be that the 8.25 has to be a train before it can be the 8.25: nobody will remark, 'There goes the

8.25 to Paris' if a flock of pigeons emerges from under the station canopy: likewise, it is true to say that a given street has a largely relational identity – you define 'X' Street by saying that it's the one that runs at right angles between 'Y' Street and 'Z' Street. All the same, a piece of string stretched between the two will not be mistaken for the street.

The scope of structuralism

But structualism is not just about language and literature. When Saussure's work was 'co-opted' in the 1950s by the people we now call structuralists, their feeling was that Saussure's model of how language works was 'transferable', and would also explain how all signifying systems work. The anthropologist Claude Lévi-Strauss applied the structuralist outlook to the interpetation of myth. He suggested that the individual tale (the *parole*) from a cycle of myths did not have a separate and inherent meaning but could only be understood by considering its position in the whole cycle (the *langue*) and the similarities and difference between that tale and others in the sequence.

So in interpreting the Oedipus myth, he placed the individual story of Oedipus within the context of the whole cycle of tales connected with the city of Thebes. He then began to see repeated motifs and contrasts, and he used these as the basis of his inter-pretation. On this method the story and the cycle it is part of are reconstituted in terms of basic oppositions: animal/human, rela-tion/stranger, husband/son and so on. Concrete details from the story are seen in the context of a larger structure, and the larger structure is then seen as an overall network of basic 'dyadic pairs' which have obvious symbolic, thematic, and archetypal resonance (like the contrast between art and life, male and female, town and country, telling and showing, etc., as in the 'worked example' later).

This is the typical structuralist process of moving from the par-ticular to the general, placing the individual work within a wider structural context. The wider structure might also be found in, for instance, the whole corpus of an author's work; or in the genre conventions of writing about that particular topic (for instance, discussing Dickens's novel *Hard Times* in terms of its deviations from novelistic conventions and into those of other more popular genres, like melodrama or the ballad); or in the identification of sets of underlying fundamental 'dyads'. A signifying system in this sense is a very wide concept: it means any organised and structured set of signs which carries cultural meanings. Included in this category would be such diverse phenomena as: works of literature, tribal rituals (a degree ceremony, say, or a rain dance), fashions (in clothing, food, 'life-style', etc.), the styling of cars, or the contents of advertisements. For the structuralist, the culture we are part of can be 'read' like a language, using these principles, since culture is made up of many structural networks which carry significance and can be shown to operate in a systematic way. These networks operate through 'codes' as a system of signs; they can make statements, just as language does, and they can be read or decoded by the structuralist or semiotician.

Fashion, for instance, can be 'read' like a language. Separate items or features are added up into a complete 'outfit' or 'look' with complex grammatical rules of combination: we don't wear an evening dress and carpet slippers: we don't come to lectures in military uniform, etc. Likewise, each component sign derives its meaning from a structural context. Of course, many fashions in clothing depend on breaking such rules in a 'knowing' way, but the 'statement' made by such rule-breaks (for instance, making outer garments which look like undergarments, or cutting expensive fabrics in an apparently rough way) depends upon the prior existence of the 'rule' or convention which is being conspicuously flouted. In the fashion world today, for instance, (late 1994) the combination of such features as exposed seams, crumpled-looking fabrics, and garments which are too big or too small for the wearer signifies the fashion known (confusingly, in this context) as deconstruction. Take any one of these features out of the context of all the rest, however, and they will merely signify that you have your jacket on inside out or don't believe in ironing. Again, these individual items have their place in an overall structure, and the structure is of greater significance than the individual item.

The other major figure in the early phase of structuralism was

Roland Barthes, who applied the structuralist method to the general field of modern culture. He examined modern France (of the 1950s) from the standpoint of a cultural anthropologist in a little book called *Mythologies* which he published in France in 1957. This looked at a host of items which had never before been subjected to intellectual analysis, such as: the difference between boxing and wrestling; the significance of eating steak and chips; the styling of the Citroën car; the cinema image of Greta Garbo's face; a magazine photograph of an Algerian soldier saluting the French flag. Each of these items he placed within a wider structure of values, beliefs, and symbols as the key to understanding it. Thus, boxing is seen as a sport concerned with repression and endurance, as distinct from wrestling, where pain is flamboyantly displayed. Boxers do not cry out in pain when hit, the rules cannot be disregarded at any point during the bout, and the boxer fights as himself, not in the elaborate guise of a make-believe villain or hero. By contrast, wrestlers grunt and snarl with aggression, stage elaborate displays of agony or triumph, and fight as exaggerated, larger than life villains or super-heroes. Clearly, these two sports have quite different functions within society: boxing enacts the stoical endurance which is sometimes necessary in life, while wrestling dramatises ultimate struggles and conflicts between good and evil. Barthes's approach here, then, is that of the classic structuralist: the individual item is 'structuralised', or 'contextualised by structure', and in the process of doing this layers of sigificance are revealed.

Roland Barthes in these early years also made specific examinations of aspects of literature, and by the 1970s, structuralism was attracting widespread attention in Paris and world wide. A number of English and American academics spent time in Paris in the 1970s taking courses under the leading structuralist figures (and these included Colin MacCabe) and came back to Britain and the USA fired up to teach similar ideas and approaches here. The key works on structuralism were in French, and these began to be translated in the 1970s and published in English. A number of Anglo-American figures undertook to read material not yet translated and to interpret structuralism for English-speaking readers; these important mediators included: the American,

Jonathan Culler, whose book *Structuralist Poetics* appeared in 1975: the English critic Terence Hawkes whose book *Structuralism and Semiotics* came out in 1977 as the first book in a new series published by Methuen called 'New Accents'. Hawkes was the general editor of the series, and its mission was 'to encourage rather than resist the process of change' in literary studies. Another influential figure was the British critic Frank Kermode, then professor at University College, London, who wrote with enthusiasm about Roland Barthes, and set up graduate seminars to discuss his work (though he has now in the 1990s become identified, in retirement, with much more traditional approaches). Finally, there was David Lodge, Professor of English at Birmingham, who tried to combine the ideas of structuralism with more traditional approaches. This attempt is typified by his book *Working with Structuralism* (1980).

What structuralist critics do

1. They analyse (mainly) prose narratives, relating the text to some larger containing structure, such as:
   (a) the conventions of a particular literary genre, or
   (b) a network of intertextual connections, or
   (c) a projected model of an underlying universal narrative structure, or
   (d) a notion of narrative as a complex of recurrent patterns or motifs.
2. They interpret literature in terms of a range of underlying parallels with the structures of language, as described by modern linguistics. For instance, the notion of the 'mytheme', posited by Lévi-Strauss, denoting the minimal units of narrative 'sense', is formed on the analogy of the morpheme, which, in linguistics, is the smallest unit of grammatical sense. An example of a morpheme is the 'ed' added to a verb to denote the past tense.
3. They apply the concept of systematic patterning and structuring to the whole field of Western culture, and across cultures, treating as 'systems of signs' anything from Ancient Greek myths to brands of soap powder.

Structuralist criticism: examples

I will base these examples on the methods of literary analysis described and demonstrated in Barthes's book *S/Z*, published in 1970. This book, of some two hundred pages, is about Balzac's thirty-page story 'Sarrasine'. Barthes's method of analysis is to divide the story into 561 'lexies', or units of meaning, which he then classifies using five 'codes', seeing these as the basic underlying structures of all narratives. So in terms of our opening statement about structuralism (that it aims to understand the individual item by placing it in the context of the larger structure to which it belongs) the individual item here is this particular story, and the larger structure is the system of codes, which Barthes sees as generating all possible actual narratives, just as the grammatical structures of a language can be seen as generating all possible sentences which can be written or spoken in it. I should add that there is a difficulty in taking as an example of structuralism material from a text by Barthes published in 1970, since 1970 comes within what is usually considered to be Barthes's post-structuralist phase, always said to begin (as in this book) with his 1968 essay 'The Death of the Author'. My reasons for nevertheless regarding *S/Z* as primarily a structuralist text are, firstly, to do with precedent and established custom: it is treated as such, for instance, in many of the best known books on structuralism (such as Terence Hawkes's *Structuralism and Semiotics*, Robert Scholes's *Structuralism in Literature*, and Jonathan Culler's *Structuralist Poetics*). A second reason is that while *S/Z* clearly contains many elements which subvert the confident positivism of structuralism, it is nevertheless essentially structuralist in its attempt to reduce the immense complexity and diversity possible in fiction to the operation of five codes, however tongue-in-cheek the exercise may be taken to be. The truth, really, is that the book sits on the fence between structuralism and post-structuralism: the 561 lexies and the five codes are linked in spirit to the 'high' structuralism of Barthes's 1968 esssay 'Analysing Narrative Structures', while the ninety-three interspersed digressions, with their much more free-wheeling comments on narrative, anticipate the 'full' post-structuralism of his 1973 book *The Pleasure of the*

Text.

The five codes identified by Barthes in *S/Z* are:

1. *The proairetic code*   This code provides indications of actions.
   ('The ship sailed at midnight' 'They began again', etc.)
2. *The hermeneutic code*   This code poses questions or enigmas
   which provide narrative suspense. (For instance, the sentence
   'He knocked on a certain door in the neighbourhood of Pell
   Street' makes the reader wonder who lived there, what kind
   of neighbourhood it was, and so on).
3. *The cultural code*   This code contains references out beyond
   the text to what is regarded as common knowledge. (For
   example, the sentence 'Agent Angelis was the kind of man
   who sometimes arrives at work in odd socks' evokes a pre-
   existing image in the reader's mind of the kind of man this is
   – a stereotype of bungling incompetence, perhaps, contrasting
   that with the image of brisk efficiency contained in the notion
   of an 'agent'.).
4. *The semic code*   This is also called the connotative code. It is
   linked to theme, and this code (says Scholes in the book mentioned above) when organised around a particular proper
   name constitutes a 'character'. Its operation is demonstrated
   in the second example, below.
5. *The symbolic code*   This code is also linked to theme, but on
   a larger scale, so to speak. It consists of contrasts and pairings
   related to the most basic binary polarities – male and female,
   night and day, good and evil, life and art, and so on. These
   are the structures of contrasted elements which structuralists
   see as fundamental to the human way of perceiving and
   organising reality.

As the last two codes have generated the greatest difficulty
(especially in distinguishing one from the other) I will use each
in turn as the basis of an example, beginning with the symbolic
code, which I will illustrate in use as the organising principle for
the interpretation of an entire tale, the story being 'The oval portrait' (reproduced in Appendix 1), by the early nineteenth-century American writer Edgar Allan Poe, an author who has
received considerable attention from both structuralists and post-

structuralists. In terms of the 'What structuralists do' list of activities above, this is an example of category 1.(d), treating narrative structure as a complex of recurrent patterns and motifs.

In discussing it I will enlist your help as a co-writer of this structuralist critique. The points at which your help is requested are indicated by the 'STOP and SHINK' heading.

A brief working summary of the plot may be useful. During what appears to be a civil war in an unnamed European country a wounded officer (as we may assume him to be) takes refuge in a recently abandoned chateau. The room he sleeps in contains an extremely lifelike portrait of a young woman, and a written account of this portrait, which he finds in the room, tells how the artist was her husband, who had become so carried away with the creation of the portrait that he failed to notice that as 'life' was kindled in the painting it simultaneously drained away from the sitter. At the end of the tale the placing of the final touch of colour which renders the portrait perfect coincides with the death of the sitter.

The most basic difference between liberal humanist and structuralist reading is that the structuralist's comments on structure, symbol, and design, become paramount, and are the main focus of the commentary, while the emphasis on any wider moral significance, and indeed on interpretation itself in the broad sense, is very much reduced. So instead of going straight into the content, in the liberal humanist manner, the structuralist presents a series of parallels, echoes, reflections, patterns, and contrasts, so that the narrative becomes highly schematised, is translated, in fact, into what we might call a verbal diagram. What we are looking for, as we attempt a structuralist critique, and where we expect to find it, can be indicated as in the diagram below. We are looking for the factors listed on the left, and we expect to find them in the parts of the tale listed on the right:

Parallels		Plot
Echoes		Structure
Reflections/Repetitions	in	Character/Motive
Contrasts		Situation/Circumstance
Patterns		Language/Imagery

Listing some of the parallels, etc., which might be picked out in Poe's tale is perhaps the best way of illustrating all this. Firstly, then, the tale itself has a binary structure (a structure of paired opposites) made up of two contrasting halves: the first part is a 'framing' narrative, containing the first-person account of the wounded officer, while the second is the story-within-the-story which he reads in the commentary on the painting. There is a very marked difference in narrative pace between these two halves, the first being leisurely, ponderous even, reflecting the down-to-earth, rationalistic mind of the officer, while the second moves with increasingly disjointed rapidity, reflecting the frenzy of artistic creation, and the rapid downward spiral of the victim/sitter's health.

A second contrast within the tale is that the chateau itself performs very different functions in the two halves. In the first half it is a place of refuge and recuperation for the officer, where he finds safety from his enemies and, we may assume, recovers his health. In the second half, by contrast, it is a place of danger and ultimately destruction for the sitter, where she is delivered to the whims of her artist-husband and her life is drained away.

STOP and THINK

Now, look for other contrasts between the two halves. For instance, each half features a relationship between two people (the officer and the valet in the first part and the artist and his wife in the second): how do these two relationships differ? There is an unequal distribution of power within each relationship, but the effects are different. How, exactly? Is there a similarity in what the members of each couple do to and for each other?

The main 'actors' in the two halves are (respectively) the wounded officer and the artist. What contrasts are observable in the mental state of these two?

Both the officer in the first part and the artist in the second are, in a sense, engrossed in a painting, but the role of art in the two halves is very different. What exactly is the contrast?

All these are contrasts, parallels, etc., between the two halves. There are also many more *within* the two halves. Firstly, there is a strongly implied contrast between the husband's self-absorbed artistic frenzy on the one hand, and a more conventional outwardly directed sexual passion of the kind which might be expected in a husband for a new bride. Instead of being fascinated by her, this husband is 'entranced before his work' in auto-erotic contemplation. Indeed, the marriage is in a sense bigamous, since the husband is described as 'having already a bride in his art'. The several weeks he spends alone with his new bride executing the painting are a kind of sustained negative parody of a honeymoon. Locked up together for several weeks, the husband painter 'took a fervid and burning pleasure in his task and wrought day and night', and towards the end 'the painter had grown wild with the ardour of his work'. In fact, he has spent this 'honeymoon' in passionate involvement with the first bride rather than the second.

A third level of contrasts and parallels are those which concern narrative mechanisms such as presentation and language, as well as content. One such, for instance, is the parallel between the narrators of the two halves. Both have a degree of anonymity, and in the second case the anonymity is complete, since we are given no information at all about the identity of the author of the 'vague and quaint words' of the story-within-the-story. (The only named character is Pedro the valet, the least important figure in the tale.) But structuralists are encouraged by Roland Barthes to ask of a text the question '*qui parle*?' – 'Who is speaking?' and if we ask that question of the second part of the tale, then the answer will involve dislodging the narrator from the position of a neutral spectatorial recorder, for this account must have been written by someone who witnessed these events without attempting any intervention. At the very least, this witness is someone without insight, indistinguishable from those who, having seen the portrait, 'spoke of its resemblance in low words, as of a mighty marvel, and a proof not less of the power of the painter than of his deep love for her whom he depicted so surpassingly well'.

STOP and THINK

The first narrator, too, can be seen as to some degree culpable, and as wilfully blind to the events witnessed. Could we go further? Is there a parallel between the two narrators, such that the first is aligned, through the language used, with the attitudes of the artist-husband?

For instance, what do you make of his prolonged contemplation of the painting? Are there elements in that part of the text which parallel the displaced eroticism of the artist's protracted gazing on his wife as he makes the painting? There are two examples, not just one, of an intense masculine gaze in the story. Look at the distribution of the words 'gaze' and 'glory' (or 'gloriously') in the text. Look at the way the passing of time is depicted in each of these cases. In both cases there is a moment when the gaze is averted: what is the significance of this parallelism?

All these contrasts are of a very particular kind, proper to just this one tale. We may then perform a simplifying move which is rather like finding the lowest common denominator of a set of numbers, for these items might be reduced to a set of more generalised ones: the contrast and conflict between *life* and *art*, *male* and *female*, *light* and *dark* (in the sense of enlightenment and moral benightedness, as well as in purely physical terms), *looking* and *doing*, *reality* and *representation*. The thesis of the structuralist is that narrative structures are founded upon such underlying paired opposites, or dyads, so that contrasts such as these are the skeletal structure on which all narratives are fleshed out. If we had to reduce even this list of dyads, to achieve a single pair, then it would have to be the art/life contrast, since the tale seems most to be about life and art viewed as factors in an overall psychic economy.

The obvious final question is to ask which side of this dichotomy the tale is on. There can surely be little doubt that it is on the side of art, for it is the act of artistic creation, and, to a lesser extent, that of contemplating a work of art, which is most vividly and passionately described in the tale, rather than any sense of the waste of a young life. The frenzy of this 'passionate, wild, and moody man' produces a work of art so lifelike that it seems the product of a divine being. This is no way to champion 'life'. 'Officially' the story is a pious protest at the sacrifice of a young life, but in practice the making of the sacrifice is presented with a kind of loving envy. As D. H. Lawrence didn't quite say, never trust the moral, trust the tale.

So much, then, for the symbolic code. The second example centres on the operation within a text of the *semic code*. This code, as we have said, is linked with the process of characterisation and thematicisation but operates on a smaller scale than the symbolic code. For Hawkes, in the book mentioned earlier, it 'utilises hints or "flickers of meaning"', and given that it operates through the nuances of individual words and phrases, the best way to appreciate it in action is to use a variation of what educationalists call 'cloze procedure', which involves deleting words from a text and having readers fill these gaps by drawing inferences from context and overall structure.

The passage below is the opening of a novel by Mervyn Jones. The central character, Mr Armitage, is presented in the opening scene and his character immediately established. I have left gaps in the text and have listed at the end of the relevant sentences several words which might fill that gap (one of which, in each case, is the word actually used by the author). You will see that the character is decisively altered, according to the word you choose to fill the gap, enabling us to feel the semic code actually at work. The paragraphs have been numbered for ease of reference. In terms of the 'What structuralists do' list, this is an example of 1.(c), that is, of relating the text to a projected model of an underlying universal narrative structure, since the critic would assume that the five Barthesian codes are fundamental to the workings of all narratives. Spend time now selecting a word for each gap before going on to my commentary.

STOP and THINK

1. John Edward Scott Armitage: fifty-five years old, five feet eleven inches tall, weight thirteen stone three ____.
   [*pounds, ounces*]

2. June the eighth: a fine morning, nine-fifteen by the programme change on the car radio, also nine-fifteen exactly as he checked the time on his ____ watch.
   [*multi-function, Swiss, Swatch, Timex, Pocket, Mickey Mouse*]

3. Hendon Way, north-bound. Armitage was driving a Jaguar, just run in. Its newness pleased him – the ____ smell of the leather, the neat zeros on the mileage dial. He was among those men whose car is never more than a year old.
   [*rich, sweet, heady, sexy, opulent*]

There is further description, then Armitage slows the car to look at two hitch-hikers. They meet his standards of acceptability, and he offers them a lift, but the response to his offer is a momentary hesitation. The text resumes:

4. The boy still presented his pleasant smile, but did not get into the car. Now he seemed to be considering, not only the directions, but also the car, and even Armitage himself. The hitch-hiker, in fact, was deciding whether to accept the driver instead of the other way round. Armitage was ____. In a few seconds more he might have been indignant. But the girl said: 'This is fine – yes it is – super, really'.
   [*baffled, stumped, gob-smacked*]

5. She spoke eagerly, indeed with some impatience at the boy's hesitation. And she too smiled at Armitage, but more than pleasantly, ____, he thought. Of course, they were lucky to get a long ride in a new Jaguar. The girl clearly realised this; she seemed, moreover, to be happy to travel with Armitage. As soon as this notion occurred to him Armitage saw that it was absurd. Yet it was an attractive thing for her to give such an impression.
   [*happily, cheerfully, invitingly, gleefully*]

6. She ____ into the front seat, and the boy got into the back. Armitage pulled away quickly to get ahead of a removal van. He drove in a thrusting style, seizing every opportunity, overtaking in roaring third gear. He met, and then dismissed, the thought that the girl's presence beside him had made him show off his skill.

   [*jumped quickly, plumped heavily, slid seductively, slid easily, squeezed awkwardly, slipped quietly*]

I'll comment briefly on the gaps in each of these paragraphs.

In the first the word in the published text is 'ounces', the precision of which immediately suggests a man with a very precise and ordered attitude to life. (How many people know their weight to the nearest ounce?)

In the second paragraph the character of Armitage is completely changed if we change his watch. In the text his 'Swiss' watch reinforces the image of the well-ordered, well-to-do life already established in the first few lines of the book. But the semic code's 'flicker of meaning' can instantly change him into an ageing gadget-faddist with a multi-function digital timepiece, or a dedicated follower of fashion with a trendy Swatch Watch, or an old fogey with a pocket watch, or a hearty life-and-soul-of-the-party type with a jokey Mickey Mouse watch.

In the third paragraph the words 'sweet', 'heady', and 'sexy' all come close to turning Armitage into a leather fetishist, while 'rich' has a certain directness and vulgarity which implies that his pleasure in things is in direct proportion to their cost. The text's 'opulent' retains an element of this but seems to imply an appreciation of quality and craftsmanship for its own sake.

In the fourth paragraph (as often in fiction) the kind of word used by the narrating voice reflects the character being described. 'Stumped' suggests an undignified cluelessness, as, even more so, does 'gob-smacked', whereas the text's 'baffled' implies the offended dignity of a man of some standing accustomed to a degree of respect.

In the fifth paragraph Armitage's perception of the nature of the girl's smile is a crucial element in his characterisation. The text has him seeing her as smiling 'cheerfully', indicating that he is pleased to perceive a positive reaction towards him. If she were smiling, in his view, 'invitingly', then the implication would be that his motives were entirely sexual. 'Gleefully', on the other hand, would make her into a child rather than an adult.

In the final paragraph the missing phrase indicates that, all the same, Armitage finds the girl attractive and is physically aware of her. The text tells us that she 'slid easily' into the front seat, implying a certain slender gracefulness. Armitage's attention is less directed towards the boy, so he simply 'got into' the back. If we reverse these two phrases the implication is that Armitage is more interested in the boy than the girl, thus: 'She got into the front seat, and the boy slid easily into the back'. This has the effect of tending to construct Armitage as homosexual, even though no such explicit statement is made.

This simple 'cloze' exercise, then, indicates something of the small-scale, but none the less crucial, workings of the semic code in the construction of character, while also showing how, in sequence, this code can begin to activate thematic motifs, such as the notion of orderliness and control associated with Armitage.

The operation of two other codes could easily be illustrated from the same passage. The *hermeneutic code*, for instance, is obviously important in it. Right at the beginning of a novel the reader has to be drawn into the process of speculating about possible outcomes, working out enigmas, and predicting the possible patterns of events and motives. Thus, with this example we are immediately involved in answering questions like 'What is going to happen as a result of this meeting?' 'Are the hitch-hikers as innocent as they seem?' 'Will Armitage's confidence be shaken in some way as the novel progresses?' Finally, an example of the *cultural code* is seen in the third paragraph when we are told that Armitage 'was among those men whose car is never more than a year old', where the text appeals to our prior knowledge of this kind of man as a distinct type with a whole range of related characteristics and habits. The last code, the symbolic, would be difficult to detect in such a brief and early extract from a novel, and has already been demonstrated at length on the Poe example.

Selected reading

Barthes, Roland, *Selected Writings*, introduced by Susan Sontag (Fontana, 1983).

Barthes, Roland, *The Semiotic Challenge*, translated by Richard Howard (Blackwell, 1988).

Essays by the best-known structuralist critic; see chapter in section three 'Textual Analysis of a Tale by Edgar Allan Poe', on 'The Facts in the Case of M. Valdemar'.

Culler, Jonathan, *Barthes* (Fontana, 1983).

Culler, Jonathan, *Structuralist Poetics* (Routledge, 1975).

A book which immediately established the author's reputation as a 'mediator' of difficult theories. Thorough, but seldom succinct.

Hawkes, Terence, *Structuralism and Semiotics* (Methuen, 1977).

A pioneering book in a key series. Equivalent to Culler, but does it better, in my view, because the series format makes for brevity and tightness.

Scholes, Robert, *Structuralism in Literature: An Introduction* (Yale University Press, 1974).

An admirable book. Don't be put off by its age. You won't find anything to match it.

Sturrock, John, *Structuralism* (Paladin, 1986).

Covers structuralism in a variety of fields (language, social sciences, etc.). Chapter four is a good, succinct account of literary structuralism and its antecedents.

3

Post-structuralism and deconstruction

Some theoretical differences between structuralism and post-structuralism

Is post-structuralism a continuation and development of structuralism or a form of rebellion against it? In one important sense it is the latter, since a very effective way of rebelling is to accuse your predecessors of not having the courage of their convictions. Thus post-structuralists accuse structuralists of not following through the implications of the views about language on which their intellectual system is based. As we saw, one of structuralism's characteristic views is the notion that language doesn't just reflect or record the world: rather, it shapes it, so that *how* we see is *what* we see. The post-structuralist maintains that the consequences of this belief are that we enter a universe of radical uncertainty, since we can have no access to any fixed landmark which is beyond linguistic processing, and hence we have no certain standard by which to measure anything. Without a fixed point of reference against which to measure movement you cannot tell whether or not you are moving at all. You have probably at some time had the experience of sitting in a stationary train with another train between yourself and the far platform. When that train begins to move you may have the sensation that it is *your* train which is moving and only realise this isn't so when the other train has gone and you again see the fixed point of the platform. Post-structuralism says, in effect, that fixed intellectual reference points are permanently removed by properly taking on board what structuralists said about language. Or, to change the analogy, in space, where there is no gravity, there is no up and down, and these pronoucements about language send us into a gravity-free universe, without upside down or right way up. This situation, of being without intellectual reference points, is one way of describing what post-structuralists call the *decentred universe*, one in which, by definition, we cannot know where we are, since all the concepts which previously defined the centre, and hence also the margins, have been 'deconstructed', or undermined, in the manner described later.

The characteristic concerns of post-structuralism, as hinted at here, may at first seem pretty remote. Why this constant high anxiety about language, we might ask, when it seems to work perfectly well most of the time for day-to-day purposes? But on reflection we may find that it is precisely on this matter of anxiety about language that we can most easily identify with post-structuralist concerns, for these anxious feelings seem remarkably pervasive whenever we have to use language at any level beyond that of casual daily exchange with people we know very well and whose status is the same as our own. For instance, think of any slightly less straightforward language situation, like writing to your bank, writing an essay, striking up a friendship with a stranger at a party, or sending a letter of condolence. In these cases, and many more, there is an almost universally felt anxiety that the language will express things we hadn't intended, or convey the wrong impression, or betray our ignorance, callousness, or confusion. Even when we use a phrase like 'If you see what I mean' or 'In a manner of speaking' there is the same underlying sense that we are not really in control of the linguistic system. These feelings, writ large, are really the same, or, at least, surely have the same source, as the radical linguistic scepticism which is so typical of deconstruction. Here, then, is a way into the post-structuralist frame of mind which lies very much within attitudes and anxieties which most of us experience.

However, perhaps it will be helpful simply to list some differences and distinctions between structuralism and post-structuralism, under the four headings below.

1. *Origins* Structuralism derives ultimately from linguistics. Linguistics is a discipline which has always been inherently confident about the possibility of establishing objective knowledge. It believes that if we observe accurately, collect data systematically, and make logical deductions then we can reach reliable conclusions about language and the world. Structuralism inherits this confidently scientific outlook: it too believes in method, system, and reason as being able to establish reliable truths.

By contrast, post-structuralism derives ultimately from philosophy. Philosophy is a discipline which has always tended to emphasise the difficulty of achieving secure knowledge about things. This point of view is encapsulated in Nietzsche's famous remark 'There are no facts, only interpretations'. Philosophy is, so to speak, sceptical by nature and usually undercuts and questions commonsensical notions and assumptions. Its procedures often begin by calling into question what is usually taken for granted as simply the way things are. Post-structuralism inherits this habit of scepticism, and intensifies it. It regards any confidence in the scientific method as naive, and even derives a certain masochistic intellectual pleasure from knowing for certain that we *can't* know anything for certain, fully conscious of the irony and paradox which doing this entails.

2. *Tone and style* Structuralist writing tends towards abstraction and generalisation: it aims for a detached, 'scientific coolness' of tone. Given its derivation from linguistic science, this is what we would expect. An essay like Roland Barthes's 1966 piece 'Introduction to the Structural Analysis of Narrative' (reprinted in *Image, Music, Text* ed. Stephen Heath, 1977) is typical of this tone and treatment, with its discrete steps in an orderly exposition, complete with diagrams. The style is neutral and anonymous, as is typical of scientific writing.

Post-structuralist writing, by contrast, tends to be much more emotive. Often the tone is urgent and euphoric, and the style flamboyant and self-consciously showy. Titles may well contain puns and allusions, and often the central line of the argument is based on a pun or a word-play of some kind.

Often deconstructive writing fixes on some 'material' aspect of language, such as a metaphor used by a writer, or the etymology of a word. Overall it seems to aim for an engaged warmth rather than detached coolness.

3. *Attitude to language*   Structuralists accept that the world is constructed through language, in the sense that we do not have access to reality other than through the linguistic medium. All the same, it decides to live with that fact and continue to use language to think and perceive with. After all, language is an orderly system, not a chaotic one, so realising our dependence upon it need not induce intellectual despair.

By contrast, post-structuralism is much more fundamentalist in insisting upon the consequences of the view that, in effect, reality itself is textual. Post-structuralism develops what threaten to become terminal anxieties about the possibility of achieving *any* knowledge through language. The verbal sign, in its view, is constantly floating free of the concept it is supposed to designate. Thus, the post-structuralist's way of speaking about language involves a rather obsessive imagery based on liquids – signs float free of what they designate, meanings are fluid, and subject to constant 'slippage' or 'spillage'. This linguistic liquid, slopping about and swilling over unpredictably, defies our attempts to carry signification carefully from 'giver' to 'receiver' in the containers we call words. We are not fully in control of the medium of language, so meanings cannot be planted in set places, like somebody planting a row of potato seeds; they can only be randomly scattered or 'disseminated', like the planter walking along and scattering seed with broad sweeps of the arm, so that much of it lands unpredictably or drifts in the wind.

Likewise, the meanings words have can never be guaranteed one hundred per cent pure. Thus, words are always 'contaminated' by their opposites – you can't define *night* without reference to *day*, or *good* without reference to *evil*. Or else they are interfered with by their own history, so that obsolete senses retain a troublesome and ghostly presence within present-day usage, and are likely to materialise just when we thought it was safe to use them. Thus, a seemingly innocent word like 'guest', is etymologically cognate with 'hostis', which means an enemy or a stranger, thereby inadvertently manifesting the always potentially unwelcome status of the guest (see below, page 71). Likewise, the long-dormant metaphorical bases of words are often reactiviated by their use in philosophy or literature and then interfere with literal sense, or with the stating of single meanings. Linguistic anxiety, then, is a keynote of the post-structuralist outlook.

4. *Project* By 'project' here I mean the fundamental aims of each movement, what it is they want to persuade us of. Structuralism, firstly, questions our way of structuring and categorising reality, and prompts us to break free of habitual modes of perception or categorisation, but it believes that we can thereby attain a more reliable view of things.

Post-structuralism is much more fundamental: it distrusts the very notion of reason, and the idea of the human being as an independent entity, preferring the notion of the 'dissolved' or 'constructed' subject, whereby what we may think of as the individual is really a product of social and linguistic forces – that is, not an essence at all, merely a 'tissue of textualities'. Thus, its torch of scepticism burns away the intellectual ground on which the Western civilisation is built.

Post-structuralism – life on a decentred planet

Post-structuralism emerged in France in the late 1960s. The two figures most closely associated with this emergence are Roland Barthes and Jacques Derrida (1930–). Barthes's work around this time began to shift in character and move from a structuralist phase to a post-structuralist phase. The difference can be seen by comparing two different accounts by Barthes of the nature of the narrative, one from each phase, namely the essay 'The Structural Analysis of Narrative' (first published in 1966 and reprinted in *Image, Music, Text* ed. Stephen Heath, 1970) and *The Pleasure of the Text* (1973). The former is detailed, methodological and forbiddingly technical, while the latter is really just a series of random comments on narrative, arranged alphabetically, thereby, of course, emphasising the randomness of the material. Between these two works came the crucial essay 'The Death of the Author' (1968) which is the 'hinge' round which Barthes turns from structuralism to post-structuralism. In that essay he announces the death of the author, which is a rhetorical way of asserting the independence of the literary text and its immunity to the possibility of being unified or limited by any notion of what the author might have intended, or 'crafted' into the work. Instead, the essay makes a declaration of radical textual independence: the work is not determined by intention, or context. Rather, the text is free by its very nature of all such restraints. Hence, as Barthes says in the essay, the corollary of the death of the author is the birth of the reader. So the difference between the 1966 essay and the 1973 book is a shift of attention from the text seen as something produced by the author to the text seen as something produced by the reader, and, as it were, by language itself, for as Barthes also says, in the absence of an author, the claim to decipher a text becomes futile. Hence, this early phase of post-structuralism seems to license and revel in the endless free play of meanings and the escape from all forms of textual authority. Later there is an inevitable shift from this textual permissiveness to the more disciplined and austere textual republicanism suggested in the quotation (p. 71) from Barbara Johnson. For her, deconstruction is not a hedonistic abandonment of all restraint, but a disciplined identification and dismantling of the sources of textual power.

The second key figure in the development of post-structuralism in the late 1960s is the philosopher Jacques Derrida. Indeed, the starting point of post-structuralism may be taken as his 1966 lecture 'Structure, Sign and Play in the Discourse of the Human Sciences' (variously reprinted, most recently in abbreviated form in K. M. Newton's *Twentieth Century Literary Theory: A Reader*, Macmillan, 1988). In this paper Derrida sees in modern times a particular intellectual 'event' which constitutes a radical break from past ways of thought, loosely associating this break with the philosophy of Nietzsche and Heidegger and the psychoanalysis of Freud. The event concerns the 'decentring' of our intellectual universe. Prior to this event the existence of a norm or centre in all things was taken for granted: thus 'man', as the Renaissance slogan had it, was the measure of all other things in the universe: white Western norms of dress, behaviour, architecture, intellectual outlook, and so on, provided a firm centre against which deviations, aberrations, variations could be detected and identified as 'Other' and marginal. In the twentieth century, however, these centres were destroyed or eroded; sometimes this was caused by historical events – such as the way the First World War destroyed the illusion of steady material progress, or the way the Holocaust destroyed the notion of Europe as the source and centre of human civilisation; sometimes it happened because of scientific discoveries – such as the way the notion of relativity destroyed the ideas of time and space as fixed and central absolutes; and sometimes, finally, it was caused by intellectual or artistic revolutions – such as the way modernism in the arts in the first thirty years of the century rejected such central absolutes as harmony in music, chronological sequence in narrative, and the representation of the visual world in art.

In the resulting universe there are no absolutes or fixed points, so that the universe we live in is 'decentred' or inherently relativistic. Instead of movement or deviation from a known centre, all we have is 'free play' (or 'play' as the title of the essay has it). In the lecture Derrida embraces this decentred universe of free play as liberating, just as Barthes in 'The Death of the Author' celebrates the demise of the author as ushering in an era of joyous freedom. The consequences of this new decentred universe are impossible to predict, but we must endeavour not to be among 'those who ... turn their eyes away in the face of the as yet unnameable which is proclaiming itself' (Newton, p. 154). This powerful, quasi-religious appeal to us not to turn our eyes away from the light is typical of the often apocalyptic tone of post-structuralist writing. If we have the courage, the implication is, we will enter this new Nietzschean universe, where there are no guaranteed facts, only interpretations, none of which has the stamp of authority upon it, since there is no longer any authorative centre to which to appeal for validation of our intepretations.

Derrida's rise to prominence was confirmed by the publication of three books by him in the following year (translated as *Speech and Phenomena*, *Of Grammatology*, and *Writing and Difference*). All

of these books are on philosophical rather than literary topics, but
Derrida's method always involves the highly detailed 'deconstructive' reading of selected aspects of other philosophers' works,
and these deconstructive methods have been borrowed by literary
critics and used in the reading of literary works. Essentially, the
deconstructive reading of literary texts tends to make them
emblems of the decentred universe we have been discusssing.
Texts previously regarded as unified artistic artefacts are shown
to be fragmented, self-divided, and centreless. They always turn
out to be representative of the 'monstrous births' predicted at the
end of 'Structure, Sign, and Play'.

STOP and THINK

A key text in post-structuralism is Derrida's book *Of
Grammatology*. The slogan 'There is nothing outside the text'
is the most frequently quoted line from this book, but it is
usually quoted out of context to justify a kind of extreme
textualism, whereby it is held that all reality is linguistic, so that
there can be no meaningful talk of a 'real' world which exists
without question outside language.

It is becoming common today to deny that such a view is the
one actually put forward by Derrida, and while I do not
recommend that you attempt to tackle the whole book at this
stage, you could put yourself considerably ahead of many
commentators and critics by acquiring a detailed knowledge of
the section of the book in which this remark occurs, using the
intensive reading technique I describe in the Introduction. The
section is subheaded 'The exorbitant. questions of method' (pp.
157–64).

Derrida is writing in this section about Rousseau's 'Essay on
the origin of languages', but he stops to question his own
method of interpreting this text, and hence the nature of all
interpretation. He debates the concept of the 'supplement', a
word which in French can also mean a replacement, in the
sense that language replaces or stands in for reality. (This idea
is outlined in the immediately preceding pages of *Of*

Grammatology, 141–57.) But what exactly is the nature of this 'standing in', since 'the person writing is inscribed in a determined textual system' (p. 160), which is to say that we all inherit language as a ready-made system, with its own history, philosophy, and so on already 'built in'? In this sense one might argue that we don't express ourselves in words, merely some aspect of language:

> The writer writes *in* a language and *in* a logic whose proper systems, laws, and life his discourse by definition cannot dominate absolutely. He uses them by only letting himself, after a fashion and up to a point, be governed by the system. And the reading must always aim at a certain relationship, unperceived by the writer, between what he commands and what he does not command of the patterns of the language that he uses. This relationship is not a certain quantitative distribution of shadow and light, of weakness or of force but a signifying structure that critical reading should *produce*.
>
> Derrida, *Of Grammatology*, p. 158

Reading and interpretation, then, are not just *reproducing* what the writer thought and expressed in the text. This inadequate notion of interpretation Derrida calls a 'doubling commentary', since it tries to reconstruct a pre-existing, non-textual reality (of what the writer did or thought) to lay alongside the text. Instead, critical reading must *produce* the text, since there is nothing behind it for us to reconstruct. Thus, the reading has to be *de*constructive rather than *re*constructive in this sense. This is the point where Derrida makes the remark which he later calls 'the axial proposition of this essay, that there is nothing outside the text' (*Of Grammatology*, p. 163):

> Reading ... cannot legitimately transgress the text toward something other than it ... or toward a signified outside the text whose content could take place, could have taken place, outside of language, that is to say, in the sense that we give here to that word, outside of writing in general. That is why the

methodological considerations that we risk applying here to an
example are closely dependent on general propositions that we
have elaborated above; as regards the absence of the referent
or the transcendental signified. There is nothing outside of the
text.

(*Of Grammatology*, p. 158)

He expands this further and reiterates that 'beyond and behind
what one believes can be circumscribed as Rousseau's text,
there has never been anything but writing ... what opens
meaning and language is writing as the disappearance of
natural presence' (p. 159).

You will not find these pages of Derrida by any means easy,
but they will repay some intensive work, ideally in group
discussion. Do they enable you to pin down precisely what
Derrida is saying about the relationship between word and
world, and are his views as stark and uncompromising as they
are often accused of being?

Structuralism and post-structuralism – some practical differences

An initial problem here is that post-structuralism often claims
that it is more an attitude of mind than a practical method of criticism. This is, in a sense, quite true, but perhaps no more true of
post-structuralism than of any other critical orientation. After all,
in what sense could, say, Marxist or feminist – or even liberal
humanist – criticism be called a method? Only in the loosest way,
surely, since none of these provide anything like a step by step
procedure for analysing literary works. All they offer is an orientation towards a characteristic central issue (that is, towards issues
of class, gender, and personal morality, respectively) and a body
of work which constitutes a repertoire of examples.

What, then, seem to be the characteristics of post-structuralism as a critical method? The post-structuralist literary critic is
engaged in the task of 'deconstructing' the text. This process is
given the name 'deconstruction', which can be roughly defined as
applied post-structuralism. It is often referred to as 'reading

against the grain' or 'reading the text against itself', with the purpose of 'knowing the text as it cannot know itself'. (These are
Terry Eagleton's definitions.) A way of describing this would be
to say that deconstructive reading uncovers the unconscious
rather than the conscious dimension of the text, all the things
which its overt textuality glosses over or fails to recognise. This
repressed unconscious within language might be sensed, for
instance, in the example used earlier when we said that the word
'guest' is cognate with (that is, has the same original root as) the
word 'host', which in turn comes from the Latin word *hostis*,
meaning an enemy. This hints at the potential double aspect of a
guest, as either welcome or unwelcome, or as changing from one
to the other. This notion of 'hostility', then, is like the repressed
unconscious of the word, and the process of deconstruction, in
revealing the unconscious of the text, might draw upon such disciplines as etymology in this way.

Another well-known definition of deconstructive reading is
Barbara Johnson's in *The Critical Difference* (Johns Hopkins University Press, 1980):

> Deconstruction is not synonymous with 'destruction'. It is in fact
> much closer to the original meaning of the word 'analysis', which
> etymologically means 'to undo' ... The deconstruction of a text
> does not proceed by random doubt or arbitrary subversion, but by
> the careful teasing out of warring forces of signification within the
> text.

> (Johnson, *The Critical Difference*, p. 5)

Derrida's own description of deconstructive reading has the same
purport. A deconstructive reading:

> must always aim at a certain relationship, unperceived by the
> writer, between what he commands and what he does not command
> of the patterns of language that he uses ... [It] attempts to make
> the not-seen accessible to sight.

> (*Of Grammatology*, pp. 158 and 163)

J. A. Cuddon, in his *Dictionary of Literary Terms* asserts that in
deconstruction:

a text can be read as saying something quite different from what it appears to be saying ... it may be read as carrying a plurality of significance or as saying many different things which are funda-mentally at variance with, contradictory to and subversive of what may be seen by criticism as a single 'stable' meaning. Thus a text may 'betray' itself.

(from the entry on Deconstruction)

So the deconstructionist practises what has been called textual harassment or oppositional reading, reading with the aim of unmasking internal contradictions or inconsistencies in the text, aiming to show the disunity which underlies its apparent unity. The aim of the 'New Critics' of the previous generation, by con-trast, had been precisely the opposite of this, to show the unity beneath apparent disunity. In pursuance of its aims, the decon-structive process will often fix on a detail of the text which looks incidental – the presence of a particular metaphor, for instance – and then use it as the key to the whole text, so that everything is read through it.

In talking about structuralism we discussed how structuralists look for such features in the text as parallels, echoes, reflections, and so on (p. 52). The effect of doing this is often to show a unity of purpose within the text, as if the text knows what it wants to do and has directed all its means towards this end. By contrast, the deconstructionist aims to show that the text is at war with itself: it is a house divided, and disunified. The deconstructionist looks for evidence of gaps, breaks, fissures and discontinuities of all kinds. So a diagram showing the differences between struc-turalism and post-structuralism at the practical level might look like this:

The structuralist seeks:	*The post-structuralist seeks:*
Parallels/Echoes	Contradictions/Paradoxes
Balances	Shifts/Breaks in: Tone
	Viewpoint
	Tense
	Time
	Person
	Attitude

Reflections/Repetitions	Conflicts
Symmetry	Absences/Omissions
Contrasts	Linguistic quirks
Patterns	Aporia
Effect: To show textual unity and coherence	*Effect: To show textual disunity*

In presenting the example, I will refer back to this list, and will also suggest a simple three-stage model of the deconstructive process. I will end with some questions to help you to try your own 'worked example'.

What post-structuralist critics do

1. They 'read the text against itself' so as to expose what might be thought of as the 'textual subconscious', where meanings are expressed which may be directly contrary to the surface meaning.

2. They fix upon the surface features of the words – similarities in sound, the root meanings of words, a 'dead' (or dying) metaphor and bring these to the foreground, so that they become crucial to the overall meaning.

3. They seek to show that the text is characterised by disunity rather than unity.

4. They concentrate on a single passage and analyse it so intensively that it becomes impossible to sustain a 'univocal' reading and the language explodes into 'multiplicities of meaning'.

5. They look for shifts and breaks of various kinds in the text and see these as evidence of what is repressed or glossed over or passsed over in silence by the text. These discontinuities are sometimes called 'fault-lines', a geological metaphor referring to the breaks in rock formations which give evidence of previous activity and movement.

Deconstruction – an example

I try here to give a clear example of deconstructive practice,

showing what is distinctive about it while at the same time suggesting it may not constitute a *complete* break with more familiar
forms of criticism.

The three stages of the deconstructive process described here
I have called the *verbal*, the *textual*, and the *linguistic*. They are
illustrated using Dylan Thomas's poem 'A refusal to mourn the
death, by fire, of a child in London' (Appendix 2).

The verbal stage is very similar to that of more conventional
forms of close reading, as pioneered in the 1920s and 1930s in
Empson's *Seven Types of Ambiguity*, and elsewhere. It involves
looking in the text for paradoxes and contradictions, at what
might be called the purely verbal level. For instance, the final line
of Thomas's poem reads 'After the first death there is no other'.
This statement contradicts and refutes itself: if something is
called the first then a sequence is implied of second, third, fourth,
and so on. So, the phrase 'the first death' clearly implies, at the
literal level, that there *will* be others. Internal contradictions of
this kind are indicative, for the deconstructionist, of language's
endemic unreliability and slipperiness, of which more will be said
later. There are other examples of this kind in the poem. Please
look again at the poem and see if you can identify others. You
might begin by considering the use of the word 'until' in combination with 'never'.

One other facet of post-structuralism relevant here is its tendency to reverse the polarity of common binary oppositions like
male and *female*, *day* and *night*, *light* and *dark*, and so on, so that
the second term, rather than the first, is 'privileged' and regarded
as the more desirable. Thus, in the poem it seems to be darkness,
rather than light, which is seen as engendering life, as the poet
talks of 'the mankind making / Bird beast and flower / Fathering and all humbling darkness'. This paradox reflects the way the
world of this poem is simultaneously a recognisable version of the
world we live in, and an inversion of that world. For the deconstructionist, again, such moments are symptomatic of the way language doesn't reflect or convey our world but constitutes a world
of its own, a kind of parallel universe or virtual reality. Identifying contradictory or paradoxical phrases like these, then, is the
first step in going against the grain of the poem, reading it 'against

itself', showing the 'signifiers' at war with the 'signified', and revealing its repressed unconscious. This first stage will always turn up useful material for use in the later stages.

The 'textual' stage of the method moves beyond individual phrases and takes a more overall view of the poem. At this second stage the critic is looking for shifts or breaks in the continuity of the poem: these shifts reveal instabilities of attitude, and hence the lack of a fixed and unified position. They can be of various kinds (as listed in the diagram given earlier); they may be shifts in focus, shifts in time, or tone, or point of view, or attitude, or pace, or vocabulary. They may well be indicated in the grammar, for instance, in a shift from first person to third, or past tense to present. Thus, they show paradox and contradiction on a larger scale than is the case with the first stage, taking a broad view of the text as a whole. In the case of the 'A refusal to mourn', for instance, there are major time shifts and changes in viewpoint, not a smooth chronological progression. Thus, the first two stanzas imagine the passing of geological aeons and the coming of the 'end of the world' – the last light breaks, the sea finally becomes still, the cycle which produces 'Bird beast and flower' comes to an end as 'all humbling darkness' descends. But the third stanza is centred on the present – the actual death of the child, 'The majesty and burning of the child's death'. The final stanza takes a broad vista like the first two, but it seems to centre on the historical progression of the recorded history of London, as witnessed by 'the unmourning water / Of the riding Thames'. Hence, no single wider context is provided to 'frame' and contextualise the death of the child in a defined perspective, and the shifts in Thomas's poem make it very difficult to ground his meaning at all.

Look again at the poem to see if you can detect other examples of this larger scale 'textual' level of breaks and discontinuities. Note that *omissions* are important here, that is, when a text doesn't tell us things we would expect to be told. You might begin by asking whether the poet tells us why he refuses to mourn, or rather, why the expressed intention of not doing so is not carried out.

The 'linguistic' stage, finally, involves looking for moments in the poem when the adequacy of language itself as a medium of communication is called into question. Such moments occur when, for example, there is implicit or explicit reference to the unreliability or untrustworthiness of language. It may involve, for instance, *saying* that something is unsayable; or saying that it is impossible to utter or describe something and then doing so; or saying that language inflates, or deflates, or misrepresents its object, and then continuing to use it anyway. In 'A refusal to mourn', for instance, the whole poem does what it says it *won't* do: the speaker professes his refusal to mourn, but the poem itself constitutes an act of mourning. Then in the third stanza the speaker says that he will not 'murder / The mankind of her going with a grave truth'. This condemns all the accepted ways of speaking about this event, and the poet professes to stand outside the available range of clichéd, elegiac stances or 'discursive practices', as if some 'pure' stance beyond these necessarily compromised forms of utterance were possible. Yet this is followed, not by silence, but by the solemn, quasi-liturgical pronouncements of the final stanza: 'Deep with the first dead lies London's daughter', the speaker proclaims, which sounds very like traditional panegyrical oratory, with the dead person transformed into some larger than life heroic figure, becoming 'London's daughter' (an impossible designation for her in life), 'robed' as for some great procession of the dead of all the ages, and now reunited with Mother Earth in the form of the London clay in which she is now buried.

In this poem, we might say, Thomas identifies the language trap, and then falls into it. Look again at the poem with this 'textual' level in mind. Are there other examples of Thomas's being forced to use the rhetorical strategies he has just exposed? You might start by looking at his use of the words 'mother' and 'daughter' and thinking about the nature of the metaphorical 'family' implied by these words. Other metaphorical constructs to look at are those entailed in the word 'murder' and in the notion of the 'unmourning' Thames.

Once the grain of the poem is opened up, then, it cannot long survive the deconstructive pressures brought to bear upon it, and reveals itself as fractured, contradictory, and symptomatic of a cultural and linguistic malaise. A three-step model like this will lend itself to applications to other material; it gives this approach something distinctive as a critical practice, and lays the strengths and weaknesses of deconstruction open to scrutiny, just as other methods are open. The deconstructive reading, then, aims to produce *dis*unity, to show that what had looked like unity and coherence actually contains contradictions and conflicts which the text cannot stabilise and contain. We might characterise it as waking up the sleeping dogs of signification and setting them on each other. In contrast, more conventional styles of close reading had the opposite aim: they would take a text which appeared fragmented and disunified and demonstrate an underlying unity, aiming to separate the warring dogs and soothe them back to sleep with suitable blandishments. Yet the two methods, far apart though they would see themselves as being, suffer from exactly the same drawback, which is that both tend to make all poems seem similar. The close reader detects miracles of poised ambiguity alike in Donne's complex metaphysical lyrics, and simple poems like Robert Frost's 'Stopping by woods on a snowy evening', which receive the full-scale explicatory treatment of the ten- or twenty-page article, so that the experience of reading them loses all its particularity. Similarly, after the deconstructionist treatment all poems tend to emerge as angst-ridden, fissured enactments of linguistic and other forms of indeterminacy.

I'll comment further on some of the characteristics listed on the post-structuralist side of the diagram on page 72, using as an example 'The castaway' (Appendix 3), a well-known poem by the eighteenth-century poet William Cowper. As all critics recognise, this poem works at two levels: on the 'surface' it is an account of the death of a man washed overboard from a ship, who speaks in the poem in his own voice and laments his fate. At a 'deeper' level the poem is about Cowper's own fear of and isolation within his incipient mental breakdown.

For the deconstructionist, firstly, exposing contradictions or paradoxes might involve showing that the feelings *professed* in a poem can be at odds with those *expressed*. For instance, in 'The castaway' (p.224) the speaker *says* that he does not blame his ship-mates for his plight, but even saying this raises the possibility that

he does. Thus, at one point he says that his friends did all they
could to save him, but elsewhere he implies that they desert him
and hurry off to save themselves. Look again at the poem to identify the points where these inferences might be drawn.

Secondly, pointing to breaks, gaps, fissures, discontinuities is a
way of implying that the text lacks unity and consistency of purpose. There may, for instance, be changes in tone, or perspective,
or point of view. In 'The castaway', for instance, the text sometimes uses 'I' and sometimes 'he' for the man lost overboard:
('such a destin'd wretch as I' but '*His* floating home for ever left'
– my italics). Look again at the poem and see if you can identify
other examples of this. As I have already indicated, at one level
it is an imaginative retelling of the death of a sailor lost overboard
during one of the expeditions of the explorer George Anson,
based on the account of the incident in Anson's published journals. At another level this is merely a metaphor for the isolation
and depression felt by Cowper himself. But the relationship
between these two levels is very 'unsettled': for instance, all the
specific details about Anson and his expedition distract from the
generalised notion of loss, abandonment, and isolation, and we
shift erratically from one to the other.

Thirdly, the 'linguistic quirks' which seem relevant include
several kinds of linguistic oddity or *non sequitur* of the kind which
undermine secure meanings. There are many of these in 'The
castaway'. In the final stanza the poet says that no divine assis-
tance came when '*We* perished, each alone' – my italics – but the
poem has shown the death of only one person. On the other hand,
if the statement is a general one about how we all have to face
death alone, then we would expect the present tense rather than
the past ('We perish' rather than 'We perish'd').

The term 'aporia', finally, is a popular one in deconstructive
criticism. It literally means an *impasse*, and designates a kind of
knot in the text which cannot be unravelled or solved because
what is said is self-contradictory. It perhaps corresponds, therefore, to what the British critic William Empson, in his book *Seven
Types of Ambiguity* (1930) designated as the seventh type of verbal
difficulty in literature, namely that which occurs when 'there is
an irreconcilable conflict of meaning within the text'. For

instance, at the start of the third stanza we are told of the drowned man that 'No poet wept him', but the existence of the poem we are reading contradicts this. There seems to be no way out of this 'bind'. It is often said that Roland Barthes's 1968 essay 'The Death of the Author' marks the transition from structuralism to post-structuralism, and in that essay Barthes says that in the text 'everything must be disentangled, nothing deciphered'. The aporia, though, is a textual knot which resists disentanglement, and several of the elements discussed above as contradictions, paradoxes, or shifts might equally be classified under the more general heading of aporia.

While it is easy to see why this process might be called reading against the grain, it is misleading to suggest that the poem has an obvious 'grain' or overt meaning which the critic has merely to routinely counteract. Reading this poem will also have shown, I hope, that structuralist and post-structuralist reading practices are much at odds with each other: identifying patterns and symmetries in the structuralist manner discovers a unified text which is, so to speak, happy with itself, whereas 'reading the text against itself' produces a sense of disunity, of a text engaged in a civil war with itself.

Selected reading

Barthes, Roland, *The Pleasure of the Text* trans. R. Miller (Hill & Wang, 1975).

This book represents the 'playful' side of Barthes: it is brief, enigmatic, and entertaining.

Derrida, Jacques, 'Structure, Sign and Play in the Discourse of the Human Sciences', reprinted in abbreviated form in K. M. Newton's *Twentieth Century Literary Theory: A Reader* (Macmillan, 1988).

Derrida, Jacques, 'The exorbitant. question of method', pp. 157–64 in *Of Grammatology*, translated by Gayatri Chakravorty Spivak (Johns Hopkins University Press, 1976).

Derrida, Jacques, 'The purveyor of Truth', pp. 173–212 in *The Purloined Poe: Lacan, Derrida, and Psychoanalytic reading* ed. John P. Muller and William J. Richardson (Johns Hopkins University Press, 1988).

This essay is Derrida's response, fully introduced within the volume, to Lacan's reading of Poe's story 'The Purloined Letter'. This and the two previous items constitute suggested initial reading of Derrida.

Derrida, Jacques, *A Derrida Reader: Between the Blinds* ed. Peggy Kamuf (Harvester, 1991).

An 'assisted introduction' – a substantial selection of Derrida's essays, each with its individual introduction. A very useful book for sustained engagement with Derrida.

Jefferson, Ann & Robey, David eds, *Modern Literary Theory: A Comparative Introduction* (Batsford, 2nd edn, 1986).

See chapter four, 'Structuralism and post-structuralism'.

Norris, Christopher, *Deconstruction: Theory and Practice* (Routledge, 2nd edn, 1991).

A standard introductory account.

Norris, Christopher, *Derrida* (Fontana, 1987).

A brief guide ...

Sarup, Madan, *An Introductory Guide to Post-structuralism and Postmodernism* (Harvester, 1988).

Expanded and updated in 1993. See the chapter 'Derrida and Deconstruction'.

4

Postmodernism

What is postmodernism? What was modernism?

As with structuralism and post-structuralism, there is a great deal of debate about how exactly modernism and postmodernism differ. The two concepts are of different vintage, 'Modernism' being a long-standing category which is of crucial importance in the understanding of twentieth-century culture, whereas the term 'postmodernism', as is well known, has only become current since the 1980s. 'Modernism' is the name given to the movement which dominated the arts and culture of the first half of the twentieth century. Modernism was that earthquake in the arts which brought down much of the structure of pre-twentieth-century practice in music, painting, literature, and architecture. One of the major epicentres of this earthquake seems to have been Vienna, during the period of 1890–1910, but the effects were felt in France, Germany, Italy and eventually even in Britain, in art movements like Cubism, Dadaism, Surrealism, and Futurism. Its after-shocks are still being felt today, and many of the structures it toppled have never been rebuilt. Without an understanding of modernism, then, it is impossible to understand twentieth-century culture.

In all the arts touched by modernism what had been the most fundamental elements of practice were challenged and rejected: thus, melody and harmony were put aside in music; perspective and direct pictorial representation were abandoned in painting, in favour of degrees of abstraction; in architecture traditional forms and materials (pitched roofs, domes and columns, wood, stone, and bricks) were rejected in favour of plain geometrical forms, often executed in new materials like plate glass and concrete. In literature, finally, there was a rejection of traditional realism (chronological plots, continuous narratives relayed by omniscient narrators, 'closed endings', etc.) in favour of experimental forms of various kinds.

The period of high modernism was the twenty years from 1910 to 1930 and some of the literary 'high priests' of the movement (writing in English) were T. S. Eliot, James Joyce, Ezra Pound, Wyndham Lewis, Virginia Woolf, Wallace Stevens, and Gertrude Stein, and (writing in French or German) Marcel Proust, Stéphane Mallarmé, André Gide, Franz Kafka, and Rainer Maria Rilke. Some of the important characteristics of the literary modernism practised by these writers include the following:

1. A new emphasis on impressionism and subjectivity, that is, on *how* we see rather than *what* we see (a preoccupation evident in the use of the stream-of-consciousness technique).
2. A movement (in novels) away from the apparent objectivity provided by such features as: omniscient external narration, fixed narrative points of view and clear-cut moral positions.
3. A blurring of the distinctions between genres, so that novels tend to become more lyrical and poetic, for instance, and poems more documentary and prose-like.
4. A new liking for fragmented forms, discontinuous narrative, and random-seeming collages of disparate materials.
5. A tendency towards 'reflexivity', so that poems, plays and novels raise issues concerning their own nature, status, and role.

The overall result of these shifts is to produce a literature which seems dedicated to experimentation and innovation. After its high point, modernism seemed to retreat considerably in the 1930s, partly, no doubt, because of the tensions generated in a decade of political and economic crisis, but a resurgence took place in the 1960s (a decade which has interesting points of similarity with the 1920s, when modernism was at its height). However, modernism never regained the pre-eminence it had enjoyed in the earlier period.

This gives us a rough indication of what and when modernism was. Does postmodernism, then, continue it or oppose it? To decide this we need to attempt a working definition of this second term. As a starting-point, we can take a selection of the most readily available descriptions of postmodernism. J. A. Cuddon's entry in his *Dictionary of Literary Terms and Literary Theory* describes postmodernism as characterised by 'an eclectic approach, [by a liking for] aleatory writing, [and for] parody and pastiche'. So far, this doesn't really put much daylight between modernism and postmodernism, since the word 'eclectic' suggests the use of the fragmented forms which, as we have just said, are characteristic of modernism. (Eliot's *The Waste Land*, for instance, is a collage of juxtaposed, incomplete stories, or fragments of stories.) Also 'aleatory forms', meaning those which incorporate an element of randomness or chance, were important to the Dadaists of 1917, who, for instance, made poems from sentences plucked randomly from newspapers. The use of parody and pastiche, finally, is clearly related to the abandonment of the divine pretensions of authorship implicit in the omniscient narratorial stance, and this too was a vital element in modernism. It could be said, then, that one way of establishing the distinction between modernism and postmodernism is to dissolve the sequential link between them, by retrospectively redefining certain aspects of modernism as postmodernist. According to this view, they are not two successive stages in the history of the arts, but two opposed moods or attitudes, differing, as suggested in the next paragraph.

The nature of the distinction between modernism and postmodernism is summarised in the excellent joint entry on the two terms in Jeremy Hawthorn's *Concise Glossary of Contemporary Literary Theory* (Edward Arnold, 1992). Both, he says, give great prominence to fragmentation as a feature of twentieth-century art and culture, but they do so in very different moods. The modernist features it in such a way as to register a deep nostalgia for an earlier age when faith was full and authority intact. Ezra Pound, for instance, calls his major work, *The Cantos*, a 'rag-bag', implying that this is all that is possible in the modern age, but also implying regret about that fact. In his poem 'Hugh Selwyn

Mauberley' he speaks of the First World War being fought 'For two gross of broken statues, For a few thousand battered books', and is evidently pained, in lines from the same poem like 'a tawdry cheapness / Shall outlast our days ' and 'We see *to kalon* [beauty] / Decreed in the market place' by the rise of commercialism at the expense of 'eternal verities'. In *The Waste Land*, too, the persona says, as if despairingly of the poem, 'These fragments I have shored against my ruins'. In instances like this there is a tone of lament, pessimism, and despair about the world which finds its appropriate representation in these 'fractured' art forms (the collages of Kurt Switters, for example, which mix painted areas of canvas with random clippings from newspapers, timetables, and advertisements). For the postmodernist, by contrast, fragmentation is an exhilarating, liberating phenomenon, symptomatic of our escape from the claustrophobic embrace of fixed systems of belief. In a word, the modernist laments fragmentation while the postmodernist celebrates it.

A second, and related, difference between the two is also a matter of tone or attitude. An important aspect of modernism was a fierce asceticism which found the over-elaborate art forms of the nineteenth century deeply offensive and repulsive. This asceticism has one of its most characteristic and striking manifestations in the pronouncements of modernist architects, such as Adolf Loos's proclamation that 'decoration is a crime', or Miës van der Rohe's that 'less is more', or Le Corbusier's that 'a house is a machine for living in'. These pronouncements resulted in the 'shoe box' and 'carbuncle' buildings which have generated such hatred and opposition, particularly through the 1980s, but the high idealism they represent retains its power to move. The same refined asceticism is seen in literature in the minimalism which (for instance) shrinks poems to narrow columns of two-word lines registering rigorously sparse, pared-down observations, or in the drama of Samuel Beckett, in which a play may be reduced to a running time of thirteen minutes, with a single speaker, no set, and language which is sparse in the extreme. By contrast, again, postmodernism rejects the distinction between 'high' and 'popular' art which was important in modernism, and believes in excess, in gaudiness, and in 'bad taste' mixtures of qualities. It disdains the modernist asceticism as elitist and cheerfully mixes, in the same building, bits and pieces from different architectural periods – a mock-Georgian pediment here, a tongue-in-cheek classical portico there. A similar postmodernist 'edifice' in literature would be the 'Martian' poetry of writers like Craig Raine or Christopher Reid, where bizarrely colourful mixtures of imagery, viewpoint, and vocabulary jostle on a surface which seems happy to be nothing *but* surface, without the depths of significance which a literary education trains us to seek out. Nothing could be further in spirit from that austere modernist asceticism.

'Landmarks' in postmodernism – Habermas, Lyotard and Baudrillard

A major 'moment' in the history of postmodernism is the influential paper 'Modernity – an Incomplete Project' delivered by the contemporary German theorist Jürgen Habermas in 1980. For Habermas the modern period begins with the Enlightenment, that period of about one hundred years, from the mid-seventeenth to the mid- eighteenth century, when a new faith arose in the power of reason to improve human society. Such ideas are expressed or embodied in the philosophy of Kant in Germany, Voltaire and Diderot in France, and Locke and Hume in Britain. In Britain the term 'The Age of Reason' was used (till recently) to designate the same period. The so-called Enlightenment 'project' is the fostering of this belief that a break with tradition, blind habit, and slavish obedience to religious precepts and prohibitions, coupled with the application of reason and logic by the disinterested individual can bring about a solution to the problems of society. This outlook is what Habermas means by 'modernity'. The French Revolution can be seen as a first attempt to test this theory in practice. For Habermas this faith in reason and the possibility of progress survived into the twentieth century, and even survives the catalogue of disasters which makes up this century's history. The cultural movement known as modernism subscribed to this 'project', in the sense that it constituted a lament for a lost sense of purpose, a lost coherence, a lost system of values. For Habermas, the French post-structuralist thinkers of the 1970s, such as

Derrida and Foucault, represented a specific repudiation of this kind of Enlightenment 'modernity'. They attacked, in his view, the ideals of reason, clarity, truth, and progress, and as they were thereby detached from the quest for justice, he identified them as 'young conservatives'.

The term 'postmodernism' was used in the 1930s, but its current sense and vogue can be said to have begun with Jean-François Lyotard's *The Postmodern Condition: A Report on Knowledge* (Manchester University Press, 1979). Lyotard's essay 'Answering the Question: What is Postmodernism?', first published in 1982, added in 1984 as an appendix to *The Postmodern Condition* and included in Brooker's *Modernism/Postmodernism, 1992*, takes up this debate about the Enlightenment, mainly targeting Habermas, in a slightly oblique manner. Lyotard opens with a move which effectively turns the debate into a struggle to demonstrate that one's opponents are the real conservatives (a familiar 'bottom line' of polemical writing on culture). From every direction', he says, 'we are being urged to put an end to experimentation', and after citing several other instances he writes (obviously of Habermas):

> I have read a thinker of repute who defends modernity against those he calls the neo-conservatives. Under the banner of postmodernism, the latter would like, he believes, to get rid of the uncompleted project of modernism, that of the Enlightenment.
>
> (Brooker, p. 141)

Habermas's is simply one voice in a chorus which is calling for an end to 'artistic experimentation' and for 'order ... unity, for identity, for security' (Brooker, p. 142). In a word, these voices want 'to liquidate the heritage of the avant-gardes'. For Lyotard the Enlightenment whose project Habermas wishes to continue is simply one of the would-be authoritative 'overarching', 'totalising' explanations of things – like Christianity, Marxism, or the myth of scientific progress. These 'metanarratives' ['super-narratives'], which purport to explain and reassure are really illusions, fostered in order to smother difference, opposition, and plurality. Hence Lyotard's famous definition of postmodernism, that it is, simply, 'incredulity towards metanarratives'. 'Grand Narratives' of progress and human perfectability, then, are no longer tenable, and the best we can hope for is a series of 'mininarratives', which are provisional, contingent, temporary, and relative and which provide a basis for the actions of specific groups in particular local circumstances. Postmodernity thus 'deconstructs' the basic aim of the Enlightenment, that is 'the idea of a unitary end of history and of a subject'.

Another major theorist of postmodernism is the contemporary French writer Jean Baudrillard, whose book *Simulations* (1981, translated 1983) marks his entry into this field. Baudrillard is associated with what is usually known as 'the loss of the real', which is the view that in contemporary life the pervasive influence of images from film, TV, and advertising has led to a loss of the distinction between real and imagined, reality and illusion, surface and depth. The result is a culture of 'hyperreality', in which distinctions between these are eroded. His propositions are worked out in his essay 'Simulacra and Simulations' reprinted in abridged form in Brooker, 1992. He begins by evoking a past era of 'fullness', when a sign was a surface indication of an underlying depth or reality ('an outward sign of inward grace', to cite the words of the Roman Catholic Catechism). But what, he asks, if a sign is not an index of an underlying reality, but merely of other signs? Then the whole system becomes what he calls a *simulacrum*. He then substitutes for *representation* the notion of *simulation*. The sign reaches its present stage of emptiness in a series of steps, which I will try to illustrate by comparing them to different kinds of paintings.

Firstly, then, the sign represents a basic reality: let's take as an example of this the representations of the industrial city of Salford in the work of the twentieth-century British artist L. S. Lowry. Mid-century life for working people in such a place was hard, and the paintings have an air of monotony and repetitiveness – cowed, stick-like figures fill the streets, colours are muted, and the horizon filled with grim factory-like buildings. As signs, then, Lowry's paintings seem to represent the basic reality of the place they depict.

The *second* stage for the sign is that it misrepresents or distorts the reality behind it. As an example of this let's take the glamourised representations of cities like Liverpool and Hull in the paintings of the Victorian artist Atkinson Grimshaw. These paintings show the cities at night, wet pavements reflecting the bright lights of dockside shops, the moon emerging from behind clouds, and a forest of ships' masts silhouetted against the sky. Life in these places at that time was presumably grim, too, but the paintings offer a romantic and glamourised image, so the sign can be said to misrepresent what it shows.

The *third* stage for the sign is when the sign disguises the fact that there is no corresponding reality underneath. To illustrate this, take a device used in the work of the surrealist artist René Magritte, where, in the painting, an easel with a painter's canvas on it is shown standing alongside a window: on the canvas in the painting is painted the exterior scene which we can see through the window. But what is shown beyond the window is not reality, against which the painting within the painting can be judged, but simply another sign, another depiction, which has no more authority or reality than the painting within the painting (which is actually a representation of a representation).

The *fourth* and last stage for the sign is that it bears no relation to any reality at all. As an illustration of this stage we have simply to imagine a completely abstract painting, which is not representional at all, like one of the great purple mood canvases of Mark Rothko, for instance. I should emphasise that I'm not suggesting that these four paintings are examples of the four stages of the sign, merely that the four stages can be thought of as analogous to the four different ways in which these paintings signify or represent things.

The first two of these stages are fairly clear, the second two perhaps less so. Baudrillard's own example of the third stage (when the sign hides an absence) is Disneyland. In one way, of course, it is a sign of the second type, a mythologised misrepresentation of the United States:

> All its [the USA's] values are exalted here, in miniature and comic-strip form. Embalmed and pacified ... digest of the American way of life, panegyric to American values, idealised transposition of a contradictory reality.
>
> (Brooker, *Modernism/ Postmodernism*, p. 154)

But Disneyland is actually a 'third-order simulation' (a sign which conceals an absence):

> Disneyland is there to conceal the fact that it is the 'real' country, all of 'real' America, which *is* Disneyland (just as prisons are there to conceal the fact that it is the social in its entirety, in its banal omnipresence, which is carceral. Disneyland is presented as imaginary in order to make us believe that the rest is real.

In a word, Disneyland has the effect of 'concealing the fact that the real is no longer real, and thus of saving the reality principle'. Within postmodernism, the distinction between what is real and what is simulated collapses: *everything* is a model or an image, all is surface without depth; this is the *hyperreal*, as Baudrillard calls it.

The grand sweep of this kind of rhetoric has a strong appeal. One might see it as a kind of latter-day Platonism, its devotees enjoying the mystical insight that what is normally taken as a solid and real world is actually just a tissue of dreamlike images. If this second aspect of the postmodern condition, this loss of the real, is accepted as a fact, then it is hard to see a ground for literary theory to occupy, since all methods of literary interpretation – Marxist, feminist, structuralist, and so on – depend upon the making of a distinction between surface and depth, between what is *seen* in the text and some *underlying* meaning. Once we accept that what we see is all we get, then there is, clearly, very little which a literary critic or theorist can claim to be doing.

More generally, for postmodernism there are certain ever-present questions and provisos. In this extreme Baudrillardian form, the 'loss of the real' may seem to legitimise a callous indifference to suffering. In a now notorious pronouncement Baudrillard maintained that the Gulf War never happened, that what 'really' took place was a kind of televisual virtual reality. (See the book by Christopher Norris in the Selected reading section.) Likewise, if we accept the 'loss of the real' and the collapsing of reality and simulation into a kind of virtual reality, then what of the Holocaust? Could this, too, be part of the reality 'lost' in the image networks? In other words, without a belief in some of the concepts which postmodernism undercuts – history, reality, and truth, for instance – we may well find ourselves in some pretty repulsive company.

STOP and THINK

The crucial category in Baudrillard's four-stage model is the third one, the sign which conceals an absence, which conceals the fact that the supposedly 'real' which it represents is no longer there, that beyond the play of surfaces there is nothing else.

It is not easy to achieve a precise understanding of this concept. It may help in doing so if you try to think of examples other than Disneyland. The idealised images of masculinity or femininity presented in advertisements, for instance, may be helpful: these also are copies or representations for which no original exists – no actual people are quite like these, though people might strive to become like them. In this way the image tends to become the reality, and the two tend to become indistinguishable.

Further, if we agree that the real has indeed been lost then we need to decide how we react to this fact. If we are to revel in the boundary-free zone which results, we will need to be sure that the 'real' is a concept we can do without. Perhaps recent events suggest otherwise. In the television coverage of the Gulf War we saw computer-image film of high-tech 'smart' weapons homing in on Iraqi targets, while the commentary spoke of 'surgical strikes' which could 'take out' key enemy installations. News bulletins also included footage of pilots who spoke of what they were doing in the same 'unreal' terms, using the terminology of video combat games, for instance. Perhaps these things are symptomatic of what can happen when the category of the real is eroded. Likewise, could we condemn the Holocaust without the category of the real, or campaign against (say) racial discrimination or environmental pollution?

What postmodernist critics do

1. They discover postmodernist themes, tendencies, and attitudes within literary works of the twentieth century and explore their implications.
2. They foreground fiction which might be said to exemplify the notion of the 'disappearance of the real', in which shifting postmodern identities are seen, for example, in the mixing of literary genres (the thriller, the detective story, the myth saga, and the realist psychological novel, etc.).
3. They foreground what might be called 'intertextual elements' in literature, such as parody, pastiche, and allusion, in all of which there is a major degree of reference between one text and another, rather than between the text and a safely external reality.
4. They foreground irony, in the sense described by Umberto Eco, that whereas the modernist tries to destroy the past, the postmodernist realises that the past must be revisited, but 'with irony' (*Modernism/Postmodernism* ed. Peter Brooker, p. 227.
5. They foreground the element of 'narcissism' in narrative technique, that is, where novels focus on and debate their own ends and processes, and thereby 'de-naturalise' their content.
6. They challenge the distinction between high and low culture, and highlight texts which work as hybrid blends of the two.

Postmodernist criticism: an example

A useful example of postmodernist criticism, which makes a straightforward application of ideas derived from Lyotard, is Jeffrey Nealon's 'Samuel Beckett and the Postmodern: Language games, Play, and *Waiting for Godot*' (reprinted in the Macmillan 'New Casebook' on *Waiting for Godot* and *Endgame* ed. Steven

Connor, 1992). This mainly shows the first of the six postmodernist critical activities listed above, but also has elements of the
second, in the sense that the notion of language as a self-contained
system relates closely to Lyotard's idea of the 'disappearance of
the real'. Nealon first explains the notion of 'language games',
derived from Wittgenstein, whereby when we claim that something is true we are not measuring it against some external
absolute standard, but by internal rules and criteria which operate only within that designated sphere and have no 'transcendent'
status beyond that. These have a restricted applicability, just like
the rules which govern moves in a game. Thus, *Knight to King's
Rook Four* might be a winning move in a chess game, but would
carry no weight at all in a game of football, say, or an argument
about who should do the washing-up. Likewise, the 'move' in a
philosophical discussion which establishes a proposition as true or
valid has its validity only within the 'language game' of philosophy. For Nealon, Vladimir and Estragon in Beckett's play, *Waiting for Godot*, engage in 'language games' of this type, but without
realising their full significance. Actually, such language games,
the postmodernists agree, are all we have; there is no transcendent reality behind them and they are actually self-validating, and
provide us with the social identity we seek. But Vladimir and
Estragon hanker for some deeper or 'transcendent' reality over
and above this. Thus, says Nealon, 'it is the play of Vladimir and
Estragon's words, not any agreed-upon meaning for them, which
constitutes their social bond. Waiting for legitimation of their
society in Godot is, from the beginning, unnecessary'.

Vladimir and Estragon, then, have difficulty in accepting this
postmodern view that 'gaming' is enough (*Just Gaming* is the title
of one of Lyotard's books): they wish to have the security provided by some 'Grand Narrative' of guarantee and absolute validation. This desired comprehensive reassurance is linked in the
play with Christian notions of redemption, which 'recuperate'
(meaning, roughly, explain and give significance to) the apparently meaningless details and trials of daily life. ('Offer it up', my
Catholic teachers would say in response to any minor complaint
about unfairness or injustice.) Vladimir and Estragon, then, are
trapped at the 'modernist' stage, and hence riven with nostalgia

for the lost wholeness of the past. For Nealon, the kind of legit-imating discourse which Vladimir and Estragon seek is parodied in Lucky's 'think' near the end of the first act. This is a parody of the 'totalising' 'metadiscourse' of philosophy and religion, a practical demonstration of the 'language game of truth' which is all that is available to us. It is, says Nealon, a narrative that disrupts and deconstructs all notions of universal, ahistorical, consistent metanarrative – *all* Godots. Had Godot turned up, the implication is, what could he have offered but pious and pedantic gibberish of this kind?

Lucky has perceived this, hence his exuberant and joyous parody, but the others resist it, so his speech is met with violence. The modernist, that is, wishes to go on believing in the toppled gods and Godots. Vladimir and Estragon, for Nealon, are, throughout the play, on the verge of a 'deconstructive break-through'. When they forget about Godot they are happy and inventive in their language games, revelling, we might say, in the openness and uncertainties of 'the postmodernist condition'. But repeatedly they come back to Godot, and the supposed restraints and imperatives he places upon them. 'Let's go far away from here', Vladimir proposes at one point, to which the response is 'We can't … We have to come back tomorrow … To wait for Godot'. We might characterise this view by saying that Vladimir and Estragon prove themselves in the end to have a modernist attitude to the fragmentation of truths and values which we have seen in the twentieth century. They long for a return to the lost fullness of purpose of the past, so their experience of fragmentation is nostalgic and angst-ridden. At times they seem on the verge of making a transition (or 'breakthrough', as Nealon calls it) to a postmodern attitude, in which fragmentation becomes a condition welcomed and enjoyed, but in the end they fail to do this.

The modernist/postmodernist dichotomy that underpins this reading could be applied to many other works. Are there any which stand out in your mind? Waiting, for instance, seems to be an important activity in twentieth-century drama, notably in the plays of Harold Pinter – *The Dumb Waiter* would be a very obvious example. You might like to consider the value or otherwise of using the ideas of postmodernism in the explication of any of his plays with which you are familiar. Another 'waiting' play on which a very similar reading might be attempted is Anton Chekhov's *The Three Sisters* (1901), in which the sisters of the title, Olga, Masha, and Irina, are stranded in lives of bourgeois respectability in northern Russia, twenty-three hours by train from the next town of any size (see Michael Frayn's introduction to the Methuen edition of Chekhov's plays). The sisters wait in vain – like Vladimir and Estragon – for some external force to enter their provincial lives and transform them, and the ideals for which each pines can be seen as personal 'metanarratives', such as an ideal of social progress, or the notion that their sufferings will in some way contribute to a better human life in the future. Irina, for instance, says near the end of the play that 'A time will come when people will understand what it was all for, what the purpose was of all this suffering, and what was hidden from us will be hidden no more'. For the sisters, too, the actually self-sufficient reality of their condition is provided by the language games they play endlessly, and the image of the capital city of Moscow, a glittering amalgam of memory and desire, which constitutes for them a kind of hyperreality or simulacrum.

Selected reading

Benjamin, Andrew, ed. *The Lyotard Reader* (Blackwell, 1989).
A very useful source.

Brooker, Peter, ed. *Modernism/Postmodernism* (Longman, 1992).
A general reader on the topic to examine alongside Docherty's and Waugh's. I find the introduction makes heavy going of the modernism/postmodernism distinction, but this is a compact collection of the key items by Habermas, Lyotard, Baudrillard, Jameson, Eco, Hutcheon, etc., as well as earlier material.

Connor, Steven, *Postmodernist Culture: An Introduction to Theories of the Contemporary* (Blackwell, 1989).
Connor's has been an important voice in this field, stating issues and dilemmas with clarity and force.

Docherty, Thomas, ed. *Postmodernism: A Reader* (Harvester, 1992).
Monumental. The rival reader to Waugh's. A very useful collection of material, with sub-sections, each with its own introduction, but I

prefer Waugh for its overall clarity and convenience.

Norris, Christopher, *Uncritical Theory: Postmodernism, Intellectuals and the Gulf War* (Lawrence & Wishart, 1992).

A difficult but timely 'exposé of some postmodernist excesses.

Sarup, Madan, *An Introductory Guide to Post-Structuralism and Postmodernism* (Harvester, 2nd edn, 1993).

A helpful section on postmodernism, including Lyotard and Baudrillard, and considerations of selected postmodernist 'cultural practices' such as video and architecture.

Waugh, Patricia, ed. *Postmodernism: A Reader* (Arnold, 1992).

A valuable collection of material, which includes relevant American essays (such as Susan Sontag's seminal 'Against Interpretation') which pre-date the general use of the term 'postmodern' – as well as key pieces by Lyotard, Baudrillard, and Habermas: also essays from the Marxist debate on postmodernism between Jameson and Eagleton, where postmodernism is reluctantly accepted as the inevitable 'cultural logic of late capitalism'. Essays too from prominent theorists of postmodernism like Linda Hutcheon and Brian McHale.

5
Psychoanalytic criticism

Introduction

Psychoanalytic criticism is a form of literary criticism which uses some of the techniques of psychoanalysis in the interpretation of literature. Psychoanalysis itself is a form of therapy which aims to cure mental disorders 'by investigating the interaction of conscious and unconscious elements in the mind' (as the *Concise Oxford Dictionary* puts it). The classic method of doing this is to get the patient to talk freely, in such a way that the repressed fears and conflicts which are causing the problems are brought into the conscious mind and openly faced, rather than remaining 'buried' in the unconscious. This practice is based upon specific theories of how the mind, the instincts, and sexuality work. These theories were developed by the Austrian, Sigmund Freud (1856–1939). There is a growing consensus today that the therapeutic value of the method is limited, and that Freud's life-work is seriously flawed by methodological irregularities. All the same, Freud remains a major cultural force, and his impact on how we think about ourselves has been incalculable.

Freud's major ideas include those italicised in the next three paragraphs. All of Freud's work depends upon the notion of the *unconscious*, which is the part of the mind beyond consciousness which nevertheless has a strong influence upon our actions. Freud was not the discoverer of the unconscious: his uniqueness lies in his attributing to it such a decisive role in our lives. Linked with this is the idea of *repression*, which is the 'forgetting' or ignoring of unresolved conflicts, unadmitted desires, or traumatic past events, so that they are forced out of conscious awareness and into the realm of the unconscious. A similar process is that of *sublimation*, whereby the repressed material is 'promoted' into something grander or is disguised as something 'noble'. For instance, sexual urges may be given sublimated expression in the form of intense religious experiences or longings. Later in his career Freud suggested a three-part, rather than a two-part, model of the psyche, dividing it into the *ego*, the *super-ego*, and the *id*, these three 'levels' of the personality roughly corresponding to, respectively, the consciousness, the conscience, and the unconscious.

Many of Freud's ideas concern aspects of sexuality. *Infantile sexuality*, for instance, is the notion that sexuality begins not at puberty, with physical maturing, but in infancy, especially through the infant's relationship with the mother. Connected with this is the *Oedipus complex*, whereby, says Freud, the male infant conceives the desire to eliminate the father and become the sexual partner of the mother. Many forms of inter-generational conflict are seen by Freudians as having Oedipal overtones, such as professional rivalries, often viewed in Freudian terms as reproducing the competition between siblings for parental favour. (As the very idea of the Oedipal complex would suggest, Freudian theory is often deeply masculinist in bias.) Another key idea is that of the *libido*, which is the energy drive associated with sexual desire. In classic Freudian theory it has three stages of focus, the *oral*, the *anal*, and the *phallic*. The libido in the individual is part of a more generalised drive which the later Freud called *Eros* (the Greek word for 'love') which roughly means the life instinct, the opposite of which is *Thanatos* (the Greek word for 'death') which roughly means the death instinct, a controversial notion, of course.

Several key terms concern what might be called psychic processes, such as *transference*, the phenomenon whereby the patient under analysis redirects the emotions recalled in analysis towards the psychoanalyst: thus, the antagonism or resentment felt towards a parental figure in the past might be reactivated, but directed against the analyst. Another such mechanism is *projection*, when aspects of ourselves (usually negative ones) are not recognised as part of ourselves but are perceived in or attributed to another; our own desires or antagonisms, for instance, may be 'disowned' in this way. Both these might be seen as *defence mechanisms*, that is, as psychic procedures for avoiding painful admissions or recognitions. Another such is the *screen memory*, which is a trivial or inconsequential memory whose function is to obliterate a more significant one. A well-known example of these mechanisms is the *Freudian slip*, which Freud himself called the 'parapraxis', whereby repressed material in the unconscious finds an outlet through such everyday phenomena as slips of the tongue, slips of the pen, or unintended actions.

A final example of important Freudian terminology is the *dream work*, the process by which real events or desires are transformed into dream images. These include: *displacement*, whereby one person or event is represented by another which is in some way linked or associated with it, perhaps because of a similar-sounding word, or by some form of symbolic substitution; and *condensation*, whereby a number of people, events, or meanings are combined and represented by a single image in the dream. Thus, characters, motivation, and events are represented in dreams in a very 'literary' way, involving the translation, by the dream work, of abstract ideas or feelings into concrete images. Dreams, just like literature, do not usually make explicit statements. Both tend to communicate obliquely or indirectly, avoiding direct or open statement, and representing meanings through concrete embodiments of time, place, or person.

How Freudian interpretation works

Freudian interpretation is popularly thought to be a matter of attributing sexual connotations to objects, so that towers and ladders, for instance, are seen as phallic symbols. This kind of thing had become a joke even in Freud's own lifetime, and we should remember that he once said, 'Sometimes a cigar is just a cigar'. (Freud was a heavy cigar smoker, mind you, so he had a vested interest in saying that.) In reality, Freudian interpretation is often highly ingenious, rather than highly simplistic. For example, let's

imagine how a dream featuring a Roman soldier might be interpreted. Freud believes that a dream is an escape-hatch or safety-
valve through which repressed desires, fears, or memories seek an
outlet into the conscious mind. The emotion in question is cen-
sored by the conscious mind and so has to enter the dream in disguise, like a person barred from a club who gets in by dressing
up as somebody else. The Roman soldier might be connected
with the real subject of the dream by a chain of associations. Let's
say that the dreamer is a young adult still under the thumb of an
authoritarian father but wanting to break away from his influence,
and experience adult life to the full. The Roman soldier might
represent the father by a process of *association:* the father is associated with ideas of strictness, authority, and power in the domestic sphere; the Roman soldier is linked to the same things in the
political sphere; so the one is substituted for the other. So the soldier in the dream is a symbolic representation of the father.

But several meanings might be condensed into this symbol.
Suppose the dreamer is tempted to rebel against the father by
entering into a sexual liaison of which the father would certainly
disapprove. The Roman soldier might also represent this person,
the envisaged lover; perhaps the clichéd phrase 'Latin lover'
might have prompted this. Thus, both the feared father and the
desired lover are *condensed* into the single dream figure of the
Roman soldier.

The purpose of devices like displacement and condensation is
two-fold. Firstly, as we said, they disguise the repressed fears and
wishes contained in the dream so that they can get past the censor
which normally prevents their surfacing into the conscious mind.
Secondly, they fashion this material into something which can be
represented in a dream, that is, into images, symbols, and
metaphors. Material has to be turned into this form for dreams,
since dreams don't *say* things, they *show* things. In this sense
especially, as we have indicated, they are very like literature.
Hence the interest of literary critics in Freudian methods of interpretation.

This should raise questions in your mind about how we decide
when a Freudian interpretation is plausible and when not. I want
to take one more example, this time from a book by Freud called

The Psychopathology of Everyday Life. In spite of its title, this is one of Freud's most enjoyable and accessible publications. Its subtitle explains what it's about: 'Forgetting, slips of the tongue, bungled actions, superstitions and errors'. (Bungled actions are when you do things like unwrapping a sweet, putting the paper in your mouth, and throwing away the sweet.) The underlying assumption is that when some wish, fear, memory, or desire is difficult to face we may try to cope with it by repressing it, that is, eliminating it from the conscious mind. But this doesn't make it go away: it remains alive in the unconscious, like radioactive matter buried beneath the ocean, and constantly seeks a way back into the conscious mind, always succeeding eventually. As Freud famously said, 'There is always a return of the repressed'. Slips of the tongue or pen, the forgetting of names, and similar 'accidents' show this repressed material in the act of seeking a way back.

The example is from Freud's own experience and it attributes significance to the forgetting of a word from a quotation. It is worth spending a little time on, since it typifies the quality of complexity and ingenuity which I have suggested is common in Freudian interpretation. Freud explains that while on holiday with his family he met an academic young man who, like Freud, was Jewish and they discussed the anti-semitism which might hinder their careers. The young man voiced strong feelings on this matter, expressing the wish that such wrongs might be put right by a future generation. He made this point with a quotation from the Latin poet Virgil, using words spoken by Dido, Queen of Carthage, when she is abandoned by Aeneas. Her words are '*Exoriare aliquis nostris ex ossibus ultor*', meaning 'May someone arise from our bones as an avenger', but in quoting the line in Latin the young man accidently leaves out the word 'aliquis' (which means 'somebody'). Freud corrects the quotation, and the young man (who has read Freud's books) challenges him to explain the significance of this simple act of forgetting. Freud accepts the challenge, and asks the young man to say 'candidly and uncritically whatever comes into your mind if you direct your attention to the forgotten word without any definite aim'. This produces the following sequence of associations:

Firstly, similar-sounding words like *relics*, *liquefying*, *fluidity*, and *fluid*.

Secondly, St Simon of Trent, whose relics he saw some years ago.

Thirdly, an article in an Italian newspaper called 'What St Augustine says about women'.

Fourthly, St Januarius, whose blood is kept in a phial in a church at Naples and on a particular holy day it miraculously liquefies. He says 'the people get very agitated if it is delayed'.

Freud points out that two of these saints (*Januarius* and *Augustine*) have names which link them closely with the calendar, and he has already worked out why the young man forgot the word 'aliquis'. The young man has been uneasy about a certain event, and if he had said the word 'aliquis' that would have reminded him again of this anxiety: so the unconscious protects him by deleting the word from his conscious memory. Perhaps you can already work out what the event is which the young man is worried about. He breaks off and says in some embarrassment 'I've suddenly thought of a young lady from whom I might easily hear a piece of news that would be very awkward for both of us'. He hesitates, and Freud asks 'That her periods have stopped?' The young man is astonished, and Freud explains how he knew: 'Think of the calendar saints, the blood that starts to flow on a particular day, the disturbance when the event fails to take place.'

STOP and THINK

In its elaborateness, and its use of what literary critics would call 'symbolism', this example is fairly typical of aspects of psychoanalytic interpretation. How convincing do you find it?

Try to pin-point your own reaction in a specific way. What is your judgement based upon? Do you distrust the example because of its elaborateness? (I am assuming some degree of distrust, since that is what I have encountered whenever I have used it.) Should there be a limit to the number of associative steps allowable between the slip and its interpretation? Without some such limit, could not the chain of associations be made to stretch to almost any interpretative destination? Or is it the nature of the steps, rather than their number, which makes the example finally unconvincing? If so, what is it about them which has this effect?

Note that the example seems to require the unconscious to anticipate the flow of conscious thought, to see that any word suggesting liquid will act as a reminder of the feared pregnancy, and then to eliminate the Latin word 'aliquis', pre-emptively, from the conscious mind.

My own feeling about it is that there is an attractive complexity about this example, far removed from the banalities of interpretations which are popularly called 'Freudian'. The anxiety felt by the young man is shown to suffuse the mind, in what seems to me a very plausible way, rather than being locked away in some specific compartment; hence, it is likely to surface anywhere at all. But perhaps this is simply to say that the elaborateness is what I like about this example.

Freudian interpretation, then, has always been of considerable interest to literary critics. The basic reason, again, is that the unconscious, like the poem, or novel, or play, cannot speak directly and explicitly but does so through images, symbols, emblems, and metaphors. Literature, too, is not involved with making direct explicit statements about life, but with showing and expressing experience through imagery, symbolism, metaphor and so on. However, because the 'statements' made are not explicit there is an inevitable 'judgemental' element involved, and in consequence psychoanalytic interpetations of literature are often controversial.

Freud and evidence

Distrust of Freud has been growing in recent years, partly as a result of his mainly negative views on women, as seen in the notion that women's sexuality is based upon feelings of narcissism, masochism, and passivity, and the idea that they suffer from an innate form of inferiority complex known as 'penis envy'. Recent work seems to show that these views were maintained by misreading, or even misrepresenting, the evidence presented to him by his patients; for instance by taking accounts of sexual abuse in childhood as fantasies rather than reality. Freud's wilful misreading is seen in the case study usually known simply as 'Dora', but officially entitled 'Fragment of an Analysis of a Case of Hysteria' (volume 8 in the Pelican Freud Library). Feminist critics, and others, have read this case study as a means of psychoanalysing Freud. For instance, a collection of essays on the case appeared in 1985 under the title *In Dora's Case: Freud, Hysteria, and Feminism* (ed. Charles Bernheimer and Claire Kahane, Virago, 1985). 'Dora' was brought to Freud for treatment in the autumn of the year 1900, by her father, as an eighteen-year-old. Her parents had found a note threatening suicide, which was the culmination of a period of withdrawal and difficulty. Dora broke off the treatment before it reached any conclusion, so Freud calls the case '*Fragment* of an Analysis of a Case of Hysteria'. The bulk of the material is Freud's analysis and interpretation of two dreams which she related to him in the course of the treatment, and we'll concentrate on one of these.

The family situation at the time the analysis took place is that Dora's wealthy parents were unhappy in their marriage, but they had formed a close friendship with another couple, Mr and Mrs K. A sexual relationship developed between Dora's father and Mrs K, which went on for several years. Mr K knew of this, and all three adults seemed to have an unspoken agreement that in exchange, as it were, Dora should be made available to Mr K. Mr K made approaches to her on two occasions, the first in his office, when she was fourteen; in a state of obvious excitement he suddenly took hold of her and began to kiss her. She reacted with a violent feeling of disgust and ran out. Freud considered this reaction neurotic: in his view 'this was surely just the situation to call up a distinct feeling of sexual excitement in a girl of fourteen', since Mr K, as he explains in a footnote, was 'still quite young and of prepossessing appearance' (p. 60).

The second occasion happened when Dora was sixteen. She and Mr K were walking together beside a lake, and he 'had the audacity to make a suggestion to her'. She slapped his face and hurried away. Freud is puzzled by the 'brutal form' of her refusal, and again sees her reaction as neurotic. When Dora told her father about what had happened he asked Mr K for an explanation, but Mr K denied that the incident had ever taken place. Her father believed him rather than Dora. Given these circumstances, Freud's view of the situation seems remarkably perverse. The first of the two dreams on which much of the analysis centres was a recurrent one, which first happened when they were staying in a house by the lake where Mr K made his indecent proposal:

> A house was on fire. My father was standing beside my bed and woke me up. I dressed quickly. Mother wanted to stop and save her jewel-case, but father said 'I refuse to let myself and my two children be burnt for the sake of your jewel-case'. We hurried downstairs, and as soon as I was outside I woke up.
>
> (The Pelican Freud Library, vol. 8, p. 99)

Freud comments, *firstly*, that the immediate trigger of the dream is that when they arrived at this small wooden house her father said he was afraid of what would happen if there was a fire there. *Secondly*, in the afternoon Dora had woken up from an afternoon nap on the sofa to find Mr K standing over her. In the dream the father and Mr K are transposed. *Thirdly*, some years before she had heard her mother and father having a serious argument about jewels. *Fourthly*, Freud points out that the German word 'jewel-case' is a slang term for the female genitals. According to Freud, therefore, the dream expresses Dora's repressed wish to give Mr K what he wants (that is, her jewel-case): the fire represents her own repressed passion. The figure of Mr K is transposed with that of the father to express the wish that her former Oedipal love for her father will protect her from the temptation to yield to Mr K's advances. Freud sees in Dora's resentment of the relationship between her father and Mrs K a residual trace of this Oedipus complex, a feeling that Mrs K is her successful rival for her father's love. Against the combined male forces of her father, Mr K, and Freud it would seem that Dora has little chance, and the whole case study certainly shows Freud and psychoanalysis at their weakest. (Psychoanalysis in relation to feminism is further discussed in Chapter 6 on feminism.)

What Freudian psychoanalytic critics do

1. They give central importance, in literary interpretation, to the distinction between the conscious and the unconscious mind. They associate the literary work's 'overt' content with the former, and the 'covert' content with the latter, privileging the latter as being what the work is 'really' about, and aiming to disentangle the two.
2. Hence, they pay close attention to unconscious motives and feelings, whether these be (a) those of the author, (b) those of the characters depicted in the work.
3. They demonstrate the presence in the literary work of classic psychoanalytic symptoms, conditions, or phases, such as the oral, anal, and phallic stages of emotional and sexual development in infants.
4. They make large-scale applications of psychoanalytic concepts to literary history in general, for example, Harold Bloom's book *The Anxiety of Influence* (1973) sees the struggle for identity by each generation of poets, under the 'threat' of the greatness of its predecessors, as an enactment of the Oedipus complex.
5. They identify a 'psychic' context for the literary work, at the expense of social or historical context, privileging the individual 'psycho-drama' above the 'social drama' of class conflict. The conflict between generations or siblings, or between competing desires within the same individual looms much larger than conflict between social classes, for instance.

Freudian psychoanalytic criticism: examples

What kind of literary problem can Freudian psychoanalytic theories help with? Let's start with Shakespeare's *Hamlet*, an example which is so well-known that it has become a cliché. The relevant items in the above list of what Freudian critics do are:

1. the distinction between conscious and unconscious, 2. uncovering the unconscious motives of characters, and 3. seeing in the literary work an embodiment of classic psychoanalytic conditions. In the play Hamlet's father is murdered by his own brother, Hamlet's uncle, who then marries Hamlet's mother. The ghost of Hamlet's father appears to Hamlet and tells him to avenge the murder by killing his uncle. There is no obvious difficulty about doing this, but Hamlet spends most of the play delaying and making excuses. Why? He is not particularly squeamish, as he kills other people in the course of the play. Also, what the ghost reveals merely confirms suspicions Hamlet had independently formed himself, and he gathers other external evidence that the ghost is telling him the truth. So why the delay? Critics have long debated the question without coming to any generally accepted conclusions. Psychoanalytic criticism offers a neat and simple solution: Hamlet cannot avenge this crime because he is guilty of wanting to commit the same crime himself. He has an Oedipus complex, that is, a repressed sexual desire for his own mother, and a consequent wish to do away with his father. Thus, the uncle has merely done what Hamlet himself secretly *wished* to do: hence the difficulty for him of being the avenger. This view of the play was first sketched out by Freud in *The Interpretation of Dreams* (1900). As Freud summarises the matter, Hamlet is unable to

> take vengeance on the man who did away with his father and took that father's place with his mother, the man who shows him the repressed wishes of his own childhood realized. Thus the loathing which should drive him on to revenge is replaced in him by self-reproaches, by scruples of conscience, which remind him that he himself is literally no better than the sinner he is to punish.
>
> (Pelican Freud Library, vol. 4, p. 367)

As evidence for this view of the play, the psychoanalytic critic points to the bedroom scene in which Hamlet shows an intense and unusual awareness of his mother's sexuality. Freud links the situation of Hamlet in the play to that of Shakespeare himself ('It can, of course, only be the poet's own mind which confronts us in *Hamlet*'.) He cites the view that it was written immediately after the death of Shakespeare's own father in 1601 ('while his childhood feelings about his father had been freshly revived') and he adds, 'It is known, too, that Shakespeare's own son who died at an early age bore the name of "Hamnet", which is identical with "Hamlet"' (p. 368). All the same, it is Hamlet the character in whom the Oedipal conflict is detected, not Shakespeare the author. Here, then, is a famous problem in literature, to which psychoanalysis can offer the basis of a solution. The sketch for an interpretation of the play put forward by Freud was later developed by his British colleague Ernest Jones in *Hamlet and Oedipus* (1949). There is a famous sustained literary pastiche of this psychoanalytical-autobiographical view of *Hamlet* in James Joyce's *Ulysses* (1922).

Another example of a puzzling play with which the psychoanalytic critic can offer help is Harold Pinter's *The Homecoming*. This example illustrates the third item in the list of what psychoanalytic critics do, the classic Freudian condition embodied in the play being that of the mother fixation. *The Homecoming* centres on an East End of London all-male household consisting of an autocratic father and two grown-up sons. The mother has been dead for some years but her memory is worshipped by the widower and her sons. There is a third son who has emigrated to America where he is a college professor. He comes back on a visit to his family, bringing his wife (this being the literal homecoming of the title). During the visit the sons and the father have the idea of setting their brother's wife up as a prostitute in a Soho flat, and living off the proceeds. Their brother agrees to this, and the wife accepts it calmly when it is put to her, having first extracted the best possible financial terms, and made it clear that she will be in many ways the boss of this new household. Her husband goes back to America without her, and to their three children (all boys). These events seem so bizarre that the play is often performed as a kind of surreal farce.

But, again, the psychoanalytic critic is able to offer an explanation which makes some sense of them. In her article 'Pinter's Freudian Homecoming' (*Essays in Criticism*, July 1991, pp. 189–207) M. W. Rowe suggests that the underlying explanation is to be found in Freud's essay, 'The most prevalent form of degradation in erotic life'. The all-male family shown in the play suffers from a classic condition known as a mother fixation, in which there is an exaggerated reverence for the mother. Such people are attracted only to women who resemble the mother, but because of this the shadow of the incest taboo makes the expression of sexual feelings towards them difficult or impossible. Hence, their only way out is to seek sexual relationships with women who do not resemble the mother, and whom they therefore despise. So in order to generate sexual excitement such men have to degrade the love object, since if they are not so degraded they will resemble the mother, and hence, in the man's mind, not be available as a sexual partner. Thus, women are polarised into idealised maternal figures on the one hand and prostitute figures on the other. The exaggerated reverence for the mother is usually much diluted by adolescence, but if the mother has died before the child reached adolescence, as in the household shown in the play, then a damaging, idealised image of her can live on, and eclipse that of all possible sexual partners. Hence, when the brothers propose the prostitute plan the husband accepts this because that is how he himself has thought about or fantasised about his wife in order to make a sexual relationship with her possible. Again, then, the action which we see presented in the play turns out to be an enacting of the suppressed desires of one of the central characters.

Lacan

Jacques Lacan (1901–1981) was a French psychoanalyst whose work has had an extraordinary influence upon many aspects of recent literary theory. Lacan began his career by taking a medical degree and then training in psychiatry in the 1920s. In the 1930s he worked on paranoia, publishing his thesis on his patient Aimée. His famous theory of the 'mirror stage' (explained later) was first presented at a conference in 1936. Subsequently his ideas were influenced by figures who successively dominated Parisian intellectual life, such as the anthropologist Claude Lévi-Strauss (1908–), and the linguists Ferdinand de Saussure (1857–1913), and Roman Jakobson (1896–1982). Only in the 1950s did Lacan begin to challenge the orthodoxies of his subject field. In 1955 at a conference in Vienna he called for a new 'back-to-basics' Freudianism. But he meant, not a new attempt to understand the 'conscious personality' (the 'ego') and interpret its behaviour in the light of an understanding of the workings of the unconscious (which many would take to be the whole point of Freudianism), but rather a new emphasis on the the unconscious itself, as 'the nucleus of our being'. In 1959 these unorthodox views resulted in his expulsion from the International Psychoanalytic Association (a kind of World Congress of Freudian analysts) and in 1964 in Paris he set up his own breakaway Ecole Freudienne and published a section of his training sessions under the title *Ecrits*. By this time he himself was one of the most prominent Parisian intellectuals.

Lacan's reputation, then, rests on the published 'seminars', the *Ecrits*. A French seminar is not a group discussion but a kind of extended lecture for graduate-level students. The intense atmosphere of these occasions is suggested in an eyewitness account of Lacan's seminars in the 1950s:

> He speaks in a wavering, syncopated or thundering voice, spiced with sighs and hesitations. He notes down in advance what he is going to say, then, before the public, he improvises like an actor from the Royal Shakespeare Company ... he fascinates his audience with his impressive language ... Lacan does not analyse, he associates. Lacan does not lecture, he produces resonances. At each session of this collective treatment, the pupils have the impression that the master speaks about them and for them in a coded message secretly destined for each one.
>
> (Quoted by John Lechte in *Julia Kristeva* Routledge, 1990, pp. 36-7)

Note here the emphasis on showmanship, on improvisation, on by-passing the formally structured presentation of ideas usual in lectures, and on the transmission of information in a coded form as part of an initiation process. Lacan says, in the piece discussed below, that the only teaching worthy of the name is teaching you can only come to terms with in its own terms. I emphasise all this to prepare you for the initial strangeness of Lacan's writing, all of which was based on the semi-improvised meditations which occupied the two to three hours of these weekly occasions.

The vast output of Lacan has not all been of equal interest to literary critics. The major interest has been in the following:

1. The essay 'The insistence of the letter in the unconscious', reprinted in David Lodge, ed. *Modern Criticism and Theory* (Longman, 1988), pp. 79–106.
2. The seminar on Edgar Allan Poe's story 'The Purloined Letter', reprinted in *The Purloined Poe: Lacan, Derrida, and Psychoanalytic Reading* ed. John P. Muller and William J. Richardson (Johns Hopkins University Press, 1988), pp. 28–54, with extensive editorial commentary and annotations.
3. The seminar on *Hamlet*, 'Desire and the Interpretation of desire in *Hamlet*', reprinted in *Literature and Psychoanalysis: the Question of Reading: Otherwise* Shoshana Felman, ed. (Johns Hopkins University Press, 1982), pp. 11–52.

Lacan's own explication of his ideas is often intimidatingly obscure. I would suggest that in reading him you should devote some study time to reading the same piece several times, rather than reading through a great deal of his work once only. In grappling with Lacan I have found the following particularly helpful:

1. David Lodge's pre-summary of the argument of Lacan's 'The insistence of the letter in the unconscious', pp. 79–80 in *Modern Criticism and Theory*.
2. John Lechte's account of Lacan's thinking, chapter two 'The effect of the unconscious' in his book *Julia Kristeva*, pp. 13–64. I have also drawn upon this for the biographical details given above.
3. A summary by Toril Moi, pp. 99–101 in *Sexual/Textual Politics* (Methuen, 1985).
4. The critique of Lacan, chapter five 'The mirror stage – a critical reflection', pp. 131–63, in Raymond Tallis's *Not Saussure: A Critique of Post-Saussurean Literary Theory* (Macmillan, 1988).

The most important Lacanian text for literary students is 'The insistence of the letter', first delivered in 1957 to a 'lay' audience of philosophy students, rather than to trainee psychiatrists, but using material from the professional seminars. In what follows I attempt a summary of the argument, trying to show why these ideas have been used so intensively by literary critics.

Lacan begins the piece by paying allegiance to the intellectual dominance of language studies: he asks (rhetorically) 'how could a psychoanalyst of today not realise that his realm of truth is in fact the word?' Language, then, is central, and this is so because in investigating the unconscious the analyst is always both using and examining language – in effect, Freudian psychiatry is entirely a verbal science. And the unconscious is not a chaotic mass of disparate material, as might formerly have been thought, but an orderly network, as complex as the structure of a language: 'what the psychoanalytic experience discovers in the unconscious is the whole structure of language'.

So the unconscious, in Lacan's famous slogan, is structured like a language. But how is a language structured? Modern language studies, he goes on, begin with Saussure, who shows that meaning in language is a matter of contrasts between words and other words, not between words and things. Meaning, that is to say, is a network of differences. There is a perpetual barrier between signifier (the word) and signified (the referent). He demonstrates this built-in separation with a diagram showing two identical lavatory doors, one headed 'Ladies' the other 'Gentlemen'. This purports to show that the same signifier may have different signifieds, so that (Lodge, p. 86) 'only the correlations between signifier and signifier supply the standard for all research into meaning'. Hence, 'we are forced to accept the notion of an incessant sliding of the signified under the signifer' (Lodge, p. 87). That is, words and meanings have a life of their own and constantly override and obscure the supposed simplicities and clarity of external reality. If signifiers relate only to one another, then language is detached from external reality, and becomes an independent realm, a crucial notion in post-structuralist thinking (see Chapter 3, pp. 64–5).

But what evidence is there that the unconscious is 'linguistic' in structure as Lacan alleges? He argues that the two 'dream work' mechanisms identified by Freud, *condensation* and *displacement* (Chapter 5, pp. 98–9) correspond to the basic poles of language identified by the linguist Roman Jakobson, that is, to *metaphor* and *metonymy*, respectively. The correspondence is that:

1. In metonymy one thing represents another by means of the part standing for the whole. So twenty sail would mean twenty ships. In Freudian dream interpretation an element in a dream might stand for something else by *displacement*: so, a person might be represented by one of their attributes; for instance, a lover who is Italian might be represented in a dream by, let's say, an Alfa Romeo car. Lacan says this is the same as *metonymy*, the part standing for the whole.
2. In *condensation* several things might be compressed into one symbol, just as a *metaphor* like 'the ship ploughed the waves' condenses into a single item two different images, the ship cutting through the sea and the plough cutting through the soil.

The use by the unconscious of these linguistic means of self-expression is part of Lacan's evidence for the claim that the unconscious is structured like a language. He goes on to emphasise the linguistic aspect of Freud's work: whenever the unconscious is being discussed the amount of linguistic analysis increases, since puns, allusions, and other kinds of word play are often the mechanisms which make manifest the content of the unconscious – think back to the 'aliquis' example, for instance.

The transition section of the essay moves attention again from the conscious self, which has always been regarded as the primary self, to the unconscious as 'the kernel of our being'. In Western philosophy the conscious mind has long been regarded as the essence of selfhood. This view is encapsulated in the proclamation by the philosopher Descartes, 'I think, therefore I am'. Lacan lays down a dramatic challenge to this philosophical consensus (remember that he is addressing an audience of philosophy students) when he reverses this into 'I am where I think not' (Lodge, p. 97), that is, in the unconscious, where my true selfhood lies. Lacan insists, then, that the Freudian discovery of the unconscious be followed through to its logical conclusion, which is 'the self's radical ex-centricity to itself' (Lodge, p. 101). And he asks 'who is this other to whom I am more attached than to myself, since at the heart of my assent to my own identity it is still he who wags me?' (Lodge, p. 102). Hence, the self is 'deconstructed', shown to be merely a linguistic effect, not an essential entity. The unconscious, then, is the 'kernel of our being', but the unconscious is like a language, and language exists as a structure before the individual enters into it. Hence, the liberal humanist notion of unique, individual selfhood is deconstructed. The argument, then, is extremely ambitious and wide-ranging in its effects. In a few pages Lacan seeks to alter nothing less than our deepest notions of what we are.

But why, in particular, is it of such interest to literary critics? I think the answer to this question is a consequence of the relentless logic of the views put forward in the essay. Thus, Lacan says that the unconscious is the 'kernel of our being', but since the unconscious is linguistic, and language is a system already complete and in existence before we enter into it, then it follows that the notion of a unique, separate self is deconstructed. If this is so, the idea of 'character', which rests in turn on the notion of a unique separate self, becomes untenable. So a major consequence of accepting the Lacanian position would be to reject the conventional view of characterisation in literature. Since Lacan deconstructs the idea of the subject as a stable amalgam of consciousness, we can hardly accept novelistic characters as people but must hold them in abeyance, as it were, and see them as assemblages of signifiers clustering round a proper name. Hence, a wholly different reading strategy is demanded.

Further, the view of language offered by Lacan sees it as fundamentally detached from any referent in the world. Accepting this view leads to a rejection of literary realism, since in realist novels the underlying assumption is that the text figures forth the real world for us. Hence, adopting the Lacanian outlook would involve valuing instead the modernist or postmodernist experimental, fragmented, allusive text, where, for instance, a novel plays with the devices of the novel, alludes to other novels, and so on, just as, for Saussure, the signifiers which make up a language refer only to one another, and interact with one another, but do not figure forth a world. Hence, a wholly different set of literary preferences is also demanded.

Lacan's foregrounding of the unconscious leads him to specu-
late about the mechanism whereby we emerge into consciousness.
Before the sense of self emerges the young child exists in a realm
which Lacan calls the Imaginary, in which there is no distinction
between self and Other and there is a kind of idealised
identification with the mother. Then, between six months and
eighteen months comes what he calls the 'mirror-stage', when the
child sees its own reflection in the mirror and begins to conceive
of itself as a unified being, separate from the rest of the world. At
this stage the child enters into the language system, essentially a
system which is concerned with lack and separation – crucial
Lacanian concepts – since language names what is not present and
substitutes a linguistic sign for it. This stage also marks the beginning of socialisation, with its prohibitions and restraints, associated with the figure of the father. The new order which the child
now enters is called by Lacan the Symbolic. This distinction
between the Imaginary and the Symbolic has been used exten-
sively in literary studies, for instance, by French feminist critics
(see Chapter 6, pp.129–30). In terms of the literary polarisation
between the realist and the anti-realist text, the Symbolic realm
would have to be seen as the one found in realist literature, a
world of patriarchal order and logic. By contrast, the anti-realist
text represents the realm of the Imaginary, a world in which language gestures beyond itself, beyond logic and grammar, rather
in the way that poetic language often does. Indeed, the contrast
between the Imaginary and the Symbolic might be seen as analogous to that between poetry and prose. In practice the two
realms, and the two kinds of language, must always co-exist, and
the critical stance which follows from an acceptance of the Lacanian outlook will involve a preference for the kind of literary text
in which there are constant irruptions of the Imaginary into the
Symbolic, as in the kind of 'metafiction' or 'magic realism' in
which the novel undercuts and queries its own realism. A fine
example of this kind of work would be that of the British novelist B. S. Johnson whose constant textual inventiveness takes the
form, for instance, of moments when the characters cross-ques-
tion the author, taking issue with his version of their motives, or
his handling of the plots in which they figure. Hence, apparently

abstract Lacanian notions, such as the constructedness and insta-
bility of the subject (the self), or the subject as a linguistic construct, or language as a self-contained universe of discourse can
be seen in action in the texture of the work of fiction.

What Lacanian critics do

1. Like Freudian critics they pay close attention to unconscious
   motives and feelings, but instead of excavating for those of the
   author or characters, they search out those of the text itself,
   uncovering contradictory undercurrents of meaning, which lie
   like a subconscious beneath the 'conscious' of the text. This
   is another way of defining the process of 'deconstruction'.
2. They demonstrate the presence in the literary work of Lacanian psychoanalytic symptoms or phases, such as the mirror-
   stage or the sovereignty of the unconscious.
3. They treat the literary text in terms of a series of broader
   Lacanian orientations, towards such concepts as lack or desire,
   for instance.
4. They see the literary text as an enactment or demonstration
   of Lacanian views about language and the unconscious, particularly the endemic elusiveness of the signified, the centrality of the unconscious. In practice, this results in favouring
   the anti-realist text which challenges the conventions of literary representation.

Lacanian criticism: an example

To illustrate some of the concerns of a Lacanian approach to literature we can now look briefly at Lacan's well-known interpretation of Edgar Allan Poe's pioneering detective story 'The
Purloined Letter'. (The tale is included in the Penguin *Edgar
Allan Poe: Selected Writings*, ed. David Galloway, and also
reprinted in *The Purloined Poe*.) Lacan analysed this story in a
series of 'seminars', as part of the induction process for trainee
analysts. In the 1980s several post-structuralist essays were written in response to the publication of these seminars, and much of
the material has usefully been collected and republished in *The*

Purloined Poe. Also, Newton's *Theory into Practice* contains an essay on the topic by the Lacanian psychoanalytic critic Shoshana Felman. Since it is by Lacan himself, this example demonstrates the fourth of the Lacanian critical activities listed above, Lacan finding in it evidence of his own views on language, and on the process of psychoanalysis.

Poe's story has about it an archetypal air which lends itself well to psychoanalytic interpretation. There is no in-depth character-isation, the characters being suggestive of chess pieces which are moved about by the author in a ritualistic combat of bluff, counter-bluff, and subterfuge. They are named the Queen, the King, the Minister, the Chief of Police and Dupin, the detective. What happens can be divided into four phases:

1. The Minister is in discussion with the Queen in her appart-ments when the King enters unexpectedly. He notices that she is anxious the King should not see a letter which is on the desk, but she can't conceal it as this would draw his atention to it. When the attention of both is distracted the Minister removes it, substituting a letter from his own pocket which has a similar appearance.

2. When she discovers the theft the Queen realises who is responsible, and when the Minister is away she gets the Chief of Police and his men to search his apartments. In spite of employing the most thorough and scientific methods he finds nothing.

3. In desperation she asks for Dupin's help. He visits the Min-ister and reasons that carrying the letter on his person would be too great a risk, but its usefulness lies in his being able to produce it at any time, so it can't be hidden outside the house. But if it had been *hidden* inside the house the search would have discovered it, so it must be in the house but not hidden. Sure enough, he sees the letter above the mantelpiece, care-lessly pushed in amongst other items of correspondence.

4. He visits again, and having arranged a distraction in the street, substitutes a fake letter for it. The letter is returned to the Queen, and the Minister, unaware that he no longer pos-

sesses it, brings about his own downfall. A note inside the fake reveals that this is Dupin's revenge for being duped by the Minister in a love affair in earlier life.

Lacan's account of the tale is lengthy, but of markedly different character from the conventional Freudian criticism of Poe, which is best represented by the work of Freud's 1930s disciple Marie Bonaparte (also extracted in *The Purloined Poe*). In Bonaparte the tale is read, as are all Poe's works, as a symptom of the author's neurotic inner life. Thus, she reads beyond the text to the author, identifying in him a mother fixation and necrophilia on the basis of the content of the tales. Lacan, by contrast, does not talk about the psychology of the individual author, but sees the text as a metaphor which throws light upon aspects of the unconscious, on the nature of psychoanalysis, and on aspects of language. We can summarise these as follows:

1. *The stolen letter is an emblem of the unconscious itself.* In the story we find out nothing about the *content* of the letter: we merely see it affecting the actions of every person in the tale. Likewise, the content of the unconscious is, by definition, unknowable, but everything we do is affected by it: we can guess at the nature of this content by observing its effects, just as we can deduce the general nature of the letter's contents from the anxiety it generates. Freud's investigations resulted in confident assertions about the precise nature of the content of the unconscious, but Lacan is much more sceptical about the possibility of such certainties. Like the letter, the pieces which might make sense of our inner mental universe have been purloined, and we have to learn to operate without them. We have, that is, to use the code without having the key.

2. *Dupin's investigation of the crime of the stolen letter enacts the process of psychoanalysis.* The analyst in psychoanalysis uses repetition and substitution: in getting the patient to verbalise painful repressed memories, the original event is repeated in verbal form, but the verbal account is then substituted in the conscious mind for the repressed memory in the unconscious. Once it is conscious and verbalised, the memory is disempowered and mental well-being is restored. Likewise, Dupin's

investigative process in the story centres on repetition and substitution: his theft of the letter from the Minister is a repetition of the Minister's theft of it from the Queen, and the theft is achieved by substitution, a false letter being used as a replacement for the real one.

3. *The letter with the unknown content is an embodiment of aspects of the nature of language.* In language there is an endless play of signifiers, but no simple connection with any signified content beyond language. The signified is always lost or purloined. In the same way, we see the significance of the letter throughout the story, but we never find out precisely what is signified within it. It is an example of signification itself, not a sign of some specific thing. Likewise, all words are purloined letters: we can never open them and view their content unambiguously; we have the signifiers, which are the verbal envelopes of concepts, so to speak, but these envelopes cannot be unsealed, so that the signifieds will always remain hidden, just like the content of the purloined letter in Poe's tale.

Comparing the Freudian and Lacanian examples discussed in this chapter will make it immediately apparent that there is an immense gulf between these two approaches, even though – paradoxically – they both stem from the same original body of Freudian theory.

Selected reading

General

Felman, Shoshana, ed. *Literature and Psychoanalysis – The Question of Reading: Otherwise* (Johns Hopkins University Press, 1982).

An important collection of essays. Felman's own 'Turning the screw of interpretation' is about Henry James's story 'The Turn of the Screw', one of the earliest texts to be subjected to psychoanalytic criticism (by the critic Edmund Wilson in 1934).

Jefferson, Ann & Robey, David, eds. *Modern Literary Theory: A Comparative Introduction* (Batsford, 2nd edn, 1986). Chapter five 'Modern Psychoanalytic Criticism'.

A useful general account, not restricted to Freud.

Kurzweil, Edith, ed. *Literature and Psychoanalysis* (Columbia University Press, 1983).

A very useful collection with good editorial commentary. The first section is on early psychoanalytic theory, the third on literary applications, including essays on Keats, on Henry James's disturbing ghost story 'The Jolly Corner', on Kafka, and on Lewis Carroll. The final section is on French psychoanalytic theory.

Wright, Elizabeth, *Psychoanalytic Criticism: Theory in Practice* (Methuen, 1984).

Short and wide-ranging, dealing with Freudian and Lacanian approaches, as well as others not discussed here, but not an easy read.

Freud

Bernheimer, Charles & Kahane, Claire, *In Dora's Case: Freud, Hysteria, and Feminism* (Virago, 1985).

A critique of Freud's handling of this case, by various commentators, including Jacques Lacan (briefly and incisively), Jacqueline Rose, Toril Moi, and Jane Gallop. This book works beyond the traditional (but now outmoded) antagonism between feminism and psychoanalysis by moving towards Lacanian and post-structuralist re-readings of Freud.

Freud, Sigmund, *The Interpretation of Dreams* (first published in 1900. Volume four in the Penguin Freud).

A key work in the creation of twentieth-century sensibility. Explains the basic dream mechanisms, 'Condensation', VIa; 'Displacement', VIb; also the Oedipus complex and *Hamlet* 363–8.

Freud, Sigmund, *The Psychopathology of Everyday Life* (first published in 1901. Volume five in the Penguin Freud).

Very readable and interesting, in spite of the title. Either this book or the case histories would be the best place to begin with Freud.

Freud, Sigmund, *Case Histories I: 'Dora' and 'Little Hans'* (Volume eight in the Penguin Freud).

Detailed records of Freudian interpretation. The element of ingenuity and complexity emphasised above is very evident in these accounts.

Timpanaro, Sebastiano, *The Freudian Slip: Psychoanalysis and textual Criticism* (Verso Paperback, 1985).

I list this fascinating and readable book by a noted Italian Marxist partly because it is illustrative of the traditional antagonism between

Marxism and psychoanalysis. Timpanaro 'deconstructs' many of the slips in Freud's *Psychopathology* on the grounds that they are explicable in terms of incidental verbal similarities. See, for instance, his discussion of the 'aliquis' example, pp. 19–28.

Wolheim, Richard, *Freud* (Fontana Modern Masters, 1971).

Still the best introduction. But read some of Freud himself first.

Lacan

Lacan, Jacques, 'Desire and the interpretation of desire in *Hamlet*', reprinted in *Literature and Psychoanalysis: the Question of Reading: Otherwise*, Shoshana Felman, ed. (Johns Hopkins University Press, 1982), pp. 11–52.

Lacan, Jacques, Seminar on 'The Purloined Letter', reprinted in *The Purloined Poe: Lacan, Derrida, and Psychoanalytic Reading*, ed. John P. Muller and William J. Richardson (Johns Hopkins University Press, 1988), pp. 28–54, with extensive editorial commentary and annotations.

Lacan, Jacques, 'The insistence of the letter in the unconscious', reprinted in David Lodge, ed. *Modern Criticism and Theory* (Longman, 1988), pp. 79–106.

Mitchell, Juliet & Rose, Jacqueline, eds, *Feminine Sexuality: Jacques Lacan and the Ecole Freudienne* (Macmillan, 1982).

Key Lacanian texts translated and discussed.

Sarup, Madan, *Jacques Lacan* (Harvester, 1992).

A volume in the Modern Cultural Theorists series by an able explainer of difficult material. Begins with an account of Freudian ideas and ends with a discussion of Lacan and feminism.

6

Feminist criticism

Feminism and feminist criticism

The 'women's movement' of the 1960s was not, of course, the start of feminism. Rather, it was a renewal of an old tradition of thought and action already possessing its classic books which had diagnosed the problem of women's inequality in society, and (in some cases) proposed solutions. These books include Mary Woll-stonecraft's *A Vindication of the Rights of Women* (1792), which discusses male writers like Milton, Pope, and Rousseau; Olive Schreiner's *Women and Labour* (1911); Virginia Woolf's *A Room of One's Own* (1929), which vividly portrays the unequal treatment given to women seeking education and alternatives to marriage and motherhood; and Simone de Beauvoir's *The Second Sex* (1949), which has an important section on the portrayal of women in the novels of D. H. Lawrence. Male contributions to this tradition of feminist writing include John Stuart Mill's *The Subjection of Woman* (1869) and *The Origin of the Family* (1884) by Friedrich Engels.

The feminist literary criticism of today is the direct product of the 'women's movement' of the 1960s. This movement was, in important ways, literary from the start, in the sense that it realised the significance of the images of women promulgated by literature, and saw it as vital to combat them and question their authority and their coherence. In this sense the women's movement has always been crucially concerned with books and literature, so that feminist criticism should not be seen as an off-shoot or a spin-off from feminism which is remote from the ultimate aims of the movement, but as one of its most practical ways of influencing everyday conduct and attitudes.

The concern with 'conditioning' and 'socialisation' underpins a crucial set of distinctions, that between the terms 'feminist', 'female', and 'feminine'. As Toril Moi explains, the first is 'a political position', the second 'a matter of biology', and the third 'a set of culturally defined characteristics'. Particularly in the distinction between the second and third of these lies much of the force of feminism (see Moi's essay in *The Feminist Reader*, ed. Catherine Belsey and Jane Moore). Other important ideas are explained in the appropriate part of the remainder of this section.

The representation of women in literature, then, was felt to be one of the most important forms of 'socialisation', since it provided the role models which indicated to women, and men, what constituted acceptable versions of the 'feminine' and legitimate feminine goals and aspirations. Feminists pointed out, for example, that in nineteenth-century fiction very few women work for a living, unless they are driven to it by dire necessity. Instead, the focus of interest is on the heroine's choice of marriage partner, which will decide her ultimate social position and exclusively determine her happiness and fulfilment in life, or her lack of these.

Thus, in feminist criticism in the 1970s the major effort went into exposing what might be called the mechanisms of patriarchy, that is, the cultural 'mind-set' in men and women which perpetuated sexual inequality. Critical attention was given to books by male writers in which influential or typical images of women were constructed. Necessarily, the criticism which undertook this work was combative and polemical. Then, in the 1980s, in feminism as in other critical approaches, the mood changed. *Firstly*, feminist criticism became much more *eclectic*, meaning that it began to draw upon the findings and approaches of other kinds of criticism – Marxism, structuralism, linguistics, and so on. *Secondly*, it switched its focus from attacking male versions of the world to exploring the nature of the female world and outlook, and reconstructing the lost or suppressed records of female experience. *Thirdly*, attention was switched to the need to construct a new canon of women's writing by rewriting the history of the novel and of poetry in such a way that neglected women writers were given new prominence.

Such distinct phases of interest and activity seem characteristic of feminist criticism. Elaine Showalter, for instance, described the change in the late 1970s as a shift of attention from 'androtexts' (books by men) to 'gynotexts' (books by women). She coined the term 'gynocritics', meaning the study of gynotexts, but gynocriticism is a broad and varied field, and any generalisations about it should be treated with caution. The subjects of gynocriticism are, she says, 'the history, styles, themes, genres, and structures of writing by women; the psychodynamics of female creativity; the trajectory of the individual or collective female career; and the evolution or laws of a female literary tradition'.

Showalter also detects in the history of women's writing a *feminine phase* (1840-80), in which women writers imitated dominant male artistic norms and aesthetic standards; then a *feminist phase* (1880-1920), in which radical and often separatist positions are maintained; and finally a *female phase* (1920 onwards) which looked particularly at female writing and female experience. The reasons for this liking for 'phasing' are complex: partly, it is the result of the view that feminist criticism required a terminology if it was to attain theoretical respectability. More importantly, there is a great need, in all intellectual disciplines, to establish a sense of progress, enabling early and cruder examples of (in this case) feminist criticism to be given their rightful credit and acknowledgement while at the same time making it clear that the approach they represent is no longer generally regarded as a model for practice.

But feminist criticism since the 1970s has been remarkable for the wide range of positions that exist within it. Debates and disagreements have centred on three particular areas, these being: 1. the role of theory; 2. the nature of language, and 3. the value or otherwise of psychoanalysis. The next three sections will look at each of these in turn.

Feminist criticism and the role of theory

A major division within feminist criticism has concerned disagreements about the amount and type of theory that should feature in it. What is usually called the 'Anglo-American' version of
feminism has tended to be more sceptical about recent critical
theory, and more cautious in using it, than have the 'French' feminists, who have adopted and adapted a great deal of (mainly)
post-structuralist and psychoanalytic criticism as the basis of
much of their work. The 'Anglo-Americans' (not all are English
or American) maintain a major interest in traditional critical concepts like theme, motif, and characterisation. They seem to accept
the conventions of literary realism, and treat literature as a series
of representations of women's lives and experience which can be
measured and evaluated against reality. They see the close reading and explication of individual literary texts as the major business of feminist criticism. Generally, this kind of feminist
criticism has a good deal in common with the procedures and
assumptions of the liberal humanist approach to literature,
although feminists also place considerable emphasis on the use of
historical data and non-literary material (such as diaries, memoirs,
social and medical history) in understanding the literary text. The
American critic Elaine Showalter is usually taken as the major
representative of this approach, but other exemplars would be
Sandra Gilbert and Susan Gubar, Patricia Stubbs, and Rachel
Brownstein.

However, most of these are in fact American rather than
'Anglo', and this should make us question the usefulness of this
widely accepted category. English feminist criticism is, after all,
often distinctly different from American: it tends to be 'socialist
feminist' in orientation, aligned with cultural materialism or
Marxism, so that it is obviously unsatisfactory to try to assimilate
it into a 'non-theoretical' category. The existence of this kind of
feminism has been rather obscured by the fact that certain popular books summarising feminist criticism (like K. K. Ruthven's
Feminist Literary Studies: An Introduction and Toril Moi's
Sexual/Textual Politics) do not discuss it as a distinct category.
Examples of this kind of work are: Terry Lovell's *Consuming*

Fiction (1987), Julia Swindells's *Victorian Writing and Working Women* (1985), and *Sea Changes: Culture and Feminism* (1986) by Cora Kaplan, an American who worked in Britain for many years. Kaplan was a member of the Marxist Feminist Literature Collective, an important group whose very existence indicates the strong political and theoretical interests of this kind of feminist criticism. A similarly important group was the Literature Teaching Politics Collective, which was also a series of conferences and an associated journal. An important figure associated with this group is Catherine Belsey, whose books, (such as *The Subject of Tragedy* (1985), and *John Milton: Language, Gender, Power* (1988), are part of this same socialist feminist British tradition. While the definitive works in the so-called 'Anglo-American' tradition appeared in the late 1970s, the British 'socialist feminist' tradition produced its key works in the mid-1980s and remains active and influential.

In contrast to the Americans (if not, as we have just argued, to the British) the work of 'French' feminism is more overtly theoretical, taking as its starting-point the insights of major post-structuralists, especially Lacan, Foucault and Derrida. For these feminist critics, the literary text is never primarily a representation of reality, or a reproduction of a personal voice expressing the minutiae of personal experience. Indeed, the French theorists often deal with concerns other than literature: they write about language, representation, and psychology as such and often travel through detailed treatments of major philosophical issues of this kind before coming to the literary text itself. The major figures on this 'French' side of the divide are Julia Kristeva (actually Bulgarian, though regarded abroad – as she has ruefully said – as a kind of embodiment of French intellectualism), Hélène Cixous (Algerian-born), and Luce Irigaray.

All three are best encountered initially in the various feminist readers now available. For instance, Kristeva's 1974 interview 'Woman can never be defined' is in *New French Feminisms* (Marks & Courtivron), as are sections from 'Sorties' and 'The Laugh of the Medusa' by Cixous, and sections from Irigaray's *The Sex Which is not One*. Extracts from the same Cixous and Irigaray pieces are also in *Feminisms: A Reader* (Maggie Humm). A sustained discussion of the differences between 'Anglo-American' and 'French' feminisms (though one which is much on the side of the latter) is Toril Moi's *Sexual/Textual Politics*. For a more recent account see the chapter 'Imaginary Gardens with Real Frogs in them: feminist euphoria and the Franco-American divide, 1976–1988' by Ann Rosalind Jones in *Changing Subjects: The Making of Feminist Literary Criticism* (Greene and Kahn). These French feminists are particularly concerned with language and psychology, which are considered in the two following sections.

Feminist criticism and language

Another fundamental issue, on which opinion is just as polarised, is the question of whether or not there exists a form of language which is inherently feminine. There is a long-standing tradition of debate on this issue within feminism. For instance, Virginia Woolf, (in sections four and five of her extended polemical essay *A Room Of One's Own*) suggests that language use is gendered, so that when a woman turns to novel writing she finds that there is 'no common sentence ready for her use'. The great male novelists have written 'a natural prose, swift but not slovenly, expressive but not precious, taking their own tint without ceasing to be common property'. She quotes an example and says 'That is a man's sentence'. She doesn't make its qualities explicit, but the example seems to be characterised by carefully balanced and patterned rhetorical sequences. But 'it was a sentence unsuited for a woman's use', and women writers trying to use it (Charlotte Brontë, George Eliot) fared badly. Jane Austen rejected it and instead 'devised a perfectly natural, shapely sentence proper for her own use', but this is not described or exemplified. Presumably, though, the characteristics of a 'woman's sentence' are that the clauses are linked in looser sequences, rather than carefully balanced and patterned as in male prose.

Generally, then, the female writer is seen as suffering the handicap of having to use a medium (prose writing) which is essentially a male instrument fashioned for male purposes. This thesis that the language is 'masculine' in this sense is developed by Dale

Spender in the early 1980s in her book *Man Made Language* (1981) which also argues that language is not a neutral medium but one which contains many features which reflect its role as the instrument through which patriarchy finds expression. (This view that the language is man-made is challenged from within feminism by Sandra Gilbert and Susan Gubar in the essay 'Sexual Linguistics: Gender, Language, Sexuality', reprinted in *The Feminist Reader* ed. Catherine Belsey and Jane Moore (Macmillan, 1989). If normative language can be seen as in some way male-oriented, the question arises of whether there might be a form of language which is free from this bias, or even in some way oriented towards the female. French theorists, therefore, have posited the existence of an *écriture féminine*, (the term is that of the French theorist Hélène Cixous, from her essay 'The Laugh of the Medusa'), associated with the feminine, and facilitating the free play of meanings within the framework of loosened grammatical structures. The heightened prose of the Cixous essay both demonstrates and explains it:

> It is impossible to define a feminine practice of writing, and this is an impossibility which will remain, for this practice can never be theorized, enclosed, coded ... it will always surpass the discourse that regulates the phallocentric [male-dominated] system; it does and will take place in areas other than those subordinated to philosophico-theoretical domination. It will be conceived of by subjects who are breakers of automatisms, by peripheral figures that no authority can ever subjugate.
>
> (Marks & de Courtivron, *New French Feminisms* Harvester, 1981)

Here the user of *écriture féminine* seems to exist in a realm beyond logic ('this practice can never be theorized ... and will take place in areas other than those subordinated to philosophical-theoretical domination'.) The user of such language is seen as a kind of perennial freedom-fighter in an anarchic realm of perpetual opposition ('peripheral figures that no authority can ever subjugate') sniping at the centres of power. For Cixous (though not for other theorists) this kind of writing is somehow uniquely the product of female physiology, which women must celebrate in their writing:

Women must write through their bodies, they must invent the impregnable language that will wreck partitions, classes, and rhetorics, regulations and codes, they must submerge, cut through, get beyond the ultimate reserve-discourse, including the one that laughs at the very idea of pronouncing the word 'silence' ... Such is the strength of women that, sweeping away syntax, breaking that famous thread (just a tiny little thread, they say) which acts for men as a surrogate umbilical cord.

(Marks & Courtivron, p. 256)

Ecriture féminine, then, is by its nature transgressive, rule-transcending, intoxicated, but it is clear that the notion as put forward by Cixous raises many problems. The realm of the body, for instance, is seen as somehow immune ('impregnable') to social and gender conditioning ('rhetorics, regulations, codes') and able to issue forth a pure essence of the feminine. Such 'essentialism' is difficult to square with a feminism which emphasises femininity as a social construct, not a given entity which is somehow just mysteriously 'there'. And if femininity is socially constructed then it must follow that it differs from one culture to another, so that such overarching generalisations about it are impossible. Who, we might ask, are these women who 'must' write through their bodies? Who imposes this coercive 'must' upon them, and (above all) why?

Further expression of the notion of the *écriture féminine* is found in the writing of Julia Kristeva. Kristeva uses the terms the *symbolic* and the *semiotic* to designate two different aspects of language. In her essay 'The System and the Speaking Subject' the symbolic aspect is associated with authority, order, fathers, repression and control ('the family, normalcy, normative classico-psychological-tending discourse, all of which are just so many characteristics of fascist ideology'). This symbolic facet of language maintains the fiction that the self is fixed and unified (what she describes as 'a language with a foreclosed subject or with a transcendental subject-ego'). By contrast, the semiotic aspect of discourse is characterised not by logic and order, but by 'displacement, slippage, condensation', which suggests, again, a much looser, more randomised way of making connections, one which increases the available range of possibilities. She quotes Plato in the *Timaeus* invoking 'a state of language anterior to the Word ... Plato calls this the *chora*', and, again, it is linked with the maternal rather than the paternal. All this is presented at a fairly generalised level, but Kristeva sees the semiotic as the language of poetry as opposed to prose, and examines its operation in the work of specific poets. Though it is linked conceptually with the feminine, the poets who use it are not all female, and in fact Kristeva's major exemplars are male writers.

It should be stressed, though, that the symbolic and the semiotic are not two different *kinds* of language, but two different *aspects* of language, both of which are always present in any given sample. The model, again, is that of the unconscious and the conscious, and the Lacanian re-use of these notions. The symbolic is the orderly surface realm of strict distinctions and laid-down structures through which language works: this aspect of language is the side stressed by the structuralists, the Saussurean 'network of differences'. But ever-present is the linguistic 'unconscious', a realm of floating signifiers, random connections, improvisations, approximations, accidents, and 'slippage' – everything, that is, entailed in the post-structuralist view of language. Indeed, one way of characterising the process of deconstruction (whereby contradictory cross-currents of meaning are discovered in texts) is to see it as the 'unconscious' of the text emerging into and disrupting the 'conscious' or 'surface' meaning. These disruptive incursions into rational, previously stable structures are seen, for instance, in dreams, in poetry, and in modernist, experimental writing which distorts the surface of language (for example, the poetry of e. e. cummings). This 'random' element can never be escaped by even the most meticulous and painfully deliberate composer of prose. Clearly, since language is by definition an inventive and improvisatory practice, if cut off from Kristeva's realm of the semiotic it would instantly perish.

For her notion of the basic opposition between the semiotic and the symbolic Kristeva is indebted to Jacques Lacan and his distinction between two realms, the *Imaginary* and the *Symbolic*. The Imaginary realm is that of the young child at the pre-linguistic, pre-Oedipal stage. The self is not yet distinguished from

what is other than the self, and the body's sense of being separate from the rest of the world is not yet established. The child
lives in an Eden-like realm, free of both desire and deprivation.
The semiotic is seen as inherently subversive politically, and
always threatens the closed symbolic order embodied in such conventions as governments, received cultural values, and the grammar of standard language.

For some feminists this visionary 'semiotic' female world and
language evoked by Cixous and Kristeva is a vital theatre of possibilities, the value of which is to entertain the imagining of alternatives to the world which we now have, and which women in
particular now have. For others, it fatally hands over the world of
the rational to men and reserves for women a traditionally emotive, intuitive, trans-rational and 'privatised' arena. Not surprisingly, therefore, the language question is one of the most
contentious areas of feminist criticism.

Feminist criticism and psychoanalysis

The story so far of feminism's relationship with psychoanalysis is
simple in outline but complex in nuance. The story can be said
to begin, like so much else, with Kate Millett's *Sexual Politics* in
1969 which condemns Freud as a prime source of the patriarchal
attitudes against which feminists must fight. The influence of this
view within feminism is still very strong, but Freud was defended
in a series of important books in subsequent years, notably Juliet
Mitchell's *Psychoanalysis and Feminism* in 1974. This book
defends Freud against Millett by, in effect, using Millett's own
terms and concepts, especially the distinction, so crucial to feminism, between sex and gender, the former being a matter of biology, the latter a construct, something learned or acquired, rather
than 'natural'. This distinction is what Simone de Beauvoir
invokes in the famous first sentence of her book *The Second Sex*
(1949) when she writes 'One is not born a woman; rather, one
becomes a woman'. The project of de Beauvoir's book is one which
Sexual Politics sees itself as continuing. Mitchell's defence of
Freud, then, is to argue that Freud doesn't present the feminine
as something simply 'given and natural'. Female sexuality

(indeed, heterosexuality in general) isn't just there 'naturally' from the start, but is formed by early experiences and adjustments, and Freud shows the process of its being produced and constructed, particularly in the *Three Essays on the Theory of Sexuality* (in volume seven of the Penguin Freud, entitled *On Sexuality*). It follows that gender roles must be malleable and changeable, not inevitable and unchangeable givens.

Thus, the argument runs, the notion of penis envy need not be taken as simply concerning the male physical organ itself (whatever might have been Freud's intentions), but as concerning that organ as an emblem of social power and the advantages which go with it. (I am reminded of an advertisement – which was banned – showing a photograph of a nude woman with the caption 'What women need to succeed in a man's world'. The woman shown had male sexual organs crudely drawn in over her own.) In the reading discussed in the next section, Sandra Gilbert and Susan Gubar use the idea of 'social castration', which amounts to the same thing, for this term signifies women's lack of social power, this lack being represented, by means of the word 'castration', as a male possession, though not as in any sense a male attribute.

Jane Gallop's 1982 book *Feminism and Psychoanalysis* continues the rehabiliation of psychoanalysis, but by switching from the Freudian to the Lacanian variety, partly on the grounds that what is often implicit in Freud is explicit in Lacan's system, namely that the phallus is not the physical biological object but a symbol of the power which goes with it. While men, of course, come out of Lacan's writings better advantaged than women, none the less Lacan shows men too as powerless, since the fullness of signification, which the phallus also represents in Lacan's work, is not attainable by either men or women. Also, Lacan's way of writing – notoriously abstruse, playful, punning, and 'paralogical' (meaning beyond or above logic) seems to embody the 'feminine' or 'semiotic' aspect of language, rather than the 'masculine' or 'symbolic' aspect.

Another significant name in the rehabilitation of Freud is the British critic Jacqueline Rose whose book *The Haunting of Sylvia Plath* is an example of an applied feminist-psychoanalytic approach. Rose's project is to combine the insights of feminism, psychoanalysis and politics. She is joint editor, with Juliet Mitchell, of *Feminine Sexuality: Jacques Lacan and the école freudienne* (1982). The argument in favour of Lacan, and of Freud, is, again, that it shows sexual identity to be a 'cultural construct', gives a detailed series of 'insider' accounts of how the construction takes place, and shows examples of this conditioning being resisted.

The resulting position is (as Isobel Armstrong remarks in a article about Rose, in *The Times Higher Education Supplement* 16 July 1993, p. 15) a very complicated one. In general the defence of Freud and Lacan has been more favourably received by French and British feminists than by Americans (another interesting transgression of the usual Anglo-American versus French dichotomy). Elaine Showalter, for instance, in her essay about Ophelia (reprinted in Newton's *Theory into Practice* – see under General Readers in the Further reading section) is dismissive of Lacan's evident disregard of Ophelia – he promises to discuss her in his seminar on *Hamlet*, but somehow never gets round to it. Likewise, Jerry Aline Flieger, an American contributor to *Changing Subjects: The Making of Feminist Literary Criticism* (Greene and Kahn), sounds a note of scepticism when she writes:

> I was fascinated and troubled by Lacan's characterisation of the phallus as the Signifier of Signifiers, as well as by his infamous statements 'There is no sexual relation', and 'Woman does not exist'. Thus I was relieved and grateful when feminists such as Jacqueline Rose and Jane Gallop, in the late seventies and early eighties, performed ingenious and persuasive readings of Lacan as critic of phallocracy, rather than advocate.

(p. 267)

The effect of this comment is partly to draw attention to the ingenuity *needed* to mount such a defence.

Stephen Heath, in an essay in *Feminist Literary Criticism* (ed. Mary Eagleton) quotes Roland Barthes to the effect that 'The monument of psychoanalysis must be traversed – not bypassed' (p. 214). We might say that feminism began by trying to do the latter, then changed course and did the former. The tendency of American feminists to be unconvinced by the rehabilitation of

psychoanalysis can perhaps be explained by the fact that psychoanalysis has been more an accepted part of middle-class life in the
USA than it ever became in Europe. Hence, it is more difficult
for Americans to see it as still possessed of radical potential, least
of all for women. Further, there is a new emphasis in the 1990s
on the culturally-specific nature of psychoanalysis, and hence a
reluctance to claim any kind of universal validity for it. In Rose's
own work, as elsewhere, there is a strong and growing interest in
listening to the voices of the hitherto excluded 'Other', particularly those of the cultures and races which had no place in the
work of Freud or Lacan.

STOP and THINK

General: Within feminism there is a strong emphasis on the
'constructedness' of femininity, that is, on such matters as
conditioning and socialisation, and the influence of images and
representations of femininity in literature and culture. All
these formulations are ways of avoiding 'essentialism', which is
the contrary view that there is some natural, given essence of
the feminine, that is universal and unchangeable.

Anti-essentialism seems to me now (in the mid-1990s) the
dominant concept in critical theory, but there is some
awareness, too, that it is a notion which leaves us with certain
difficulties. For instance, does anti-essentialism, by making it
hard to make *any* generalisations about women, also make it
difficult to politicise women as a group? Does it tend to reduce
identity to the sum of circumstances, perhaps in spite of our
'instinctive' feelings that identity may be deeper than that? Is
the fact that we have such feelings admissable as evidence – on
either side? And in any case, what would consitute evidence on
either side of this question?

Specific: In the example discussed below, what are some of
the ways in which the critical assumptions and procedures
differ from those made in non-feminist approaches to the same
work? Compare it with the two essays mentioned at the start

of the example, or with the pieces in the Macmillan *Casebook on Wuthering Heights* (ed. Miriam Allott, 1970).

What feminist critics do

1. Rethink the canon, aiming at the rediscovery of texts written by women.
2. Revalue women's experience.
3. Examine representations of women in literature by men and women.
4. Challenge representations of women as 'Other', as 'lack', as part of 'nature'.
5. Examine power relations which obtain in texts and in life, with a view to breaking them down, seeing reading as a political act, and showing the extent of patriarchy.
6. Recognise the role of language in making what is social and constructed seem transparent and 'natural'.
7. Raise the question of whether men and women are 'essentially' different because of biology, or are socially constructed as different.
8. Explore the question of whether there is a female language, an *écriture féminine*, and whether this is also available to men.
9. 'Re-read' psychoanalysis to further explore the issue of female and male identity.
10. Question the popular notion of the death of the author, asking whether there are only 'subject positions ... constructed in discourse', or whether, on the contrary, the experience (e.g. of a black or lesbian writer) is central.
11. Make clear the ideological base of supposedly 'neutral' or 'mainstream' literary interpretations.

Feminist criticism: an example

As an example of feminist criticism I will take the account of *Wuthering Heights* by Sandra M. Gilbert and Susan Gubar, from their book *The Madwoman in the Attic*. The piece is reprinted in the widely-used *Debating Texts* (ed. Rick Rylance). Rylance reprints two other accounts of the same novel, one by Q. D. Leavis, which might be considered as liberal humanist, and one by Frank Kermode which might be seen as post-structuralist. Comparisons can also be made with Eagleton's Marxist account of the same novel in his book *Myths of Power: A Marxist Study of the Brontës*, to which Gilbert and Gubar refer.

Gilbert and Gubar's strategy with Brontë's novel is to see it as a female version of the male form known as the *Bildungsroman* (this German term means the 'formation' or 'education' novel) in which the hero's growth to manhood is traced, as a process of 'triumphant self-discovery', whereby an identity is discovered and a mission in life conceived and embarked upon – a classic example would be James Joyce's *A Portrait of the Artist as a Young Man*. For the heroine, however, things are different, and an equivalent novel (like *Wuthering Heights*) about the growth to womanhood records a process of 'anxious self-denial', this being the 'ultimate product of a female education'. Gilbert and Gubar say that 'What Catherine, or any girl, must learn is that she does not know her own name, and therefore cannot know either who she is or whom she is destined to be'. The process of denial involved they describe as 'social castration'. Effectively, Catherine has to leave behind all her instinctive preferences, signified by the Heights, and take on an alien attitude, signified by Thrushcross Grange. The point of the word 'castration' here is that in order to achieve acceptability and femininity Catherine has to lose the power which men take for granted, namely power over their own destiny. This is symbolised by the phallic guard-dog, 'purple tongue hanging half a foot out of its mouth' which bites Catherine's foot as she enters the Grange, a symbolic castration, they say. She then undergoes the initiation ritual of imprisonment at the Grange, similar to that undergone by traditional heroines like Persephone and Snow White.

The Grange is the home of 'concealment and doubleness'. Here she learns, as Brontë says, 'to adopt a double character without exactly intending to deceive anyone', that is, say Gilbert and Gubar, she must learn 'to repress her own impulses, must girdle her own energies with the iron stays of "reason"'. This 'education in doubleness' involves 'an actual doubling or fragmentation of her personality', as Heathcliff, 'her rebellious alter-ego' is forcibly excluded from her life. In this spirit of self-denial she agrees to marry Edgar, even though she says of Heathcliff that he is 'more myself than I am'. In this process Heathcliff too is degraded and powerless, and so 'Catherine has learned, correctly, that if it is degrading to be a woman it is even more degrading to be *like* a woman'. Hence, Gilbert and Gubar argue, against the run of *Wuthering Heights* criticism, that Edgar does not represent an image of effeminacy in contrast to the manliness of Heathcliff; on the contrary, in his ruthless employment of his social and sexual power, he is an embodiment of the patriarchal principle. The marriage 'inexorably locks her into a social system which denies her autonomy', so that Heathcliff's return, the 'return of the repressed', as we might call it in Freudian terms, 'represents the return of her true self's desires without the rebirth of her former powers', hence the inevitable descent into self-rejection (Catherine fails to recognise her own face in the mirror), self-starvation, madness, and death, 'a complex of psycho-neurotic symptoms that is almost classically associated with female feelings of powerlessness and rage'. Thus, the events of the novel are 'strongly' read as emblems of the construction of gender identity.

Selected reading

Readers

Belsey, Catherine & Moore, Jane, eds, *The Feminist Reader: Essays in Gender and the Politics of Literary Criticism* (Macmillan, 1989).
  Excellent introduction. Manageable size. Important essays on the crucial issues.
Eagleton, Mary, ed. *Feminist Literary Criticism* (Longman, 1991).
  Interesting collection, with essays paired to represent opposing views on key issues. Very good editorial commentary.
Eagleton, Mary, ed. *Feminist Literary Theory: A Reader* (Blackwell, 1986).
  Short extracts from a wide range of critical material.
Humm, Maggie, ed. *Feminisms: A Reader* (Harvester, 1992).
  An excellent book, wide-ranging and accessible, on feminisms from Woolf to the present day, including black and lesbian feminisms. Sub-

sectioned by category, with a separate introduction for each one.

Marks, Elaine & de Courtivron, Isabelle, eds, *New French Feminisms* (Harvester, 1981).

The pioneering book in introducing much of this material to English-speaking readers.

Moi, Toril, *French Feminist Thought: A Reader* (Blackwell, 1987).

General

Brownstein, Rachel, *Becoming a Heroine* (Penguin, 1982).

A readable and thoughtful account of what it takes to become a heroine in a 'classic' novel.

Gilbert, Sandra & Gubar, Susan, *The Madwoman in the Attic: The Woman Writer and the Nineteenth Century Literary Imagination* (Yale University Press, 1979).

A famous book with chapters on Austen, Brontës, George Eliot, etc.

Gilbert, Sandra & Gubar, Susan, *No Man's Land: The Place of the Woman Writer in the Twentieth Century* (Yale University Press, 1988).

Much of interest. See chapter seven, 'Women, literature and the Great War', and compare with the example of gay criticism in the next chapter.

Greene, Gayle & Kahn, Coppelia, eds, *Making a Difference: Feminist Literary Criticism* (Methuen, 1985).

Greene, Gayle & Kahn, Coppelia, eds, *Changing Subjects: the Making of Feminist Literary Criticism* (Routledge, 1993).

An interesting collection of essays in intellectual autobiography by leading figures in the field.

Jacobus, Mary, ed. *Women Writing and Writing about Women* (Croom Helm, 1979).

Chapters on *Villette*, George Eliot, Woolf, Ibsen, etc.

Jacobus, Mary, *Reading Woman: Essays in Feminist Criticism* (Methuen, 1986).

Chapters on *Villette*, *The Mill on the Floss*, Freud's case studies (see '*Dora* and the Pregnant Madonna', etc.).

Mills, Sara, *et al.*, *Feminist Readings/Feminists Reading* (Harvester, 1989). Discussions of major varieties of feminism and their application to a range of canonical literary texts. Readable, practical, and informative.

Minogue, Sally, ed. *Problems Within Feminist Criticism* (Routledge, 1993).

An interesting book which deals with some topics which have caused real difficulty.

Moi, Toril, *Sexual/Textual Politics* (Methuen, 1985).
A very influential book, though its view of the main kinds of feminist theory and criticism has been challenged.

Ruthven, K. K., *Feminist Literary Studies: An Introduction* (Cambridge University Press, 1984).
A useful overview with a bias towards 'Anglo-American' variants.

Showalter, Elaine, *A Literature of Their Own* (Princeton, 1977).

Showalter, Elaine, *The New Feminist Criticism: Essays on Women, Literature, and Theory* (Pantheon, 1985).

Stubbs, Patricia, *Women and Fiction: Feminism and the Novel 1880-1920* (Harvester, 1979).

7

Lesbian/gay criticism

Lesbian and gay theory

Lesbian and gay literary theory has emerged prominently as a distinct field only in the 1990s – there is nothing about it, for instance, in Terry Eagleton's *Literary Theory: An Introduction* (1983), or in the first edition of Raman Selden's *A Reader's Guide to Contemporary Literary Theory* (1985). As with women's studies twenty years before, the growing significance and acceptance of this new field is indicated by the presence of 'lesbian and gay studies' sections in some mainstream bookshops and publishers' academic catalogues, and by the establishment of relevant undergraduate courses, for which there is now a course reader, the *Lesbian and Gay Studies Reader*, published in 1993. There is also a relevant MA course, 'Sexual Dissidence and Cultural Change', at the University of Sussex. The field is strongly multi-disciplinary, with perhaps a predominance of cultural studies over literary material.

But lesbian/gay criticism is not of exclusive interest to gays and lesbians, and it may be helpful, in defining the nature of this field, to make an initial comparison with feminist criticism. It is obvious that not all literary criticism written by women is feminist; that not all books about women writers are feminist; that feminist writing need not be by women, and that feminist criticism is not directed exclusively at a female readership. Likewise, books about gay writers, or by gay critics, are not necessarily part of lesbian and gay studies, nor are books that are part of this field directed solely at a gay readership or relevant only to gay sexuality.

What, then, is the purpose of lesbian/gay criticism? The *Lesbian and Gay Studies Reader* tells us that 'lesbian/gay studies does for sex and sexuality approximately what women's studies does for gender', this being described a few lines earlier as establishing 'the centrality of gender as a fundamental category of historical analysis and understanding' (p. xv). In lesbian/gay criticism, the defining feature is making sexual orientation 'a fundamental category of analysis and understanding'. Like feminist criticism, then, it has social and political aims, in particular 'an oppositional design' (p. xvi) upon society, for it is 'informed by resistance to homophobia [fear and prejudice against homosexuality] and heterosexism ... [and to] the ideological and institutional practices of heterosexual privilege'.

Lesbian feminism

However, lesbian/gay criticism is not a single unified body of work. There are differences of emphasis between lesbian and gay theory, and two major strands of thinking within lesbian theory itself. The first of these is *lesbian feminism*, which is best understood by seeing it initially in the context of its own origins from within feminism, for lesbian studies emerged in the 1980s as a kind of annexe of feminist criticism, before acquiring disciplinary independence. Indeed, one reading of the academic situation in the 1990s would be that feminism has become so successful and so institutionalised that lesbian studies now occupies the radical ground vacated by feminism. On this reading of the situation, feminism found it difficult to accommodate difference, whether racial, cultural, or sexual, and tended to universalise the experience of white, middle-class, urban heterosexual women. This kind of critique of feminism originated in the work of African-American critics who pointed out that academic feminism had reproduced the structures of patriarchal inequality within itself by excluding the voices and experiences of black women. This case is memorably put, for instance, in *Ain't I a Woman: Black Women and Feminism* (Pluto Press, 1986) by bell hooks, first published in

1982. A similar accusation against feminism was made by lesbian critics: feminism assumed, they argued, that there existed an essential female identity which all women had in common irrespective of differences of race, class, or sexual orientation. Bonnie Zimmerman, among others, in a well-known essay 'What has never been: an overview of lesbian feminist criticism' attacked this 'essentialism', pointing out the way 'the perceptual screen of heterosexism' prevented any consideration of lesbian issues in pioneering feminist writing (p. 180 in the reprinting of the essay listed at the end of this chapter). Hence, a feminist literary-critical classic like Sandra Gilbert and Susan Gubar's *The Madwoman in the Attic* contains only a single passing reference to lesbianism.

'Classic' feminism, then, had marginalised or ignored lesbianism. This state of affairs was countered by arguing that, on the contrary, lesbianism should be regarded as the most complete form of feminism. This is argued in another crucial essay in the development of lesbian feminism, 'The woman identified woman', by the Radicalesbian collective, published in *Radical Feminism* (ed. Anne Koedt *et al.*, Quadrangle, 1973). The lesbian feminist position identified in this essay makes lesbianism central to feminism, since lesbianism turns away from various forms of collusion with patriarchal exploitation and instead consists of relationships among women which, by definition, constitute a form of resistance to, and a radical reorganising of, existing forms of social relations.

The conflict between heterosexual feminists and lesbians thus opened up, was partly defused in another important essay, by Adrienne Rich, which introduced the notion of the 'lesbian continuum' (in her essay 'Compulsory heterosexuality and lesbian existence', collected in her *Blood, Bread and Poetry: Selected Prose, 1979–1985*, Virago, 1987):

> I mean the term *lesbian continuum* to include a range – through each woman's life and throughout history – of woman-identified experience; not simply the fact that a woman has had or consciously desired genital sexual experience with another woman.
>
> (Quoted by Zimmerman in Greene & Kann's *Making a Difference*, p. 184)

This concept of the lesbian continuum therefore designates a wide variety of female behaviour, running, for instance, from informal mutual help networks set up by women within particular professions or institutions, through supportive female friendships and, finally, to sexual relationships. Zimmerman comments that this definition has the virtue of suggesting interconnections among the various ways in which women bond together. As Paulina Palmer points out, however, (see chapter two in her *Contemporary Lesbian Writing*) seeing lesbianism in this way has the curious effect of de-sexualising it, so that it becomes almost wholly a political act, rather than a sexual orientation, and is hence 'sanitised' and transformed into something else. Also, the corollary of the position is a moral condemnation of female heterosexuality as a betrayal of women and their interests, with the implication that women can only achieve integrity through lesbianism.

The two ideas of the 'woman identified woman' and the lesbian continuum overlap a great deal, but as ideas they have a clarity and flexibility which ensure their continued importance as personal and intellectual reference points. They introduce the notion of choice and allegiance into matters of sex and gender, so that sexuality is not seen as something merely 'natural' and unchanging, but rather as a construction and as subject to change.

As a result of these critiques, lesbian approaches separated from mainstream feminism throughout the eighties, but only in the nineties does lesbian criticism also reject the essentialism which had, so to speak, been inherited from feminism. Thus, when in 'Lesbians like this and that: some notes on lesbian criticism for the nineties' Zimmerman again surveys the field of lesbian criticism, ten years on from the earlier piece, what strikes her about her original essay is its assumption that lesbianism is a stable category, a 'transcendental signifier', which is just there as a fact, as a trans-historical constant, rather than (as it is) a late nineteenth-century construct. In the 1990s a second, less essentialist, notion of lesbianism has emerged, within the sphere of what is now known as 'queer theory'.

Queer theory

So far, then, we have discussed the nature and development of the thinking designated as lesbian feminism. The second kind of lesbian thinking, designated libertarian lesbianism by Paulina Palmer, breaks away from feminism and makes new allegiances, in particular, with gay men rather than with other women, and this kind of lesbian theory sees itself as part of the field of 'queer theory' or 'queer studies', terms increasingly used by gays, in spite of the homophobic origins of the word 'queer' as an abusive one in this context. These terms date (at least in their institutional acceptance) from the 1990 conference on 'queer theory' at the University of California, Santa Cruz. As we have said, 'queer theory' in this sense, rather than being 'woman centred', like the lesbian feminism just described, rejects female separatism and instead sees an identity of political and social interests with gay men. The key underlying question, for anyone choosing between these two possible alignments, is whether it is gender or sexuality which is the more fundamental in personal identity. Choosing the latter of course emphasises lesbianism as a form of sexuality, rather than a form of female bonding or patriarchal resistance. It tends to endorse 'experimental' forms of sexuality within lesbianism, such as sado-masochistic and butch–femme role play. However, it is sometimes argued that one of the effects of accepting the comprehensive term 'queer theory' is ultimately to perpetuate the patriarchal subservience of women's interests to men's.

How exactly, then, in theoretical terms, does queer theory differ from lesbian feminism? The answer is that like many other current critical approaches, lesbian/gay studies within this 'queer theory' ambit have drawn particularly on post-structuralist work of the 1980s. One of the main points of post-structuralism was to 'deconstruct' binary opposition (like that between speech and writing, for instance) showing, firstly, that the distinction between paired opposites is not absolute, since each term in the pairing can only be understood and defined in terms of the other, and, secondly that it is possible to reverse the hierarchy within such pairs, and so 'privilege' the second term rather than the first (See Chapter 3, pp. 74–5). Hence, in lesbian/gay studies the pair heterosexual/homosexual is deconstructed in this way. The opposition within this pair is seen, firstly, as inherently unstable: as Diana Fuss puts it, in the introduction to *Inside/outside: lesbian theories, gay theories*, much current work in the field aims 'to call into question the stability and ineradicability of the hetero/homo hierarchy' (p. 1). In an essay which we might take as a practical example of how this dichotomy can be deconstructed Richard Meyer writes, in the same volume, about the film star Rock Hudson, once the screen epitome of attractive heterosexual masculinity. In fact, Hudson was gay, but while initially shocking to some, this is less disturbing of categories than the sense that the very qualities which made his image attractive to women were related to his homosexuality, for 'Hudson promised straight women a place of sexual safety – he would acquiesce to domesticity without insisting on male domination'. (Diana Fuss, p. 282).

Likewise, straight male viewers had been relieved 'to find a role-model who did not require the exhaustive work of machismo to "measure up" to its masculinity' (p. 282). Deconstructing the hetero/homo dichotomy in this way has radical implications, since all such distinctions are constructed in the same way, so that to challenge this one is to challenge all the others too.

This anti-essentialism in relation to sexual identity is taken further by other critics. Judith Butler, a prominent contributor to *Inside/Outside*, points out in her essay that 'identity categories', like 'gay' and 'straight', 'tend to be instruments of regulatory regimes, whether as the normalizing categories of oppressive structures or as the rallying points for liberatory contestations of that very oppression' (pp. 14–15). Hence, it might be argued, she says, that the concept of homosexuality is itself part of homophobic (anti-gay) discourse, and indeed, the term 'homosexual' is a medical-legal one, first used in 1869 in Germany, and preceding the invention of the corresponding term 'heterosexual' by eleven years. In this sense, heterosexuality only comes into being as a consequence of the crystalisation of the notion of homosexuality. Thus, lesbianism, say, is not a stable, essential identity, so that, in her words, 'identity can become a site of contest and revision' (p. 19).

Taking this further, she argues that all identities, including

gender identities, are 'a kind of impersonation and approximation
... *a kind of imitation for which there is no original*' (p. 21). This
opens the way to a 'postmodernist' notion of identity as a constant switching among a range of different roles and positions,
drawn from a kind of limitless data bank of potentialities. Further, what is called into question here is the distinction between
the naturally-given, normative 'self' of heterosexuality and the
rejected 'Other' of homosexuality. The 'Other', in these formulations, is as much something within us as beyond us, and 'self' and
'Other' are always *implicated* in each other, in the root sense of
this word, which means to be intertwined or folded into each
other. As basic psychology shows, what is identified as the external 'Other' is usually part of the self which is rejected and hence
projected outwards.

Another critic who argues the fluidity of identity, including
sexual identity, is Eve Sedgwick in her highly influential *Epistemology of the Closet*. Sedgwick considers how coming 'out of the
closet' (openly revealing one's gay or lesbian sexual orientation) is
not a single absolute act. Gayness may be openly declared to
family and friends, not so comprehensively to employers and colleagues, and perhaps not at all to (say) banks or insurance com-
panies. Hence, being 'in' or 'out' is not a simple dichotomy or a
once and for all event. Degrees of concealment and openness co-
exist in the same lives. Nor will sexual orientation alone usually
make a person a complete outsider, and therefore innocent of all
patriarchal or exploitative taint. A gay person may be a comfort-
ably tenured academic, very much a privileged insider in the eyes
of, say, a factory worker, gay or not, in a small town. Sedgwick's
point, then, concerns the way subject identity is necessarily a
complex mixture of chosen allegiances, social position, and professional roles, rather than a fixed inner essence.

The consequences of this kind of argument are far-reaching,
both for politics and for literary criticism. Let's consider the
political consequences first. Drawing upon a post-structuralist
reading of Saussure, we show that such apparently elemental categories as heterosexual and homosexual do not designate fixed
essences at all – they are merely part of a structure of differences
without fixed terms, like Saussurean signifiers (see Chapter 2).

We construct instead an anti-essentialist, postmodernist concept
of identity as a series of masks, roles, and potentialities, a kind of
amalgam of everything which is provisional, contingent, and
improvisatory. The political consequence is that when we claim
that gayness, or blackness, is merely a shifting signifier, not a
fixed entity, then it becomes difficult to imagine how an effective
political campaign could be mounted on its behalf. For in the
name of anti-essentialism we have removed these bottom line concepts on which all forms of 'identity politics' depend. (By identity politics we mean those which campaign for and by groups
disadvantaged by some aspect of their identity, such as their
gender, their race, or their sexual orientation. The opposite of
identity politics would be class politics, where the campaign is on
behalf of people disadvantaged by some aspect of their situation
– (by being an under paid mine-workers, for instance).

The literary-critical consequences of anti-essentialism are two-
fold. Firstly, there is the obvious difficulty of deciding what a les-
bian/gay text is. In the list of possibilities which follow we can
take 'lesbian' to mean 'lesbian or gay'. The possibilities are (in a
slightly re-worked version of Zimmerman's formulation) that a
lesbian/gay text is:

1. One which is written by a lesbian (if so, how do we determine
    who is a lesbian, especially if we take the anti-essentialist line
    just outlined?).
2. One written about lesbians (which might be by a heterosex-
    ual woman or man, and which would also come up against the
    problem of deciding what a lesbian/gay person is in non-
    essentialist terms).
3. One that expresses a lesbian 'vision' (which has yet to be sat-
    isfactorily described).

The 1. and 2. categories here seem inadequate as they stand, since
merely writing about books by and/or about gays is clearly not
enough, since gayness is not being defined as an inherent, essential unchanging category, but as part of a complex of other factors. A solution may be to adopt an approach which is historically
specific. Thus, gayness in a novel or an author of the 1920s is not
the same as in the 1980s or 1990s, and part of the critique will

involve showing how this is so. On the 3. category, critics need
to be aware of wider metaphorical extensions of gayness, for
instance, the suggested link between lesbianism and a state of
being poised on the threshold between categories: 'In general, lesbian critical reading proposes the blurring of boundaries between
self and other, subject and object, lover and beloved as the lesbian moment in any text'. (Zimmerman, 'Lesbians like this and
that', p. 11). Thus lesbianism is theoretically linked with notions
of 'liminal' consciousness when existing categories are in process
of deconstruction.

Yet this 3. category also has obvious risks, notably that gayness
will probably assume too great an emblematic burden, since it will
tend to be romanticised and stand as a textual emblem of resistance and disruption of all kinds. Zimmerman quotes examples
from recent critical writing of this romanticising/idealising tendency. Lesbianism is a force against 'rigid definitions and polar
oppositions', expressed in terms of 'gaps', 'spaces', 'disruption',
the 'experimental', 'radical disruption', 'interrogation', and so on.
This 'heady romantic stuff' ('Lesbians like this and that', p. 4)
represents what we might call super-essentialism, since it tries to
make one kind of resistance stand for all resistance, and thus
places a political and social burden on sexual orientation which is
surely unreasonable.

A final, and more specific literary critical consequence of anti-
essentialism is a tendency to devalue literary realism, since it
tends to rely upon notions of fixed identities and stable points of
view. For instance, a realist novel typically has an omniscient narrator who presents and interprets the events from a fixed moral
and intellectual position, a linear time sequence in which events
unfold chronologically, and characters who are presented as stable
essences with a personality which develops in an orderly and
cumulative way. Hence, lesbian/gay criticism of the recent 'queer
theory' phase tends to favour (as do most other kinds of current
critical theory) texts and genres which subvert this kind of familiar literary realism, like thrillers, comic and parodic fiction, and
sexual fantasy. Thus a novel like Jeanette Winterson's *Oranges are
not the only fruit* (1985, Vintage edition 1991) is of interest to the
lesbian/gay critic not just because of its lesbian subject matter,

but also because of its many anti-realist elements. In her 1991 introduction the author says that the book is 'an experimental novel: its interests are anti-linear' and answers her own question 'Is *Oranges* an autobiographical novel?' by replying 'No not at all and yes of course'. She says (perhaps a little exaggeratedly) that the book is 'unlike any other novel' in structure, style, and content, and deliberately makes the manner of the telling draw attention to itself by her use of 'a complicated narrative structure ... a very large vocabulary and beguilingly straight-forward syntax'. The theme of a young girl's discovering her sexual identity is undercut with comic elements and details, and the narrative flow is interrupted with mythical and fantasy passages. As Paulina Palmer writes of these passages, 'the interplay of narratives which they create highlight the part which fantasy plays in the construction of the adolescent psyche and gives a more complex and multifaceted representation than is usual in the Coming out novel' (*Contemporary Lesbian Writing*, p. 101). In a basic way, then, this novel and its critical treatment, typifies the anti-realist leanings of lesbian/gay criticism.

What lesbian/gay critics do

1. Identify and establish a canon of 'classic' lesbian/gay writers whose work constitutes a distinct tradition. These are, in the main, twentieth-century writers, such as (for lesbian writers in Britain) Virginia Woolf, Vita Sackville-West, Dorothy Richardson, Rosamund Lehmann, and Radclyffe Hall.

2. Identify lesbian/gay episodes in mainstream work and discuss them as such (for example, the relationship between Jane and Helen in *Jane Eyre*), rather than reading same-sex pairings in non-specific ways, for instance, as symbolising two aspects of the same character (Zimmerman).

3. Set up an extended, metaphorical sense of 'lesbian/gay' so that it connotes a moment of crossing a boundary, or blurring a set of categories. All such 'liminal' moments mirror the moment of self-identification as lesbian or gay, which is necessarily an act of conscious resistance to established norms and boundaries.

4. Expose the 'homophobia' of mainstream literature and criticism, as seen in ignoring or denigrating the homosexual aspects of the work of major canonical figures, for example, by omitting overtly homosexual love lyrics from selections or discussions of the poetry of W. H. Auden (Mark Lilly).

5. Foreground homosexual aspects of mainstream literature which have previously been glossed over, for example the strongly homo-erotic tenderness seen in a good deal of First World War poetry.

6. Foreground literary genres, previously neglected, which significantly influenced ideals of masculinity or femininity, such as the nineteenth-century adventure stories with a British 'Empire' setting (for example those by Rudyard Kipling and Rider Haggard) discussed by Joseph Bristow in *Empire Boys* (Routledge, 1991).

STOP and THINK

General: The example at the end of this section is concerned with the second, fourth and fifth of the activities listed above. It suggests that there is a sharp difference, in terms of the sexual feelings involved, between First and Second World War poetry. How far do you feel this to be justified? Do you agree that the former is often homo-erotic while the latter seldom is? Compare two relevant anthologies in the light of this question, such as Jon Silkin's *The Penguin Book of First World War Poetry* and *The Terrible Rain* (see below).

More specific: First World War poets often use the motif of bathing with an erotic charge. Lilly quotes from 'Soldiers Bathing' by R. D. Greenway ('You strong and hairy sergeant / Stretched naked to the skies ...'). A more famous poem with the same title, by F. T. Prince, is often said to be the best-known poem of the Second World War. How would you discuss it in terms of the debate on war poetry summarised here? This poem is included in *The Terrible Rain*.

Corpses in First World War poems are often homo-eroticised. A famous corpse poem of the Second World War is Keith

Douglas's 'Vergissmieinnicht' (*The Terrible Rain: The War Poets, 1939–1945*, ed. Brian Gardner, Methuen, 1977). Illustrate and discuss some of the differences between this and 1914–18 material in the terms used in the Lilly section.

Lesbian/gay criticism: an example

As an example of this kind of criticism we can take the chapter 'The love poetry of the First World War' in Mark Lilly's *Gay Men's Literature in the Twentieth Century*. The essay is a straight-forward survey of a range of First World War poetry from this viewpoint, drawing on poems anthologised in Martin Taylor's *Lads: Love Poetry of the Trenches*, and on the views put forward in its introduction. The essay begins by commenting on the intense feelings between men evident in war conditions, and the general reluctance to admit the presence of homo-erotic under-tones, or more, in such relationships. The difficulty of admitting their existence is compounded by the fact that an army in wartime is the particular expression of the most conventionally masculine aspects of a country ('a collective symbol of the controlled viril-ity and power of the society itself', Taylor, p. 65). Hence 'the resistance amongst heterosexuals to the idea that men *upon whom otherwise they would wish to bestow their deepest admiration* might have enjoyed other men carnally' (p. 65, italics in the original). At the same time, references to armies by their own side tend to emphasise the often extreme youthfulness of those involved – the jingoistic headline of the British *Sun* newspaper during the Gulf War is quoted – 'Our boys go in'.

As well as the intensity of contact brought about by wartime circumstances, war poetry at the time functioned as a kind of licensed area in which it was possible to express male-to-male feelings in an unusually direct and open way (this had changed by the Second World War). Hence, expressing love for an (albeit usually dead) comrade-in-arms was frequent in First World War poetry, though it is difficult to know exactly what is meant by 'love' in these poems (or exactly what kind of love is meant). Most likely the poems frequently operate on a number of different levels, with the heterosexual reader able to read this 'love' simply as grief for the loss of a friend. This enables the poems to be printed and very widely circulated at the time without scandal. Very likely the poems operate in this multilayered way for the writers too, since by no means all the poets were self-acknowledged gays. Hence, 'conventions of expression sometimes make brotherly affection, physical tenderness and sexual desire all sound the same' (p. 66). If we imagine something like Rich's 'lesbian continuum' to have a male equivalent, especially in the horrific conditions of war, then we would emphasise that these would not each be distinct and separate states. Lilly makes this point, but in different terms, when he suggests that three commonly-used terms have slightly different references, so that generalised feelings of affection and physical tenderness might be described as 'homo-erotic', whereas feelings of specific sexual desire would be called 'homo-sexual' or 'gay'. Naturally, this will open up the field beyond those who were 'certainly (Sassoon) or almost certainly (Owen) gay' (p. 66).

Lilly points out that a frequent motif in these poems is to see 'same-sex love as superior to men's love for women'. One such poem is actually called 'Passing the Love of Women' and is written by army chaplain Studdert Kennedy in the persona of an ordinary soldier:

Yes, I've sat in the summer twilight,
Wiv a nice girl 'and in 'and,
But I've thought even then of the shell 'oles,
Where the boys of the old Bat. stand.
I've turned to 'er lips for 'r kisses,
And I've found them kisses cold,
Stone cold and pale like a twice-told tale,
What has gorn all stale and old.

And the poem concludes (referring to women) 'But I knows a stronger love than their's, / And that is the love of men.' It is interesting that these poems often seem unusually explicit at several levels, for instance, about physical feelings between men and women, and about the impossibility of any solace being had from religion – we might expect the poem to end (especially, perhaps,

as it is written by a parson) with the line 'And that is the love of
God', but such references seem rare. This tendency towards the
'multi-transgression' of several boundaries simultaneously lends
some weight to the contention in lesbian/gay studies that breaking the sexual norm is always potentially emblematic of norm-
breaking in general.

However, the poems cannot be seen as simply celebratory of
socially-stigmatised forms of love, since the sexual object for
whom admiration is expressed in the poems is usually dead (if a
named or specific individual). Where a generalised admiration for
the male body is expressed, the body in question is usually that
of a corpse (often an enemy corpse, it seems to me), so much so
that Lilly detects an element of necrophilia in this poetry. Sometimes the open expression of sexual desire is combined with
necrophiliac elements, as in Herbert Read's 'My Company (iii)':

> A man of mine
> Lies on the wire;
> And he will rot
> And first his lips
> The worms will eat.
> It is not thus I would hev him kissed
> But with the warm passionate lips
> Of his comrade here.
>
> (*Gay Men's Literature in the Twentieth Century*, pp. 78-9).

Hence, in order to express these homosexual feelings, the poet
first ensures that there is a barrier to their fulfilment – there is no
possibility of actual physical expression of these feelings because
the would-be recipient is dead. The exception is that there are
many poems in which the man written about is wounded – many
of these poems are gory, and Lilly makes a connection with the
homo-erotic poems about wounds and hospitals in the American
Civil War by the nineteenth-century American poet Walt Whitman. The wound is erotically charged in First World War poetry
because it allows tender physical contact between males, the war
thus becoming a 'safe' area in which feelings usually suppressed
can be openly expressed, while at the same time the intensity of
the circumstances means that the feelings evoked and expressed

are different from those felt in more ordinary circumstances. Lilly uses the parallel example of the football field, where men kiss and embrace each other passionately in public, behaviour for which they could still be arrested (in Britain) if it were happening in the street.

Hence, the poems need to be placed in their context to be properly understood. After all, the army itself exploited these feelings at the start of the war with the setting of 'Pals' regiments, in which large numbers of men from the same district enlisted and served in units together. The intention was to draw upon networks of trust and loyalty founded on school friendships, upon feelings of class solidarity, and on local identities and allegiances. (The experiment was hurriedly abandoned when whole neighbourhoods were plunged into mass mourning when an attack or bombardment took place.) Hence, it could be said (as Lilly suggests) that this kind of poetry had official sanction, since it was good for morale. Certainly combatants' poetry had ready access to publication, in newspapers, poetry journals, and school magazines. The continuum of feelings, then, expressed in this poetry, and the varying degrees of self-knowledge and self-deceiving with which it seems to be expressed, tends ultimately to 'deconstruct' the notion of gayness as (from the heterosexual point of view) a distinct 'Other' with its own stable and separate identity.

Selected reading

Abelove, Henry, Barale, Michele Aina & Halperin, David, eds, *Lesbian and Gay Studies Reader*, (Routledge, 1993).

A massive and comprehensive collection. Section one chapter two is an extract from the influential *Epistemology of the Closet*. The main literary chapters are in Section VII, 'Between the Pages', including Dollimore on Wilde and Gide. Section XII (pp. 662-5) of the invaluable 'Suggestions for further reading' contains the best bibiography there is on this field up to August 1992.

Bristow, Joseph, ed. *Sexual Sameness: Textual Difference in Lesbian and Gay Writing* (Routledge, 1992).

Contains chapters on the literary representation of same-sex love in major writers such as E .M. Forster, Walt Whitman, and Sylvia

Townsend Warner.

Dollimore, Jonathan, *Sexual Dissidence: Augustine to Wilde, Freud to Foucault* (Clarendon, 1991).

Part Three, chapters three to five inclusive, debates the issue of essentialism touched upon in the present section.

Fuss, Diana, ed. *Inside/Out: Lesbian Theories, Gay Theories* (Routledge, 1992).

I found the introduction and Section 1 chapter one (by Judith Butler) very useful, but there is otherwise little here about literature as such. Chapter ten, on Radclyffe Hall's lesbian novel *The Well of Loneliness* is actually about the various covers in which the book has been issued.

Lilly, Mark, ed. *Lesbian and Gay Writing*, (Macmillan, 1990).

Chapters five, six, and ten are about lesbian and gay poetry, very welcome in a field otherwise dominated (like so much current theory) by writing about prose.

Lilly, Mark, *Gay Men's Literature in the Twentieth Century* (Macmillan, 1993).

An accesible book which does not presuppose wide theoretical knowledge. The first chapter is a general survey of mainstream criticism of gay writers ('The Homophobic Academy'), and the rest are on major authors, including Byron, Wilde, Forster, First World War Poetry, Tennessee Williams, James Baldwin, Joe Orton, and Christopher Isherwood.

Munt, Sally, ed. *New Lesbian Criticism: Literary and Cultural Readings* (Harvester, 1992).

Contains useful general theoretical essays, pieces on major figures like the black lesbian poet and theorist Audre Lorde, and material on lesbian popular culture, lesbian utopian fiction, and lesbian pornography.

Palmer, Paulina, *Contemporary Lesbian Writing: Dreams, Desire Difference* (Open University Press, 1993).

Begins with a chapter outlining a range of theoretical perspectives and then has chapters on a variety of relevant genres, including political fictions, the thriller, the comic novel, and fantasy fiction.

Sedgwick, Eve Kosovsky, *Between Men: English Literature and Male Homosexual Desire* (Columbia University Press, 1985).

This and the following book have played an important part in laying the theoretical basis of current lesbian/gay criticism.

Sedgwick, Eve Kosovsky, *Epistemology of the Closet* (Harvester, 1991).

Taylor, Martin, *Lads: Love Poetry of the Trenches* (Constable, 1989).

An anthology of poetry, with an introduction which 're-positions' this body of work. Compare the selection and its commentary with more conventional ones, such as *The Penguin Book of First World War Poetry*, edited by Jon Silkin.

Zimmerman, Bonnie, 'What has never been: an overview of lesbian feminist criticism', reprinted in *Making a Difference: Feminist Literary Criticism*, eds, Gayle Greene and Coppelia Kahn (Methuen, 1985).

An influential survey of lesbian criticism up to the time of its publication, and a good starting point for beginners in this field.

Zimmerman, Bonnie, 'Lesbians like this and that: some notes on lesbian criticism for the nineties' in Sally Munt (see above).

Another survey of the field, written ten years after the previous item, and considering the issues and options for the nineties.

8
Marxist criticism

Beginnings and basics of Marxism

Karl Marx (1818–1883), a German philosopher, and Friedrich
Engels (1820–1895), a German sociologist (as he would now be
called), were the joint founders of this school of thought. Marx
was the son of a lawyer but spent most of his life in great poverty
as a political exile from Germany living in Britain (he was
expelled after the 1848 'year of revolutions'). Engels had left Germany in 1842 to work in Manchester for his father's textile firm.
They met after Marx had read an article by Engels in a journal
to which they both contributed. They themselves called their economic theories 'Communism' (rather than 'Marxism'), designating their belief in the state ownership of industry, transport, etc.,
rather than private ownership. Marx and Engels announced the
advent of Communism in their jointly-written *Communist Mani-
festo* of 1848.

The aim of Marxism is to bring about a classless society, based
on the common ownership of the means of production, distribution, and exchange. Marxism is a *materialist* philosophy: that is,
it tries to explain things without assuming the existence of a
world or of forces beyond the natural world around us, and the
society we live in. It looks for concrete, scientific, logical explanations of the world of observable fact. (Its opposite is *idealist* philosophy, which *does* believe in the existence of a spiritual 'world
elsewhere' and would offer, for instance, religious explanations of
life and conduct). But whereas other philosophies merely seek to

understand the world, Marxism (as Marx famously said) seeks to change it. Marxism sees progress as coming about through the struggle for power between different social classes. This view of history as class struggle (rather than as, for instance, a succession of dynasties, or as a gradual progress towards the attainment of national identity and sovereignty) regards it as 'motored' by the competition for economic, social, and political advantage. The exploitation of one social class by another is seen especially in modern industrial capitalism, particularly in its unrestricted nineteenth-century form. The result of this exploitation is *alienation*, which is the state which comes about when the worker is 'deskilled' and made to perform fragmented, repetitive tasks in a sequence of whose nature and purpose he or she has no overall grasp. By contrast, in the older 'pre-industrial' or 'cottage industry' system of manufacture, home and workplace were one, the worker completed the whole production process in all its variety, and was in direct contact with those who might buy the product. These alienated workers have undergone the process of *reification*, which is a term used in Marx's major work, *Das Kapital*, but not developed there. It concerns the way, when capitalist goals and questions of profit and loss are paramount, workers are bereft of their full humanity and are thought of as 'hands' or 'the labour force', so that, for instance, the effects of industrial closures are calculated in purely economic terms. People, in a word, become things.

There were various influences on early Marxist thinking in addition to that of the political experiences of its founders, including the work of the eighteenth-century German philosopher Hegel (especially his idea of the *dialectic*, whereby opposing forces or ideas bring about new situations or ideas). Marxism also built upon the socialist thinking which was produced in France at the time of the French Revolution, and it inverted some of the ideas of early economic theory, especially the view that the pursuit of individual economic self-interest would bring economic and social benefits to the whole of society (the belief which was and is the underlying rationale of capitalism).

The simplest Marxist model of society sees it as constituted by a *base* (the material means of production, distribution, and exchange) and a *superstructure*, which is the 'cultural' world of ideas, art, religion, law, and so on. The essential Marxist view is that the latter things are not 'innocent', but are 'determined' (or shaped) by the nature of the economic base. This belief about culture, known as *economic determinism*, is a central part of traditional Marxist thinking.

Marxist literary criticism: general

In fact, though, Marx and Engels themselves did not put forward any comprehensive theory of literature. Their views seem relaxed and undogmatic: good art always has a degree of freedom from prevailing economic circumstances, even if these economic facts are its 'ultimate determinant'. Thus, Engels, writing to the English novelist Margaret Harkness in April 1888, tells her that he is 'far from finding fault with you for not having written a point-blank socialist novel ... The more the opinions of the author remain hidden the better the work of art'. As cultured and highly-educated Germans, Marx and Engels had that reverence for 'great' art and literature which was typical of their class, and there is an obvious desire in such pronouncements to emphasise the difference between art and propaganda.

All the same, Marxist literary criticism maintains that a writer's social class, and its prevailing 'ideology' (outlook, values, tacit assumptions, half-realised allegiances, etc.) have a major bearing on what is written by a member of that class. So instead of seeing authors as primarily autonomous 'inspired' individuals whose 'genius' and creative imagination enables them to bring forth original and timeless works of art, the Marxist sees them as constantly formed by their social contexts in ways which they themselves would usually not admit. This is true not just of the *content* of their work but even of *formal* aspects of their writing which might at first seem to have no possible political overtones. For instance, the prominent British Marxist critic Terry Eagleton suggests that in language 'shared definitions and regularities of grammar both reflect and help to constitute, a well-ordered political state' (*William Shakespeare*, 1986, p. 1). Likewise, Catherine Belsey, another prominent British left-wing critic, argues that the

form of the 'realist' novel contains implicit validation of the existing social structure, because realism, by its very nature, leaves
conventional ways of seeing intact, and hence tends to discourage
critical scrutiny of reality. By 'form' here is included all the conventional features of the novel – chronological time-schemes,
formal beginnings and endings, in-depth psychological characterisation, intricate plotting, and fixed narratorial points of view.
Similarly, the 'fragmented', 'absurdist' forms of drama and fiction
used by twentieth-century writers like Beckett and Kafka are seen
as a response to the contradictions and divisions inherent in late
capitalist society.

However, it is probably true to say (as Ken Newton does, p.
244, *Theory into Practice*) that traditional Marxist criticism tends
to deal with history in a fairly generalised way. It talks about conflicts between social classes, and clashes of large historical forces,
but, contrary to popular belief, it rarely discusses the detail of a
specific historical situation and relates it closely to the interpretation of a particular literary text. As Newton implies, this suggests
one of the main differences between the Marxist criticism of the
1960s and 1970s and the cultural materialist and new historicist
criticism (Chapter 9) which came to the fore in the 1980s, since
the latter very often dealt closely with specific historical documents, attempting, in an almost archaeological spirit, to recreate
the 'state of mind' of a particular moment in history.

'Leninist' Marxist criticism

A much harder line about literature than Marx and Engels themselves would have approved of was generally pursued by officially
sanctioned Marxists, at least until the 1960s. In the 1920s, during
the early years after the revolution in Russia, the official Soviet
attitude to literature and the arts was very enlightened and 'experimental', and characteristically modern forms of art were encouraged. The 1930s saw reaction throughout the whole of Soviet
society, and the State began to exert direct control over literature
and the arts as well as everything else. At the first Soviet Writers' Congress in 1934 liberal views were outlawed and a new
orthodoxy imposed, based on the writings of Lenin rather than

those of Marx or Engels. Lenin had argued in 1905 that literature must become an instrument of the party. 'Literature', he said, 'must become Party literature ... Literature must become part of the organized, methodical, and unified labours of the social-democratic party'. Experimentation was effectively banned: writers like Proust and Joyce were stigmatised as exemplars of 'bourgeois decadence' (Joyce's *Ulysses* was denounced at the 1934 Congress as 'a heap of dung crawling with worms'), and straight realism was imposed (known as 'Socialist Realism'). In George Steiner's words, these conditions made literature impossible above the level of, say, *Uncle Tom's Cabin*. Steiner calls the two main streams of Marxist criticism, the 'Engelsian' kind, which stresses the necessary freedom of art from direct political determinism, and the 'Leninist' which insists on the need for art to be explicitly committed to the political cause of the Left. (The above discussion of the views of Engels and Lenin draws on George Steiner's chapter 'Marxism and the literary critic', pp. 271-90 in his book *Language and Silence*).

Those abroad who were sympathetic to the ideas of Communism tried to follow the 'Moscow line' on matters where an official Party policy existed, hence the international influence of the 'Leninist' views which crystalised at the 1934 Congress. Thus, in what came to be called the 'Vulgar Marxism' of the 1930s, a direct cause–effect relationship between literature and economics was assumed, with all writers seen as irrevocably trapped within the intellectual limits of their social-class position. A much-cited example of this rigid kind of Marxist literary criticism is Christopher Caudwell's *Illusion and Reality* (written in the 1930s and published in 1946). Caudwell's writing is both very generalised, in the sense that there is little detailed textual reference to the works under discussion, and very specific, in the sense that every facet of a writer is linked to some aspect of her or his social status. Thus, in Caudwell's discussion of Victorian poets (extracted in Newton's *Twentieth Century Literary Theory*) we read that '[Browning's] vocabulary has a foggy verbalism which is a reflection of his intellectual dishonesty in dealing with real contemporary problems'. Thus, a particular kind of vocabulary is the direct product of the middle-class writer's evasiveness on sensitive social issues. All poets have their own form of escape from modern reality: Tennyson laspes into a Keatsian dreamworld, Browning writes constantly on Italian medieval themes:

> To Tennyson the Keatsian world of romance, to Browning the Italian springtime; both are revolting backwards, trying to escape from the contradiction of the class for whom they speak.
>
> (Newton, p. 87).

The overall result is to provide little more than 'sound-bites' on literature for use in political argument.

'Engelsian' Marxist criticism

From the 1930s, however, a rich variety of what Steiner calls 'Engelsian' Marxist criticism flourished, either in exile, or in suppressed or underground form. The group now called the Russian Formalists had flourished in the 1920s, until disbanded by the Party, and should be mentioned here, even though their work is not strictly Marxist in spirit. The most prominent members of the group were Victor Shklovsky, Boris Tomashevsky, and Boris Eichenbaum, whose work can be sampled in *Russian Formalist Criticism: Four Essays*, edited by Lee T. Lemon and Marion J. Reis (University of Nebraska Press, 1965). Their ideas included the need for close formal analysis of literature (hence the name), the belief that the language of literature has its own characteristic procedures and effects, and is not just a version of ordinary language, and Shklovsky's idea of 'defamiliarisation' or 'making strange' (expounded in the essay 'Art as Technique', which Lemon and Reis reprint) which claims that one of the chief effects of literary language is that of making the familiar world appear new to us, as if we were seeing it for the first time, and thus laying it open to reappraisal. Another key Formalist idea is Tomashevsky's distinction (again expounded in the essay reprinted in Lemon and Reis) between story (Russian *fabula*) and plot (Russian *sjuzet*), the former being an actual sequence of (perhaps imaginary) events as they would have occurred, while the latter is the artistic presentation of these events, which might involve reorderings, juxtapositions, repetitions, and so on, in order to heighten their effect in a work of literature. As with the concept of defamiliarisation, there is a careful distinction here between reality itself and its verbal representation in a work of literature, so that we are steered away from any notion that literature simply mirrors reality in a documentary way. Later, in the early 1950s and 1960s, these Formalist ideas were of great interest to the early structuralists, partly because of their emphasis on the distinction between language and reality, and on literature as a set of systematic procedures and structures.

Some of those associated with Formalism, like Mikhail Bakhtin, remained in Russia, but others went into exile and continued their work abroad, thus sowing the seeds of the new forms of Marxist criticism which emerged in the 1960s. One such exile was the linguist Roman Jakobson (1896–1982), who continued his work in Prague, founding the Prague Linguistic Circle, the members of which included René Wellek. Wellek, like Jakobson, went to America shortly before the start of the War, and was influential in the movement known as 'New Criticism' which built upon a number of these Russian Formalist ideas, especially those concerning the need for close verbal analysis of literary texts and the special recognition of literary language as a medium with its own characteristics that set it aside from day-to-day language.

The suppressed Russian Formalists also had an influence in Germany, on the Frankfurt School of Marxist aesthetics. The school was founded in 1923, as a political research institute attached to the University of Frankfurt. They practised a form of criticism which tried to combine Freud and Marx, as well as aspects of Formalism. The best-known figures here are Walter Benjamin, who committed suicide while fleeing from the Nazis in 1940, Herbert Marcuse, a major influence on the radical thinking of the 1960s, and Theodor Adorno. Also forced to flee from Germany was the playwright Bertolt Brecht, another opponent of the simplicities of the doctrine of Socialist Realism. His notion of the 'alienation effect' in drama involves devices which draw the attention of the audience to the fact that what they see on the stage is a constructed literary image, not a natural reality. For example, a 'director' figure might sit at the side of the stage throughout a play, following the script in a book (as in Brecht's play *Galileo*).

Such a device is closely linked to the Formalists' idea of defamiliarisation, since, again, it emphasises a boundary or 'shift'
between literature and life.

The present: the influence of Althusser

Much current Marxist thinking on literature has been influenced
by the work of the French Marxist theoretician Louis Althusser
(1918–1990), and his contribution will become clear if we outline
some of the key terms and concepts he introduced. One such is
the notion of *overdeterminism*, a word borrowed from Freud,
which designates an effect which arises from a variety of causes,
that is, from several causes acting together, rather than from a
single (in this case, economic) factor. This concept of linked and
interacting causes is intended to undercut simplistic notions of a
one-to-one correspondence between base and superstructure. A
related term is the notion of *relative autonomy*, which is the view
that in spite of the connections between culture and economics,
art has a degree of independence from economic forces. This concept too is a way of attacking simplistic views of a superstructure
entirely determined by the nature of the economic base.

Ideology is a key term for Althusser, as for all Marxists. It is a
broad concept variously defined within Marxism. Althusser's
definition (quoted by Goldstein) is as follows:

> Ideology is a system (possessing its logic and proper rigour) of rep-
> resentations (images, myths, ideas or concepts according to the
> case) endowed with an existence and an historical role at the heart
> of a given society.
>
> (Philip Goldstein, *The Politics of Literary Theory: An Introduction
> to Marxist Criticism* Florida State University Press, 1990, p. 23).

We can pare this to 'a system of representations at the heart of a
given society' to give a concise definition which makes culture
(including literature) a crucial vehicle of the values which under-
pin the status quo in any society. These values and assumptions
are usually implicit, often unrecognised, but suffuse all the artefacts and all the culture of a given time. So this definition, too,
departs from the crudity of the base/superstructure model, in

which the former determines the nature of the latter. Now, says Goldstein, 'the economic infrastructure still influences ideological practices, but only in the "last instance"' (Goldstein, p. 23).

Decentering is a key term in Althusser to indicate structures which have no essence, or focus, or centre. Again, this is partly a way of avoiding the view that the economic base is the essence of society and the superstructure merely a secondary reflection. The notion of decentering implies that there is no overall unity: art has a relative autonomy and is determined by the economic level only 'in the last instance'. These 'Engelsian' pronouncements do not cancel out the Marxist tendency to imprison art within economics, but they do release literature on bail, so to speak, and allow it a high degree of day-to-day freedom.

Althusser makes a useful distinction between what we might call state power and state control. State power is maintained by what Althusser terms *repressive structures*, which are institutions like the law courts, prisons, the police force, and the army, which operate, in the last analysis, by external force. But the power of the state is also maintained more subtly, by seeming to secure the internal consent of its citizens, using what Althusser calls *ideological structures* or *State ideological apparatuses*. These are such groupings as political parties, schools, the media, churches, the family, and art (including literature) which foster an ideology – a set of ideas and attitudes – which is sympathetic to the aims of the state and the political status quo. Thus, each of us feels that we are freely choosing what is in fact being imposed upon us.

This Althusserian distinction is closely related to the notion of *hegemony*, which was given prominence by the Italian Marxist Antonio Gramsci (1891–1934). Gramsci contrasts *rule*, which is direct political control, which uses force when necessary, and *hegemony*, which is (as defined by Raymond Williams) 'the whole lived social process as practically organized by specific and dominant meanings, values and beliefs of a kind which can be abstracted as a "world-view" or "class outlook"' (Williams, *Marxism and Literature* Oxford University Press, 1977, p. 101). Williams relates hegemony to culture in general and to ideology in particular. Hegemony is like an internalised form of social control which makes certain views seem 'natural' or invisible so that they hardly seem like views at all, just 'the way things are'.

The 'trick' whereby we are made to feel that we are choosing when really we have no choice is called by Althusser *interpellation*. Capitalism, says Althusser, thrives on this trick: it makes us *feel* like free agents ('You can have any colour you like...') while actually imposing things upon us ('... as long as it's black'). Thus, democracy makes us feel that we are choosing the kind of government we have, but in practice the differences between political parties, once in power, are far fewer than the rhetorical gulfs between them. Interpellation is Althusser's term for the way the individual is encouraged to see herself or himself as an entity free and independent of social forces. It accounts for the operation of control structures not maintained by physical force, and hence for the perpetuation of a social set-up which concentrates wealth and power in the hands of the few.

The general purport of these Althusserian ideas is to enable a much more subtle view of how society works than that provided by traditional Marxism. Instead of force crudely applied from a single source, as from a lever, there is assent secured in many different and complex ways, and ideological power is shown to be of ultimately greater significance than material power. Thus, literature is shown to be of crucial importance in its own right, not just a helpless and passive reflector of the economic base where the real business of society goes on. Hence, the attraction of Althusser to recent Marxist critics is that he offers ways of by-passing the crude base/superstructure model without giving up the Marxist perspective altogether. Althusser's views represent what we might call revisionist Marxism, which is to say that they rethink and repackage the basic concepts in a form which is more subtle and more flexible. This is not to say that Althusser was a flexible thinker generally: on the contrary, he was a particularly dogmatic one, much attacked on the left for his promotion of 'theory' as a separate realm which is above experience, practice, or activism (see especially *The Poverty of Theory* by the British Marxist historian E. P. Thompson). But he did provide terms and formulae when they were needed, in the liberalising 1960s, which loosened the monolithic fabric of Marxist thinking and therefore made it acceptable to the radicals of that period. Without these 'loosening' moves Marxism might have been widely rejected as just one more form of rigid traditional thinking which the 'counter-culture' of that time needed to reject.

Since the 1970s the best-known British Marxist critic has been Terry Eagleton, whose work has reflected a wide range of influences, including for a time that of Althusser. Marxist criticism seems to conflict in its basic assumptions with those of post-structuralism and postmodernism, and the most significant Marxist writing in the 1980s and 1990s has involved a process of intricate interaction with these movements. Marxist criticism has also traditionally been opposed to psychoanalytic explanations of conduct, on the grounds that psychoanalysis falsely isolates individuals from the social structures in which they exist. All the same, the American Marxist critic Fredric Jameson (in *The Political Unconscious: Narrative as a Socially Symbolic Act*, 1981) has tried to reconcile the two. Essentially, Jameson offers political extensions of basic psychoanalytic terms like 'the unconscious' and 'repression'. Literature, in his view, often tries to *repress* historical truth, but analysis can reveal its underlying ideology (that is, its unconscious). A basic starting point on Eagleton, Jameson, and this whole area of debate would be to read Jameson's essay 'The politics of theory: Ideological positions in the postmodernism debate' and Eagleton's 'Capitalism, modernism, and postmodernism', which are reprinted as items 22 and 23 in David Lodge's *Modern Criticism and Theory: A Reader*.

STOP and THINK

General: The main tenet of Marxist criticism – that the nature of literature is influenced by the social and political cirumstances in which it is produced – might well be immediately accepted as self-evidently true.

The difficulty and controversy lie entirely in deciding how close the influence is. Are you going to adopt a 'determinist' position, and argue that literature is the passive product of socio-economic forces, or do you take a more 'liberal' line and see the socio-economic influence as much more distant and subtle?

Your main difficulty will be to show the operation of these economic forces (no matter whether you take the 'strong' or the 'weak' model) in a given literary work. What exactly do directly operating, or indirectly operating socio-economic forces look like in a literary work?

Specific: These are difficult questions to cope with in the abstract, and you will find it helpful to think about them in the context of a specific example. In the example below, therefore, is a 'determinist' or a 'liberal' line being taken, and how is this indicated? Is the socio-economic influence seen by the critic in the plot content of the play, in the characterisation, or in the literary form itself, and if so how?

What Marxist critics do

1. They make a division between the 'overt' (manifest or surface) and 'covert' (latent or hidden) content of a literary work (much as psychoanalytic critics do) and then relate the *covert* subject matter of the literary work to basic Marxist themes, such as class struggle, or the progression of society through various historical stages, such as, the transition from feudalism to industrial capitalism. Thus, the conflicts in *King Lear* might be read as being 'really' about the conflict of class interest between the rising class (the bourgeois) and the falling class (the feudal overlords).

2. Another method used by Marxist critics is to relate the context of a work to the social–class status of the author. In such cases an assumption is made (which again is similar to those made by psychoanalytic critics) that the author is unaware of precisely what he or she is saying or revealing in the text.

3. A third Marxist method is to explain the nature of a whole literary genre in terms of the social period which 'produced' it. For instance, *The Rise of the Novel*, by Ian Watt, relates the growth of the novel in the eighteenth century to the expansion of the middle classes during that period. The novel 'speaks' for this social class, just as, for instance, Tragedy

'speaks for' the monarchy and the nobility, and the Ballad 'speaks for' for the rural and semi-urban 'working class'.

4. A fourth Marxist practice is to relate the literary work to the social assumptions of the time in which it is 'consumed', a strategy which is used particularly in the later variant of Marxist criticism known as cultural materialism (see Chapter 9 pp. 182–9).

5. A fifth Marxist practice is the 'politicisation of literary form', that is, the claim that literary forms are themselves determined by political circumstance. For instance, in the view of some critics, literary realism carries with it an implicit validation of conservative social structures: for others, the formal and metrical intricacies of the sonnet and the iambic pentameter are a counterpart of social stability, decorum, and order.

Marxist criticism: an example

As an example of Marxist criticism we will take chapter five, on *Twelfth Night*, in Elliot Krieger's *A Marxist Study of Shakespeare's Comedies* (1979). As it is discussed here, the example mainly shows the first of the five Marxist critical activities just listed. The play centres on the love between the Duke Orsino and the Lady Olivia. His love is extravagantly and persistently expressed but she at first rejects him, having dedicated herself to a period of protracted mourning for her dead father. Subsequently she falls in love with Viola, a young noblewoman who is temporarily disguised as a man and acting as his servant and go-between (under the name Cesario). Olivia is also loved by her steward, the strict and punctilious Malvolio, who is tricked by her uncle, Sir Toby Belch, into believing that his love for her is returned.

The essay begins by citing the dominant critical view of the play, which is that it presents various extremes of self-indulgence (such as Orsino's wallowing in fantasies of romantic love and Toby Belch's self-abandonment to physical appetites) and contrasts these with an extreme puritanism and resistance to pleasure, as seen in Malvolio. The play is seen as recommending a balance and decorum in which these extremes are avoided and proper human fulfilment becomes possible. Krieger points out that this ignores the question of class in the play: when 'order' is restored at the end, the aristocratic characters suffer no particular ill effects, while Malvolio's fate is much more severe, yet Malvolio's self-interest differs from the obviously narcissistic preoccupations of Orsino and Olivia and the egoistic revelry of Sir Toby *only* because decorum forbids one of his rank to 'surfeit on himself' (p. 99). Thus 'only a privileged social class has access to the morality of indulgence'. Indeed, by definition, 'the members of the ruling class find their identities through excessive indulgence in appetite' (p. 100).

Each of the members of the aristocratic class, he continues, has a private 'secondary world'. For Sir Toby it is the unfettered world he reaches by drink, for he 'forces everyone to care for him while using the enforced incompetence of drunkenness and the willed oblivion of time in order to protect himself from the possibility of caring for others' (p. 102). Likewise, Olivia protects herself from the needs of others by retreating into a private world of bereavement, and Orsino into a wholly subjective world of love obsession in which everything becomes 'an adjunct of, and accompaniment to, the Duke's psychological condition' (p. 104). In these 'privatised' 'second worlds', each becomes, not part of a community, but 'one self king' (p. 103). Viola, too, attempts to retreat into one of these second worlds, but though she is actually aristocratic, the disguise she adopts enables her to choose a temporary non-aristocratic status ('I'll serve this duke'), and she thus becomes 'an object within the second worlds of Orsino, Olivia and Sir Toby' (p. 107), someone they assume is available for their use or manipulation.

Within the world of the servants in the play, there is much emphasis on 'aspiration': the new servant Cesario/Viola displaces Valentine and Curio from their positions of privileged access to Duke Orsino, and in Olivia's household there is a constant struggle for prime position between Maria (another of the servants) and Malvolio. Both, in fact, aim to marry into the family, which Maria eventually achieves by marrying Sir Toby as a reward for her decisive humiliation of Malvolio. Krieger therefore sees her as a significant element in the play:

Maria is hardly a proto-bourgeoise, in that her aspiration supports and confirms rather than challenges the continued validity of aristocratic privilege, but with her abilities to separate self from vocation, to express self apart from imposed duty, and to earn by her actions advancement in social degree, only Maria in *Twelfth Night* indicates the bourgeois and Puritan emphasis on independence, competition, and the association of stature with merit. (p. 121)

In contrast, Malvolio is much less of a representative of any kind of change in the social order, since he has an extreme reverence for all the trappings of aristocracy, and attributes the circumstances which, he thinks, have made possible his own elevation to the aristocracy to 'fortune' and his 'stars'. Thus, fortune in the play is a force, like 'nature' which is often an alibi or a rationalisation of inherited aristocratic privilege. For the Marxist critic, then, the play demonstrates the gulf which exists between masters and servants and manifests something of the state of mind that is characteristic of each class. The Marxist feature of this essay is the way it introduces the notion of social class into interpretations of the play: this is its special 'intervention' into the large body of critical writing on the play, in which the topic is never raised. Very little indeed is said in the essay about the specifics of the precise historical moment in which it was written: rather, a subtle and original reading is woven round the generalised notions of social-class conflict, class privilege, and aspirations towards what would now be called upward social mobility.

Selected reading

Dowling, William C., *Jameson, Althusser, Marx: an Introduction to The Political Unconscious* (Methuen, 1994).
   A 'contextualising introduction' to Jameson's *The Political Unconscious*. Excellent and brief, and really the best place to begin in studying the current concerns of Marxist thinking and its transforming engagements with Derrida, Lacan, and postmodernism.
Eagleton, Terry, *Marxism and Literary Criticism* (Methuen, 1976).
   A brief yet thorough introduction to this field.

Eagleton, Terry, *The Ideology of the Aesthetic* (Blackwell, 1990).

Representative of Eagleton's more recent concerns.

Goldstein, Philip, *The Politics of Literary Theory: An Introduction to Marxist Criticism* (Florida State University Press, 1990).

Useful on specific areas, such as: The Frankfurt School, pp. 17–21; post-structuralist Marxism, pp. 22–8; Terry Eagleton, pp. 59–65; Althusser, Derrida, and Foucault, pp. 164–74.

Jameson, Frederic, *The Political Unconscious: Narrative as a Socially Symbolic Act* (Cornell University Press, 1981).

The key text for Jameson, but undoubtedly difficult reading. It would be helpful to read William C. Dowling (above) first.

Krieger, Elliott, *A Marxist Study of Shakespeare's Comedies* (Macmillan, 1979).

'Applied' Marxist criticism.

Mulhern, Francis, ed. *Contemporary Marxist Criticism* (Longman, 1992).

A thoughtful and wide-ranging introduction and some key documents.

Prawer, S. S., *Karl Marx and World Literature* (Oxford University Press, 1978).

A detailed presentation and discussion of 'what Marx said about literature at various times in his life'.

'Ruis', *Marx for Beginners* (Writers & Readers Cooperative/Unwin Paperbacks, 1976/1986).

A 'documentary comic book' which summarises Marx's ideas in comic strip form. A good place to begin if you have not encountered Marx's ideas before.

Williams, Raymond, *Marxism and Literature* (Oxford University Press, 1977).

Useful on basic Marxist concepts, and Williams's adaptations of them. See 1.4 Ideology, 2.1 Base and Superstructure, 2.6 Hegemony, 2.8 Dominant, Residual, and Emergent, 2.9 Structures of feeling.

9

New historicism and cultural materialism

New historicism

The term 'new historicism' was coined by the American critic Stephen Greenblatt whose book *Renaissance Self-Fashioning: from More to Shakespeare* (1980) is usually regarded as its beginning. However, similar tendencies can be identified in work by various critics published during the 1970s, a good example being J. W. Lever's *The Tragedy of State: A Study of Jacobean Drama* (published by Methuen in 1971, and re-issued in 1987 with an introduction by Jonathan Dollimore). This brief and epoch-making book challenged conservative critical views about Jacobean theatre, and linked the plays much more closely with the political events of their era than previous critics had done.

A simple definition of the new historicism is that it is a method based on the *parallel* reading of literary and non-literary texts, usually of the same historical period. That is to say, new historicism refuses (at least ostensibly) to 'privilege' the literary text: instead of a literary 'foreground' and a historical 'background' it envisages and practises a mode of study in which literary and non-literary texts are given equal weight and constantly inform or interrogate each other. This 'equal weighting' is suggested in the definition of new historicism offered by the American critic Louis Montrose: he defines it as a combined interest in 'the textuality of history, the historicity of texts'. It involves (in Greenblatt's words) 'an intensified willingness to read *all* of the textual traces of the past with the attention traditionally conferred only on literary texts'. So new historicism (as indeed the name implies) embodies a paradox (and, for some, a scandal); it is an approach to literature in which there is no privileging of the literary (though we will see later that this statement requires some qualification).

Typically, a new historical essay will place the literary text within the 'frame' of a non-literary text. Thus, Greenblatt's main innovation, from the viewpoint of literary study, was to juxtapose the plays of the Renaissance period with 'the horrifying colonialist policies pursued by all the major European powers of the era' (Hugh Grady, in *The Modernist Shakespeare*). He draws attention to 'the marginalization and dehumanizing of suppressed Others' (Grady) usually by starting an essay with an analysis of a contemporary historical document which overlaps in some way with the subject matter of the play. Greenblatt himself refers to the appropriated historical document as the 'anecdote', and the typical new historicist essay omits the customary academic preliminaries about previously published interpretations of the play in question, and begins with a powerful and dramatic anecdote, as signalled, for instance, by Louis Montrose, in the first sentence of the essay discussed later: 'I would like to recount an Elizabethan dream – not Shakespeare's *A Midsummer Night's Dream* but one dreamt by Simon Forman on 23 January 1597'. These dramatic openings often cite date and place and have all the force of the documentary, eyewitness account, strongly evoking the quality of lived experience rather than 'history'. Since these historical documents are not subordinated as contexts, but are analysed in their own right, we should perhaps call them 'co-texts' rather than 'contexts'. The text and co-text used will be seen as expressions of the same historical 'moment', and interpreted accordingly. This process is well described by Richard Wilson and Richard Dutton in the introduction to their collection of essays *New Historicism and Renaissance Drama*:

> Where [earlier] criticism had mystified Shakespeare as an incarnation of spoken English, it [new historicism] found the plays embedded in other *written texts*, such as penal, medical and colonial documents. Read within this archival continuum, what they

represented was not harmony but the violence of the Puritan attack on carnival, the imposition of slavery, the rise of patriarchy, the hounding of deviance, and the crashing of prison gates during what Foucault called 'the Age of Confinement, at the dawn of carceral society' ['carceral' comes from the Latin word *carcer*, meaning a prison]

(Wilson & Dutton, p. 8).

This succinctly conveys the tone and ambitions of new historicism, and the phrase about reading literature 'within the archival continuum' is a vivid encapsulation of the method.

New and old historicisms – some differences

When we say that new historicism involves the parallel study of literary and non-literary texts, the word 'parallel' encapsulates the essential difference between this and earlier approaches to literature which had made some use of historical data. These earlier approaches made a hierarchical separation between the literary text, which was the object of value, the jewel, as it were, and the historical 'background', which was merely the setting, and by definition of lesser worth.

The practice of giving 'equal weighting' to literary and non-literary material is the first and major difference between the 'new' and the 'old' historicism. As representative of the 'old' historicism we could cite E. M. W. Tillyard's *The Elizabethan World Picture* (1943) and *Shakespeare's History Plays* (1944), books against which new historicism frequently defines itself. These books described the set of conservative mental attitudes (to society, to the deity, to the created universe, etc.) which Tillyard saw as typifying the Elizabethan outlook and reflected in Shakespeare's plays. The 'traditional' approach to Shakespeare (through to the 1970s) was characterised by the combination of this historical framework, with the practice of 'close reading', and the analysis of 'patterns of imagery'.

A second important difference between old and new historicisms is encapsulated in the word 'archival' in the phrase 'the archival continuum' quoted earlier, for that word indicates that new historicism is indeed a historic*ist* rather than a historic*al* movement. That is, it is interested in history as represented and recorded in written documents, in history-as-text. Historical events as such, it would argue, are irrecoverably lost. This emphasis bears the influence of the long-familiar view in literary studies that the actual thoughts, or feelings, or intentions of a writer can never be recovered or reconstructed, so that the real living individual is now entirely superseded by the literary text which has come down to us. As it were, the word of the past replaces the world of the past. Since, for the new historicist, the events and attitudes of the past now exist solely as writing, it makes sense to subject that writing to the kind of close analysis formerly reserved for literary texts.

Incorporated into this preference for the textual record of the past is the influence of deconstruction. New historicism accepts Derrida's view that there is nothing outside the text, in the special sense that everything about the past is only available to us in textualised form: it is 'thrice-processed', first through the ideology, or outlook, or discursive practices of its own time, then through those of ours, and finally through the distorting web of language itself. Whatever is represented in a text is thereby remade. New historicist essays always themselves constitute another remaking, another permutation of the past, as the play or poem under discussion is juxtaposed with a chosen document, so that a new entity is formed. In this sense the objection that the documents selected may not really be 'relevant' to the play is disarmed, for the aim is not to represent the past as it really was, but to present a new reality by re-situating it.

New historicism and Foucault

New historicism is resolutely anti-establishment, always implicitly on the side of liberal ideals of personal freedom and accepting and celebrating all forms of difference and 'deviance'. At the same time, though, it seems simultaneously to despair of the survival of these in the face of the power of the repressive state, which it constantly reveals as able to penetrate and taint the most intimate areas of personal life. This notion of the State as all-powerful and all-seeing stems from the post-structuralist cultural historian Michel Foucault whose pervasive image of the State is that of 'panoptic' (meaning 'all-seeing') surveillance. The Panopticon was a design for a circular prison conceived by the eighteenth-century utilitarian Jeremy Bentham: the design consisted of tiered ranks of cells which could all be surveyed by a single warder positioned at the centre of the circle. The panoptic State, however, maintains its surveillance not by physical force and intimidation, but by the power of its 'discursive practices' (to use Foucault's terminology – 'discursive' is the adjective derived from the noun 'discourse') which circulates its ideology throughout the body politic.

Discourse is not just a way of speaking or writing, but the whole 'mental set' and ideology which encloses the thinking of all members of a given society. It is not singular and monolithic – there is always a multiplicity of discourses – so that the operation of power structures is as significant a factor in (say) the family as in layers of government. Hence, contesting them may involve, for example, the struggle to change sexual politics just as much as party politics. Thus, the personal sphere becomes a possible sphere of political action in ways which might well interest a feminist critic. Here, then, we might see grounds for political optimism. On the other hand, when political power operates in and suffuses so many spheres, the possibility of fundamental change and transformation may come to seem very remote.

On the whole, new historicism seems to emphasise the extent of this kind of 'thought control', with the implication that 'deviant' thinking may become literally 'unthinkable' (or *only* thinkable), so that the State is seen as a monolithic structure and change becomes almost impossible. Foucault's work looks at the institutions which enable this power to be maintained, such as State punishment, prisons, the medical profession and legislation about sexuality. Foucault makes a less rigid distinction than is found in Althusser between 'repressive structures' and 'ideological structures' (see Chapter 8). All the same, there is a clear affinity between Gramsci's 'hegemony' (see Chapter 8), Althusser's 'interpellation' (see Chapter 8), and Foucault's 'discursive practices', since all of these concern the way power is internalised by those whom it disempowers, so that it does not have to be constantly enforced externally.

It should be added that new historicism, in spite of its fore-grounding of the word 'historicism', really represents a significant extension of the empire of literary studies, for it entails intensive 'close reading', in the literary-critical manner, of non-literary texts. Documents are seldom offered entire: instead an extract is made which is then subjected to intensive scrutiny. (Contextual-isation of the document is usually minimal, partly as a writerly ploy to increase its impact.) Further, little attention is paid to pre-vious writing about the same text, as if the advent of new his-toricism has wiped the academic slate clean. Hence, this is a true 'words on the page' approach in which context is dispensed with and the material then studied like the decontextualised, isolated poems which I. A. Richards offered for criticism in the 1920s. Thus, a single historical text is sometimes the sole witness, for, say, a claimed change in attitude towards some aspect of sexual-ity. The interpretative weight thus placed upon a single document is often very great. So we should not expect to find the methods of new historicism greatly valued or admired by historians. It is, on the contrary, a way of 'doing' history which has a strong appeal for non-historians.

Advantages and disadvantages of new historicism

However, the appeal of new historicism is undoubtedly great, for a variety of reasons. Firstly, although it is founded upon post-structuralist thinking, it is written in a far more accessible way, for the most part avoiding post-structuralism's characteristically dense style and vocabulary. It presents its data and draws its con-clusions, and if it is sometimes easy to challenge the way the data is interpreted, this is partly because (as in the case of Freud's the-ories) the empirical foundation on which the interpretation rests is made openly available for scrutiny. Secondly, the material itself is often fascinating and is wholly distinctive in the context of lit-erary studies. These essays look and feel different from those pro-duced by any other critical approach and immediately give the literary student the feeling that new territory is being entered.

Particularly, the 'uncluttered' 'pared-down' feel of the essays, which results from not citing previous discussions of the literary work, gives them a stark and dramatic air. Thirdly, the political edge of new historicist writing is always sharp, but at the same time it avoids the problems frequently encountered in 'straight' Marxist criticism: it seems less overtly polemical and more willing to allow the historical evidence its own voice.

STOP and THINK

'Doing' new historicism essentially involves the juxtaposition of literary material with contemporary non-literary texts. But how would you attempt to set about doing this yourself, rather than just reading published essays which use this formula?

For instance, if you wished to use the new historicist method for an essay about, say, a Shakespeare comedy where would you look for suitable historical material? Then, having found the material, what would be the format of the essay itself?

I wouldn't want to gloss over the difficulties involved, but here is a suggestion: Shakespeare's comedies are 'domestic' in theme, and concern sexual mores, courtship, relations between men and women, and inter-generational conflict. Hence, we would be looking for material on social and family history.

A well-known relevant book would be Lawrence Stone's *The Family, Sex, and Marriage in England, 1500–1800* (Penguin, 1979). Chapter five, 'The Reinforcement of Patriarchy', has useful material, such as Section 3, 'Husband and Wife', subsectioned into 'The Subordination of Wives' and 'The Education of Women'. Chapters seven and eight are on 'Marriage and Courtship', and Part five is on 'Sex'.

Less well-known, but containing data similar to that used by the major new historicists, is *Sex in Middlesex: Popular Mores in a Massachusetts County, 1649–1699*, Roger Thompson, (University of Massachusetts Press, 1986). See Section one,

'Adolescent Mores' and Section two, 'Married Mores'.

Published historical data and social history of this kind should provide an accessible source of 'co-texts' for the new historical approach. Without by-passing the problems associated with the method, you would in this way at least be able to gain 'hands-on' experience of new historicism as a practical approach to criticism.

What new historicists do

1. They juxtapose literary and non-literary texts, reading the former in the light of the latter.
2. They try thereby to 'defamiliarise' the canonical literary text, detaching it from the accumulated weight of previous literary scholarship and seeing it as if new.
3. They focus attention (within both text and co-text) on issues of State power and how it is maintained, on patriarchal structures and their perpetuation, and on the process of colonisation, with its accompanying 'mind-set'.
4. They make use, in doing so, of aspects of the post-structuralist outlook, especially Derrida's notion that every facet of reality is textualised, and Foucault's idea of social structures as determined by dominant 'discursive practices'.

New historicism: an example

As an example of new historicism in practice let us take a closer look at an essay, not by Greenblatt, but by Louis Montrose. His essay '*A Midsummer Night's Dream* and the Shaping Fantasies of Elizabethan Culture: Gender, Power, Form' appeared originally in the American journal *Representations*, the 'house magazine' of the new historicism, and is reprinted in Wilson and Dutton. Montrose's famous definition of new historicism is that it centres upon the historicity of the text and the textuality of history, and the essay might be seen as an embodiment of that pronouncement. His overall thesis is that the play 'creates the culture by which it is created, shapes the fantasies by which it is shaped' (p.

130). Thus, the cult of the Virgin Queen is both fostered by literature like Spenser's *The Faerie Queene* and a whole range of court masks and pageants, and at the same time generates such literature: life and literature stimulate and play upon each other. Elizabeth can project herself as the Queen whose virginity has mystical and magical potency because such images are given currency in court masques, in comedies, and in pastoral epic poetry. Conversely, the figure of Elizabeth stimulates the production and promotion of such work and imagery. Hence, in this sense, history is textualised and texts are historicised. A simple modern parallel would be the way images of masculinity and femininity in film pervade our lives and offer us ways of representing ourselves: they give us 'role models' which we can become trapped inside, so that real life mimics the filmic representation of life.

Montrose's essay also represents the eclecticism of new historicism, for it draws upon psychoanalysis, especially Freudian dream analysis, and feminism. It opens with an account of Simon Forman's dream, already mentioned, in which Forman describes an erotic encounter with the Queen, then an elderly woman: the dream turns on the pun of 'wait upon' the Queen and 'weight upon her'. Her dress is trailing in the mud and he offers to solve the problem by causing her belly to lift ('I mean to wait upon you not under you'). In the dream Forman has just saved the Queen from being pestered by 'a weaver, a tall man with a reddish beard', and Montrose interprets this as an Oedipal triangle. He links this to the Queen's projection of herself as mother of the nation, but also as a virgin who is openly flirtatious and provocative – Montrose quotes the French ambassador's accounts of her extremely revealing style of dress ('She kept the front of her dress open, and one could see the whole of her bosom' ... p. 111). He then relates all this to the tensions generated by the peculiar situation that a highly patriarchal society in which all power was vested in men was nevertheless ruled by a woman who therefore had absolute powers of life over all her subjects, men and women, and the power to advance or end the careers of her male courtiers. In Shakespeare's play, there are several instances of a Queen who is 'mastered', and thereby feminised – Hippolyta, the Amazonian Queen, has been defeated by Theseus, whom she must now submit to and marry: Titania, queen of the fairies, has defied her husband Oberon in her attachment to the changeling boy and hence is humiliated by him in having Puck administer the magic potion which makes her fall in love with the first being she sees on waking. Throughout the play, there is much about the rights of fathers over daughters and husbands over wives, and the precondition of male desire is female subjection. The 'happy' ending depends upon the reinforcement of patriarchy:

> The festive conclusion of *A Midsummer Night's Dream*, its celebration of romantic and generative heterosexual union, depends upon the success of a process whereby the female pride and power manifested in misanthropic warriors, possessive mothers, unruly wives, and wilful daughters are brought under the control of husbands and lords. (p. 120)

Hence, it is suggested, the play might be seen as implicitly treasonous, since:

> When a virgin ruler is ostensibly the virgin mother of her subjects, then the themes of male procreative power, autogeny, and mastery of women acquire a seditious resonance. In royal pageantry, the queen is always the cynosure; her virginity is the source of magical potency. In *A Midsummer Night's Dream*, however, such magical powers are invested in the king. (p. 127)

Hence, 'Shakespeare's comedy symbolically neutralises the royal power to which it ostensibly pays homage' (p. 127). In practice, patriarchy is maintained in spite of the presence of a woman at the pinnacle of power, by constantly insisting on Elizabeth's difference from other women. This is a familiar strategy even today, for having a female leader did not lead the Tory Party to revise its ideas about the role of women in society – on the contrary, under the rule of the 'iron lady' (an interesting locution in this context) reactionary ideas were reinforced and strengthened. Thus, 'Elizabeth's rule was not intended to undermine the male hegemony of her culture. Indeed, the emphasis upon her difference from other women may have helped to reinforce it' (p. 124). If the pageants and the encomiums constantly proclaimed her simultaneously 'Maiden, Matron and Mother' then she becomes, not a real woman, but a religious mystery. Throughout the essay, then, the account of the play entwines it with male attempts to come to terms with the simultaneous existence of a female monarch and a rigorous patriarchal structure. For male courtiers, there might seem to be a certain 'unmanning' involved in being chaste servants of the Virgin Queen, while those who sought advancement from her seemed like children seeking the favours of the nation's mother. (Montrose describes an extravagant and protracted entertainment in which Raleigh and Greville acted out this metaphor.) All this demonstrates what is meant in practice by insisting upon the historicity of the text and the textuality of history.

Cultural materialism

The British critic Graham Holderness describes cultural materialism as 'a politicised form of historiography'. We can explain this as meaning the study of historical material (which includes literary texts) within a politicised framework, this framework including the present which those literary texts have in some way helped to shape. The term 'cultural materialism' was made current in 1985 when it was used by Jonathan Dollimore and Alan Sinfield (the best-known of the cultural materialists) as the subtitle of their edited collection of essays *Political Shakespeare*. They define the term in a foreword as designating a critical method which has four characteristics: it combines an attention to:

1. historical context,
2. theoretical method,
3. political commitment, and
4. textual analysis.

To comment briefly on each of these: firstly, the emphasis on *historical context* 'undermines the transcendent significance traditionally accorded to the literary text'. Here the word 'transcendent' roughly means 'timeless'. The position taken, of course, needs to face the obvious objection that if we are today still studying and reading Shakespeare then his plays have indeed proved themselves 'timeless' in the simple sense that they are clearly not limited by the historical circumstances in which they were produced. But this is a matter of degree: the aim of this aspect of cultural materialism is to allow the literary text to 'recover its histories' which previous kinds of study have often ignored. The kind of history recovered would involve relating the plays to such phenomena as 'enclosures and the oppression of the rural poor, state power and resistance to it ... witchcraft, the challenge and containment of the carnivalesque' (Dollimore and Sinfield, p. 3). Secondly, the emphasis on *theoretical method* signifies the break with liberal humanism and the absorbing of the lessons of structuralism, post-structuralism, and other approaches which have become prominent since the 1970s. Thirdly, the emphasis on *political commitment* signifies the influence of Marxist and feminist perspectives and the break from the conservative-Christian framework which hitherto dominated Shakespeare criticism. Finally, the stress on *textual analysis* 'locates the critique of traditional approaches where it cannot be ignored'. In other words, there is a commitment not just to making theory of an abstract kind, but to practising it on (mainly) canonical texts which continue to be the focus of massive amounts of academic and professional attention, and which are prominent national and cultural icons.

The two words in the term 'cultural materialism' are further defined: 'culture' will include *all* forms of culture ('forms like television and popular music and fiction'). That is, this approach does not limit itself to 'high' cultural forms like the Shakespeare play. 'Materialism' signifies the opposite of 'idealism': an 'idealist' belief would be that high culture represents the free and independent play of the talented individual mind; the contrary 'materialist' belief is that culture cannot 'transcend the material forces and relations of production. Culture is not simply a reflection of the economic and political system, but nor can it be independent of it'. These comments on materialism represent the standard beliefs of Marxist criticism, and they do perhaps point to the difficulty of making a useful distinction between a 'straight' Marxist criticism and cultural materialism. However, it is added that the relevant history is not just that of four hundred years ago, but that of the times (including our own) in which Shakespeare is produced and reproduced. Thus, in cultural materialism there is an emphasis on the functioning of the institutions through which Shakespeare is now brought to us – the Royal Shakespeare Company, the film industry, the publishers who produce textbooks for school and college, and the National Curriculum, which lays down the requirement that specific Shakespeare plays be studied by all school pupils.

Cultural materialism takes a good deal of its outlook (and its name) from the British left-wing critic Raymond Williams. Instead of Foucault's notion of 'discourse' Williams invented the term 'structures of feeling': these are concerned with 'meanings and values as they are lived and felt'. Structures of feeling are often antagonistic both to explicit systems of values and beliefs, and to the dominant ideologies within a society. They are characteristically found in literature, and they *oppose* the status quo (as the values in Dickens, the Brontës, etc., represent human structures of feeling which are at variance with Victorian commercial and materialist values). The result is that cultural materialism is much more optimistic about the possibility of change and is willing at times to see literature as a source of oppositional values. Cultural materialism particularly involves using the past to 'read' the present, revealing the politics of our own society by what we choose to emphasise or suppress of the past. A great deal of the British work has been about undermining what it sees as the fetishistic role of Shakespeare as a conservative icon within British culture. This form of cultural materialism can be conveniently sampled in three 'New Accents' books: *The Shakespeare Myth*, Graham Holderness: *Alternative Shakespeares*, ed. John Drakakis, and *That Shakespeherian Rag*, Terence Hawkes. (This quaint title is derived from an allusion by T. S. Eliot in *The Waste Land*.) A correspondence in response to a review of the first of these ran for over a year in the *London Review of Books*, under the heading 'Bardolatry'.

How is cultural materialism different from new historicism?

Cultural materialism is often linked in discussion with new historicism, its American counterpart. Though the two movements belong to the same family, there is an ongoing family quarrel between them. *Political Shakespeare* includes new historicist essays, and the introduction explains some of the differences between the two movements.

Firstly, in a neat distinction Dollimore and Sinfield quote Marx to the effect that 'men and women make their own history but not in conditions of their own choosing' (p. 3): cultural materialists, they say, tend to concentrate on the interventions whereby men and women make their own history, whereas new historicists tend to focus on the less than ideal circumstances in which they do so, that is, on the 'power of social and ideological structures' which restrain them. The result is a contrast between political optimism and political pessimism.

Secondly, cultural materialists see new historicists as cutting themselves off from effective political positions by their acceptance of a particular version of post-structuralism, with its radical scepticism about the possibility of attaining secure knowledge. The rise of post-structuralism, problematises knowledge, language, truth, etc., and this perspective is absorbed into new historicism and becomes an important part of it. The new historicist defence against this charge would be that being aware of the in-built uncertainty of all knowledge doesn't mean that we give up trying to establish truths, it simply means that we do so conscious of the dangers and limitations involved, thus giving their own intellectual enquiries a special authority. This is rather like sailing into dangerous waters knowingly, with all sensible precautions taken, rather than blithely unaware of the dangers and with all lights blazing. Thus, when new historicists claim (in Peter Widdowson's words) that Foucault gives them entry into 'a non-truth-oriented form of historicist study of texts' (p. 161) this doesn't mean that they do not believe that what they say is true, but rather that they know the risks and dangers involved in claiming to establish truths.

A third important difference between new historicism and cultural materialism is that where the former's co-texts are documents contemporary with Shakespeare, the latter's may be programme notes for a current Royal Shakespeare Company production, quotations of Shakespeare by a Gulf War pilot, or pronouncements on education by a government minister. To put this another way: the new historicist situates the literary text in the political situation of its own day, while the cultural materialist situates it within that of ours. This is really to restate the difference in political emphasis between the two approaches. Indeed, it could be said that all three of the differences just described have this political difference as their common denominator.

STOP and THINK

The fact that we have spent time spelling out the differences between cultural materialism and new historicism indicates that there is a considerable overlap between them. Are they just two national varieties of essentially the same thing, or are the radical differences (emphasised especially by the British cultural materialists) as deep as is claimed?

Perhaps the question can only be properly answered by reading and comparing essays of each type. Allegedly, the differences lie mainly in two aspects: firstly, in political outlook, and secondly, in the degree of emphasis on the post-structralist perspective.

In thinking about the question, start by comparing the attitudes evident in the examples of each included in this book, in so far as you are able to judge from the brief accounts given. Then read and compare two further pieces (drawing on the reading suggested at the end of this section).

Of course, the differences between these two approaches are partly the result of their different intellectual frameworks. New historicism was much influenced by Foucault, whose 'discursive practices' are frequently a reinforcement of dominant ideology. Cultural materialism, on the other hand, owes much to Raymond Williams, whose 'structures of feeling' contain the seeds from which grows resistance to the dominant ideology. A sceptic about both approaches suggested that it must be hard for the new historicists to explain how the English Civil War ever got started (since they seem to envisage a pervasive State power which would make resistance virtually impossible) while for the cultural materialists it must be difficult to explain how it ever ended (since their 'structures of feeling' constantly throw up new ideas which would seem to make stasis impossible). In practice, however, the frequently evoked political difference between the two approaches is surely less uniform and predictable than such stark dichotomies would imply.

What cultural materialist critics do

1. They read the literary text (very often a Renaissance play) in such a way as to enable us to 'recover its histories', that is, the context of exploitation from which it emerged.
2. At the same time, they foreground those elements in the work's present transmission and contextualising which caused those histories to be lost in the first place, (for example, the 'heritage' industry's packaging of Shakespeare in terms of history-as-pageant, national bard, cultural icon, and so on).
3. They use a combination of Marxist and feminist approaches to the text, especially in order to do the first of these (above), and in order to fracture the previous dominance of conservative social, political, and religious assumptions in Shakespeare criticism in particular.
4. They use the technique of close textual analysis, but often employ structuralist and post-structuralist techniques, especially to mark a break with the inherited tradition of close textual analysis within the framework of conservative cultural and social assumptions.
5. At the same time, they work mainly within traditional notions of the canon, on the grounds that writing about more obscure texts hardly ever constitutes an effective political intervention (for instance, in debates about the school curriculum or national identity).

Cultural materialism: an example

An example of an informal variant of this approach is Terence

Hawkes's essay 'Telmah' (in his book *That Shakespeherian Rag*). This is the fourth piece in the book, each one being centred on the work of one of the major Shakespearian critics of the early part of the century, within an overall strategy of looking at how Shakespeare is mediated and processed to us. In this chapter the critic is John Dover Wilson, best known for his 1930s book *What Happens in Hamlet?* The opening section considers aspects of *Hamlet* , emphasising cyclic and symmetrical elements of the play, such as how the beginning echoes the end, how the same situation occurs several times in it (like the several father-son parallels) and considering how indefinite the start and end of any performance are, since the play is already culturally situated in some way in people's minds before they see it. A repeated motif of looking backwards in the play (to a past which was better than the present) leads Hawkes to imagine a 'reversed' *Hamlet* which shadows the actual play, the 'Telmah' of his title.

The second section is entitled 'To the Sunderland Station', alluding to the title of a well-known history of the Russian Revolution called *To the Finland Station*. An account is given of John Dover Wilson on the train to Sunderland in 1917, sent by the government to sort out labour problems in a munitions factory, and reading W. W. Greg's article on *Hamlet* which argues that the king's failure to react openly to the dumb show indicates that he is a figure of some complexity, not just a story-book villain. If he is this then he begins to claim some of our attention, and distract us from the exclusive focus on Hamlet himself which had been the traditional way of responding to the play, at least from the time of the Romantics. Wilson's excited outrage at this notion is related to a fanatical desire for order manifested in his published writings about Russia which see it as a picturesque 'organic' feudal state, which, in turn, looks like a version of the England which his social class regards with nostalgia and fears might be lost. Dover Wilson's rushing to the defence of Hamlet, the threatened cultural icon, in his reply to Greg, and later in his *Hamlet* book, are seen as symptomatic of this too. Shortly after the First World War Wilson was a member of the Newbolt Committee which reported on the teaching of English, and saw it as providing a form of social cohesion which might save the country from the fate which overtook Russia. Hawkes also quotes a letter from Neville Chamberlain praising *What Happens in Hamlet?*, and thus creates a pattern of appeasing and containing difference. Hence, a way of interpreting the play is placed among several co-texts from twentieth-century life, and thus the play itself is culturally transformed. Hawkes's final reading of the end of the play involves inserting an extra stage direction, and his model for a criticism of this kind is that of the jazz musician who doesn't transmit a received text, but *trans*forms what he *per*forms. That might be taken as the characteristic feature of this variant of cultural materialist criticism.

It is difficult to know how to 'place' writing of this kind. It is lively and interesting, personal and engaged in tone, and most of the formalities of academic writing are dispensed with. Openings are dramatic, transitions abrupt: suspense is maintained by holding back key details about identity or situation till the moment of maximum impact. The structure is a series of seemingly unrelated incidents or situations which turn out to be intimately intertwined. All these features are novelistic, and there is clearly a sense in which this is 'creative writing' which would not accept any absolute distinction between literature and criticism. As in new historicism, literature and history are intertwined, but the perspective and the historicising are much more those of our own day than would be the case with new historicism itself.

Selected reading

Chase, Cynthia, ed. *Romanticism*, (Longman Critical Readers, 1993).
    Contains three examples of new historicist approaches to the period, namely, the chapters by Karen Swann on Coleridge's *Christabel*, by Marjorie Levinson on Keats, and by Jerome Christensen on Byron's *Sardanapalus*.

Dollimore, Johnathan & Sinfield, Alan, eds, *Political Shakespeare: New Essays in Cultural Materialism*, (Manchester University Press, 2nd edn 1994).
    The introduction gives a useful account of new historicism and explains how it differs from cultural materialism. The book reprints Greenblatt's essay 'Invisible Bullets'.

Drakakis, John, ed. *Alternative Shakespeares* (Methuen, 1985).

The term 'cultural materialism' is not used of these essays, but they are generally representative of this approach; they seek 'to accelerate the break with established canons of Shakespeare criticism', exemplifying 'explorations of the ways in which historically specific readings are generated'.

Grady, Hugh, *The Modernist Shakespeare* (Oxford University Press, 1991).

Pages 225–35 are on the new historicism. An excellent book, always sharp and readable. Chapter four on Tillyard (the 'old historicism') is very useful. Chapter five discusses the application of contemporary critical trends to Shakespeare.

Greenblatt, Stephen, *Shakespearian Negotiations: The Circulation of Social Energy in Renaissance England* (California University Press, 1991).

The essay 'Fiction and Friction', on cross-dressing in Shakespearian comedies, is a good starting-point on new historicism. The essay 'Invisible Bullets' is the best-known piece in the book.

Hawkes, Terence, *That Shakespeherian Rag* (Methuen, 1986).

Examples of cultural materialism in practice. The whole book is a lively read which makes some startling juxtapositions of Shakespeare and the circumstances in which we encounter him.

Holderness, Graham, *The Shakespeare Myth* (Manchester University Press, 1988).

Studies of the 'culturally-produced and historically-determined Shakespeare myth', along with 'interviews with prominent mediators of Shakespeare in education, theatre, the press, and television'.

Levinson, Marjorie, ed. *Rethinking Historicism: Critical Readings in Romantic History* (Blackwell, 1989).

New historicism applied to Romanticism.

Veeser, H. Aram, ed. *The New Historicism* (Routledge, 1989).

A useful and valuable source.

Wilson, Richard & Dutton, Richard, eds, *New historicism and Renaissance Drama* (Longman, 1992).

A useful collection of key articles, well introduced.

10

Postcolonial criticism

Background

Postcolonial criticism emerged as a distinct category only in the 1990s. It is not mentioned, for instance, in the first edition of Selden's *A Reader's Guide to Contemporary Literary Theory* (1985) or Jeremy Hawthorn's *A Concise Glossary of Contemporary Literary Theory* (1992). It has gained currency through the influence of such books as: *In Other Worlds* (Gayatri Spivak, 1987); *The Empire Writes Back* (Bill Ashcroft, 1989); *Nation and Narration* (Homi Bhabha, 1990) and *Culture and Imperialism* (Edward Said, 1993). An important collection of relevant essays (though it does not use the term 'postcolonialism') is *'Race', Writing and Difference* (1986), reprinted from two issues of the journal *Critical Inquiry*, and edited by Henry Louis Gates, Jr, one of the best-known American figures in this field.

One significant effect of postcolonial criticism is to further undermine the universalist claims once made on behalf of literature by liberal humanist critics. If we claim that great literature has a timeless and universal significance we thereby demote or disregard cultural, social, regional, and national differences in experience and outlook, preferring instead to judge all literature by a single, supposedly 'universal', standard. Thus, for instance, a routine claim about the 'Wessex' setting of Hardy's novels is that it is really a canvas on which Hardy depicts and examines fundamental, universal aspects of the human condition. Thus, Hardy's books are not thought of as primarily regional or histor-

ical or masculine or white or working-class novels – they are just
novels, and built into this attitude is the assumption that this way
of writing and representing reality is the unquestioned norm, so
that the situations depicted can stand for all possible forms of
human interaction. This universalism is rejected by postcolonial
criticism; whenever a universal signification is claimed for a work,
then, white, Eurocentric norms and practices are being promoted
by a sleight of hand to this elevated status, and all others corre-
spondingly relegated to subsidiary, marginalised roles.

The ancestry of postcolonial criticism can be traced to Frantz
Fanon's *The Wretched of the Earth*, published in French in 1961,
and voicing what might be called 'cultural resistance' to France's
African empire. Fanon (a psychiatrist from Martinique) argued
that the first step for colonialised people in finding a voice and an
identity is to reclaim their own past. For centuries the European
colonising power will have devalued the nation's past, seeing its
precolonial era as a pre-civilised limbo, or even as a historical
void. Children, both black and white, will have been taught to see
history, culture and progress as beginning with the arrival of the
Europeans. If the first step towards a postcolonial perspective is
to reclaim one's own past, then the second is to begin to erode
the colonialist ideology by which that past had been devalued.

Hence, another major book, which can be said to inaugurate
postcolonial criticism proper is Edward Said's *Orientalism* (1978),
which is a specific exposé of the Eurocentric universalism which
takes for granted both the superiority of what is European or
Western, and the inferiority of what is not. Said identifies a European cultural tradition of 'Orientalism', which is a particular and
long-standing way of identifying the East as 'Other' and inferior
to the West. The Orient, he says, features in the Western mind
'as a sort of surrogate and even underground self' (*Literature in
the Modern World*, ed. Dennis Walder, p. 236). This means, in
effect, that the East becomes the repository or projection of those
aspects of themselves which Westerners do not choose to
acknowledge (cruelty, sensuality, decadence, laziness, and so on).
At the same time, and paradoxically, the East is seen as a fascinating realm of the exotic, the mystical and the seductive. It also
tends to be seen as homogenous, the people there being anony-

mous masses, rather than individuals, their actions determined by instinctive emotions (lust, terror, fury, etc.) rather than by conscious choices or decisions. Their emotions and reactions are always determined by racial considerations (they are like this because they are asiatics or blacks or orientals) rather than by apsects of individual status or circumstance (for instance, because they happen to be a sister, or an uncle, or a collector of antique pottery). As Said says, after quoting the example of a colonial administrator's 1907 account of life in Damascus, 'In such statements as these we note immediately that "the Arab" or "Arabs" have an aura of apartness, definiteness, and *collective self-consistency* [my italics] such as to wipe out any traces of individual Arabs with narratable life Histories'.

Postcolonial reading

Reading literature with the perspective of 'Orientalism' in mind would make us, for instance, critically aware of how Yeats in his two 'Byzantium' poems ('Sailing to Byzantium', 1927, and 'Byzantium', 1932) provides an image of Istanbul, the Eastern capital of the former Roman Empire, which is identified with torpor, sensuality, and exotic mysticism. At such moments Yeats adopts an ethnocentric or Eurocentric perspective, seeing the East as an exotic 'Other' which becomes the contrasting foil to his own pursuits and concerns, all of which the poem presents as normative. Interestingly, Edward Said has written an essay on Yeats which reads him in the context of postcolonialism (reprinted in Said's *Culture and Imperialism*). Said views the desire, frequently expressed in Yeats's work, to regain contact with an earlier, mythical, nationalistic Ireland as typical of writers whose own position is postcolonial, and this is closely related to Fanon's idea of the need to reclaim the past. Characteristically, postcolonial writers evoke or create a precolonial version of their own nation, rejecting the modern and the contemporary, which is tainted with the colonial status of their countries. Here, then, is the first characteristic of postcolonial criticism – an awareness of representations of the non-European as exotic or immoral 'Other'.

For Yeats, as often with the postcolonial writer, an uneasy attitude to the colonial language is evident: his injunction to Irish poets, that they should learn their craft, implies the need to serve a humble apprenticeship. This 'humble' attitude to language may remind us of Stephen Dedalus's thoughts about the English language in James Joyce's *A Portrait of the Artist as a Young Man* (published in serial form in 1914–1915), especially the early scene in which Stephen is patronised by an English priest because of his use of a local dialect word. Stephen tells himself 'the language in which we are speaking is his before it is mine ... My soul frets in the shadow of his language' (*Portrait*, chapter five). More recently, the Irish poet Seamus Heaney, in a poem entitled 'The Ministry of Fear', recalls his childhood unease and self-consciousness about his pronunciation of English ('Those hobnailed boots from beyond the mountain / Were walking, by God, all over the fine / Lawns of elocution') and remarks that 'Ulster was British, but with no rights on / The English lyric' (see the collection *North*, 1975). This linguistic deference amounts to a sense that the linguistic furniture belongs to somebody else, and therefore shouldn't be moved around without permission. Some postcolonial writers have concluded that the colonisers' language is permanently tainted, and that to write in it involves a crucial acquiescence in colonial structures. Language itself, then, is a second area of concern in postcolonial criticism. (For an essay on poetic language from this postcolonial perspective see Stan Smith's 'Darkening English: Post-imperial contestations in the language of Seamus Heaney and Derek Walcott' in *English*, Spring 1994).

As this implies, Yeats, being a member of the Protestant ruling class in Ireland, has a double identity as both coloniser and colonised, and it is the recognition of such double identities which is one of the strengths of the postcolonialist view. Thus, the Nigerian novelist Chinua Achebe, publishing his first novel, *Things Fall Apart*, in 1958, was criticised by an early reviewer for affecting to identify with African villagers when actually his university education and his broadcasting job in the capital city of Lagos should make him identify, it was implied, with the values of 'civilisation', supposedly brought to Africa by Europeans. (See Achebe's paper 'Colonialist Criticism' in *Literature in the Modern*

World, ed. Dennis Walder, Oxford University Press, 1990). This emphasis on identity as doubled, or hybrid, or unstable is a third characteristic of the postcolonial approach.

At one level Achebe's use of a village Africa corresponds to Yeats's evocation of a precolonial, mythological Ireland of heroes and heroines. At another level, the double or hybrid identity is precisely what the postcolonial situation brings into being. The shift in attitudes in the 1980s and 1990s is towards postcolonial writers seeing themselves as using primarily African or Asian forms, supplemented with European-derived influences, rather than as working primarily within European genres like the novel and merely adding to them a degree of exotic Africanisation. All postcolonial literatures, it might be said, seem to make this transition. They begin with an unquestioning acceptance of the authority of European models (especially in the novel) and with the ambition of writing works that will be masterpieces entirely in this tradition. This can be called the '*Adopt*' phase of colonial literature, since the writer's ambition is to adopt the form as it stands, the assumption being that it has universal validity. The second stage can be called the '*Adapt*' phase, since it aims to adapt the European form to African subject matter, thus assuming partial rights of intervention in the genre. In the final phase there is, so to speak, a declaration of cultural independence whereby African writers remake the form to their own specification, without reference to European norms. This might be called the '*Adept*' phase, since its characteristic is the assumption that the colonial writer is an independent 'adept' in the form, not a humble apprentice, as in the first phase, or a mere licensee, as in the second. This stress on 'cross-cultural' interactions is a fourth characteristic of postcolonialist criticism.

This notion of the double, or divided, or fluid identity which is characteristic of the postcolonial writer explains the great attraction which post-structuralism and deconstruction have proved to be for the postcolonial critic. Post-structuralism is centrally concerned to show the fluid and unstable nature of personal and gender identity, the shifting, 'polyvalent', contradictory currents of signification within texts, and the way literature itself is a site on which ideological struggles are acted out. This mind-set is admirably suited to expressing the numerous contradictions and multiple allegiances of which the postcolonial writer and critic is constantly aware. This post-structuralist perspective is seen in the work of such representative figures as Henry Louis Gates Jr, Gayatri Spivak, and Homi Bhabha. In all three of these a complex Derridean–Foucauldian notion of textuality and fields of discourse is immediately apparent. Similarly in all three, the surface of the writing is difficult and the route through to any consequent political action (or stance, even) is necessarily indirect. This kind of postcolonial criticism roughly corresponds, then, to the theoreticised 'French' feminist criticism associated with figures like Julia Kristeva or Hélène Cixous. The example of postcolonial criticism offered later is from the work of Edward Said, who is less overtly theoretical, seems to accept some of the premises of liberal humanism, and has a more 'up-front' political affiliation (his identification with the Palestinian Arab cause). His work is in this regard reminiscent of the 'Anglo-American' variety of feminist criticism, which likewise seems (to me) more overtly political and certainly more immediately accessible.

If the three stages mentioned earlier (Adopt, Adapt, and Adept) provide a way of seeing postcolonial literature, then a way of seeing the stages of postcolonial criticism would be to suggest, as we have just been doing, that they closely parallel the developmental stages of feminist criticism. In its earliest phase, which is to say before it was known as such, postcolonial criticism took as its main subject matter white representations of colonial countries and criticised these for their limitations and their bias: thus, critics would discuss the representation of Africa in Joseph Conrad's *Heart of Darkness* or of India in E. M. Forster's *A Passage to India*, or of Algeria in Albert Camus's *The Outsider*. This corresponds to the early 1970s phase of feminist criticism when the subject matter was the representation of women by male novelists like D. H. Lawrence or Henry Miller – the classic instance is Kate Millett's *Sexual Politics*. The *second* phase of postcolonial criticism involved a turn towards explorations of themselves and their society by postcolonial writers. At this stage the celebration and exploration of diversity, hybridity, and difference become central. This is the stage when, in the title of the well-known pioneering work in this field, 'the empire writes back'. This corresponds to the 'gynotext' phase of feminist criticism, when there is a turn towards the exploration of female experience and identities in books by women. The analogy between these two types of criticism might be pushed a little further, so that a parallel might also be perceived with the split in feminist criticism between 'theoretical' and 'empirical' versions, as suggested above. Thus, in postcolonial criticism we might see a split between variants very directly influenced by deconstruction and post-structuralism – such as the work of Homi Bhabha – and work like Said's which accepts a good deal from liberal humanism, is written in a more accessible way, and seems perhaps to lend itself more directly to political engagement.

STOP and THINK

Postcolonial criticism draws attention to issues of cultural difference in literary texts and is one of several critical approaches we have considered which focus on specific issues, including issues of gender (feminist criticism), of class (Marxist criticism), and of sexual orientation (lesbian/gay criticism).

This raises the possibility of a kind of 'super-reader' able to respond equally and adequately to a text in all these ways. In practice, for most readers one of these issues tends to eclipse all the rest.

For instance, the example of feminist criticism, from Gilbert and Gubar's *The Madwoman in the Attic* (Chapter 6) doesn't comment on aspects of *Wuthering Heights* which would interest postcolonial critics, such as Heathcliff's being described by Emily Brontë in terms of a racial 'Other' (a gipsy, 'a little Lascar, or an American or Spanish castaway'). He is described by Gilbert and Gubar as Catherine's 'alter-ego or Id', and contrasted in his darkness with the blond Edgar who presides over the Grange, which is presented, however ironically, as 'heaven', 'society', and 'reason'. This is a conflating of racial Otherness with the irrational forces of the id or the subconscious which might be thought insensitive.

Should we, in general, try to become super-readers, with multiple layers of sympathy and awareness, or will trying to do so merely produce blandness and superficiality?

Obviously, it is impossible for anybody to answer this question for anybody else. My own feeling is that while an even spread of awareness across all these issues is theoretically possible, in practice *aiming* for this, merely in the interests of political correctness, is almost bound to produce superficiality. A genuine interest in one of these issues can really only arise from aspects of your own circumstances. These perspectives cannot be put on and off like a suit – they have to emerge and declare themselves with some urgency.

What postcolonial critics do

1. They reject the claims to universalism made on behalf of canonical Western literature and seek to show its limitations of outlook, especially its general inability to empathise across boundaries of cultural and ethnic difference.
2. They examine the representation of other cultures in literature as a way of achieving this end.
3. They show how such literature is often evasively and crucially silent on matters concerned with colonisation and imperialism (see, for instance, the discussion of Jane Austen's *Mansfield Park* in the example described below).
4. They foreground questions of cultural difference and diversity and examine their treatment in relevant literary works.
5. They celebrate hybridity and 'cultural polyvalency', that is, the situation whereby individuals and groups belong simultaneously to more than one culture (for instance, that of the coloniser, through a colonial school system, and that of the colonised, through local and oral traditions).
6. They develop a perspective, not just applicable to postcolonial literatures, whereby states of marginality, plurality and perceived 'Otherness' are seen as sources of energy and potential change.

Postcolonial criticism: an example

Let us take the essay by Edward Said on Jane Austen's *Mansfield Park*, an essay rapidly achieving something of a definitive status and available in Mulhern's *Contemporary Marxist Criticism*, in Newton's *Theory into Practice*, in Eagleton's *Raymond Williams: Critical Perspectives* and in Said's own *Culture and Imperialism*. Under the title 'Jane Austen and the Empire' Said carefully 'foregrounds the background' of Austen's novel, which is the estate in Antigua which Sir Thomas Bertram owns, and through which the estate of Mansfield Park is maintained. The central irony, then, is that the estate in England which represents an ideal of order and civilisation is sustained by another estate a world away, so that Mansfield Park would 'not have been possible without the slave trade, sugar, and the colonial planter class' (Mulhern, p. 111), for as Said remarks, 'Sir Thomas's property in the Caribbean would have had to be a sugar plantation maintained by slave labour (not abolished until the 1830s)' (p. 106). Said thus makes central the 'moral geography' of the novel, and sees Austen as the start of a line in fiction which leads to Conrad and Kipling in which the processes of colonialisation are examined. As Mulhern puts it in his introductory note, the consequence is that the 'dating of British culture's imperial phase must be revised backwards from the beginning of formal Empire into the eighteenth century' (p. 97). Thus, Sir Thomas, returning home and rapidly re-establishing order, without ever the thought that his views and instincts could be narrow or mistaken, is the quintessential colonialising figure who takes himself as the norm of civilisation. He is, says Said, 'a Crusoe setting things in order'. Nothing prevents our assuming, he says, that he 'does exactly the same things – on a larger scale – in Antigua ... to hold and rule Mansfield Park is to hold and rule an imperial estate in association with it' (p. 104).

This reading involves 'concretising' a dimension of the novel which is largely left implicit: it involves, not necessarily arguing that all these things are 'there' in the novel, but that this is the right way to read it. All the same, Said insists, precisely, that these things *are* there: 'all these things having to do with the outside brought in, seem to me unmistakably *there* in the suggestiveness of her allusive and abstract language'. So Said invokes the processes of close reading in his support, for the most part convincingly, but in the end his appeal seems to be to the *conscience* of the (especially) white and middle-class reader:

> We cannot easily say that since Mansfield Park is a novel, its affiliations with a particularly sordid history are irrelevant or transcended, not only because it is irresponsible to say that, but because we know too much to say so without bad faith. (p. 112)

There is, I think, no doubt about the effect of reading Said's essay. Any 'innocence' we might have had about this aspect of the novel goes: it is impossible henceforth to read it without a constant awareness of that absentee settler-planter who is at the centre of everything, in one sense, and yet constantly withdrawn and marginal in another. Said's reading likewise locates the centre of the book in an absence, in things unsaid and unspecified. In this sense it is a form of Marxist criticism influenced by post-structuralist views, contrasting with Krieger's much 'straighter' Marxism. It also, like new historicism, comes closer to actually naming the details of a specific social/colonial situation (the absentee planter-landlord class of eighteenth-century Antigua) rather than just evoking a generalised notion of colonial exploitation.

Selected reading

Ashcroft, Bill, *et al.*, *The Empire Writes Back: Theory and Practice in Post-colonial Literature* (Routledge, 1989).

A readable and comprehensive book which provides an excellent start on this topic.

Bhabha, Homi K., ed. *Nation and Narration* (Routledge, 1990).

A definitive early collection in this field, with pieces by several of the major figures.

Bhabha, Homi K., *The Location of Culture* (Routledge, 1994).

Examines 'the cultural and political boundaries which exist in between the spheres of gender, race, class and sexuality'. Discusses Morrison, Gordimer and Rushdie. Not an easy writer, but (says Toni Morrison) 'any serious discussion of post-colonial/postmodern scholarship is inconceivable without referencing Mr Bhabha'.

Césaire, Aimé, *Return to My Native Land*, (Penguin Poets, 1969).

This and the next title are early founding texts of postcolonialism, their status corresponding to that of 'classics' like *The Female Eunuch* or *The Feminine Mystique* within feminism..

Fanon, Frantz, *The Wretched of the Earth* (Penguin, 1961).

Gates, Henry Louis, Jr, ed. *'Race', Writing and Difference* (Chicago, 1985).

Said, Edward, *Orientalism* (Pantheon, New York, 1978).

Said's work has been a major influence in this field, and he is a useful entry-point since his writing has an immediate accessibility and clarity of impact.

Said, Edward, *The World, the Text and the Critic* (Harvard University Press 1983).

Spivak, Gayatri Chakravorty, *In Other Worlds: Essays in Cultural Politics* (Routledge, 1987).

Spivak is another major figure, but her close involvement with post-structuralism makes her writing quite demanding. A starting point might be her essay 'Draupadi' (on a Bengali short story, which she translates and reprints) in Newton's *Theory into Practice*.

Walder, Dennis, ed. *Literature in the Modern World* (Oxford University Press, 1990).

Contains Chinua Achebe's paper 'Colonialist Criticism', and other useful material in the relevant section.

11
Stylistics

Stylistics: a theory or a practice?

Stylistics is a critical approach which uses the methods and findings of the science of linguistics in the analysis of literary texts. By 'linguistics' here is meant the scientific study of language and its structures, rather than the learning of individual languages. Stylistics developed in the twentieth century and its aim is to show how the technical linguistic features of a literary work, such as the grammatical structure of its sentences, contribute to its overall meanings and effects.

The account given below will put a good deal of emphasis on critical practice rather than critical theory, and we should ask at the outset whether stylistics is really a form of critical theory at all. The compilers of most currently available guides to literary theory assume that it is not, since they say nothing about it. But the grounds for this assumption are difficult to see. It is certainly an approach to literature which has yielded a large amount of practical work distinctly different in tone and method from what we are accustomed to. This body of practice is the product of very specific theories about literary language and how it works, and these theories are usually taught alongside the practice.

The grounds for excluding stylistics, therefore, probably lie in the nature of the theoretical outlook behind the discipline, for liberal humanism and stylistics have a good deal in common. *Firstly*, both have a strong empirical bias, that is, a bias towards detailed verbal analysis of specific canonical literary texts, rather than a commitment to establishing generalised theoretical positions. *Secondly*, both have kept aloof from the eclecticism which has led to so much cross-fertilisation between Marxist, feminist, structuralist, and post-structuralist approaches. And *thirdly*, both have generally refused to take on board the notion of the 'floating signifier' (that is, the idea that the meanings established through language are innately fluid, indeterminate, and shifting).

These similarities might lead us to expect the two to be natural allies, but in fact stylistics and liberal humanism fought with each other very bitterly, in the 1960s, at least a decade before the outbreak of hostilities between liberal humanism and theory in general. However, stylistics also has its differences from other forms of critical theory, for it has resisted the 'relativism' which permeates all other kinds of theoretical discourse. Everywhere outside stylistics indeterminacy rules: all critics scrupulously avoid 'totalising claims' and acknowledge that there can be no overviews, only viewpoints, each of which is partial. Stylistics, by contrast, remains positivist in outlook; that is, it maintains its faith in the accumulation of knowledge by empirical investigation of external phenomena carried out by disinterested enquirers. There are good reasons, then, for regarding stylistics as different, but none, in my view, for regarding it as untheoretical. Its advantage, too, for those who are just beginning theory is that it does offer a wide range of new practical methods for explicating literature, many of which can be enjoyable to practise, especially when working in class in groups.

Stylistics, it should be added, is not confined to the analysis of literature: it can be applied equally to expository prose, political speeches, advertisements, and so on. It thus assumes that the language of literature is not a 'special case': on the contrary, literary language can be analysed just like any other kind to reveal precisely how effects are created. Hence, stylistics concedes no special mysterious qualities to literary language: it is not sacred or revered; it is simply the data on which the method can be put to use. It is true, of course, that very few literary critics of any persuasion today would make semi-mystical claims that poetry is inspired, or ineffable, or operates beyond reason in a realm which analysis can never fully penetrate. But on the other hand, neither do many of them proclaim the contrary – that literary language never has any transcendent dimension which lifts it above the everyday.

A brief historical account: from rhetoric, to philology, to linguistics, to stylistics, to new stylistics

Stylistics is, in a sense, the modern version of the ancient discipline known as 'rhetoric', which taught its students how to structure an argument, how to make effective use of figures of speech, and generally how to pattern and vary a speech or a piece of writing so as to produce the maximum impact. Rhetoric in medieval times played an important part in training people for the Church, the legal profession, and political or diplomatic life, but once divorced from this vocational purpose it degenerated into a rather arid and mechanical study of the mere surface features of language which involved, for instance, identifying and classifying figures of speech. The pedantic outlook of its practitioners (for instance, their love of impressive-sounding labels) is frequently satirised by Chaucer, Shakespeare and others. Traces of this degenerate form of the discipline survived in school teaching until quite recently.

Throughout the nineteenth century, rhetoric in this medieval sense was gradually absorbed into linguistics. At this time linguistics was usually known as 'philology', and was almost entirely historical in emphasis. It involved studying the evolution of languages, and the interconnections between them, and speculating about the origins of language itself. In the twentieth century there was a movement away from this historical emphasis and a new concentration on how language as a system is structured, looking at such aspects as the way meanings are established and maintained, and the options available (and their consequences) in structuring sentences. This is where a kind of born-again form of rhetoric emerged, shortly before the First World War, with a new interest in literary style and its effects, an interest seen also in the work of the Russian Formalists (Chapter 8 pp. 161–3) in the 1920s, and in the work of the Czech linguist Roman Jakobson, leader of the Prague Linguistic Circle (Chapter 8 p. 162), who lived in America after the Second World War. A famous 'Conference on Style' was held at Indiana University in 1958, and the proceedings published in 1960 as *Style in Language*, edited by Thomas Sebeok (Technology Press of the Massachusetts Institute of Technology and John Wiley & Sons, New York). The conference was notable, among other things, for Jakobson's 'Closing Statement', which seemed to announce a takeover bid for literature on the part of linguistics:

> Poetics deals with problems of verbal structure: Since linguistics is the global science of verbal structure, poetics may be regarded as an integral part of linguistics ['Poetics' here means the study of literature in general, not just poetry].

The gist of the Sebeok collection of material is to claim that linguistics offers a more objective way of studying literature, and the book tends to set up 'a confrontation of camps' (Roger Fowler's phrase) between literary and language studies. Fowler responded to what he saw as this unhelpful polarisation by editing a collection called *Essays on Style and language: Linguistic and critical approaches to literary studies* (1966), which tried to mend the damage done by what Fowler regarded as 'an unnecessary schism between "language" and "literature"'. But the result, if anything, was to widen the gap: Fowler's collection was reviewed by Helen Vendler in the journal *Essays in Criticism*, 1966, pp. 457–63. She suggested that while linguistic study had great potential, at present linguists are 'simply under-educated in the reading of poetry' and are taking on 'documents whose primary sense and value they are not equipped to absorb' (p. 460). This stung Fowler into a riposte which inaugurated a much-cited debate between himself and F. W. Bateson, the journal's editor (see *Essays in Criticism* 1967, pp. 332–47, and 1968, pp. 164–82). The outcome of this was, again, to solidify the language–literature polarisation.

But the period up to the 1980s saw the development of what Helen Vendler had said was lacking in linguistics, namely a form of 'discourse analysis' which would enable linguistics to comment on and analyse the structure of complete pieces of writing, rather than just the isolated phrases and sentences to which it had previously been restricted. This meant that non-linguists began to take some interest in the findings of linguistic essays, while, at the same time, linguists writing such material realised the need to consult and incorporate non-linguistic material. Allegedly, this resulted, during the 1980s, in what came to be called the 'new stylistics', which had a limited degree of eclecticism (in that it drew on the findings of other new kinds of criticism – feminist, structuralist, post-structuralist, and so on) and was less likely to claim that it alone studied literature in an objective way.

In fact, however, the superiority claims from both sides continued. Fowler, for instance, in his 1986 book *Linguistic Criticism* characterises linguistic criticism as 'objective description of texts' (p. 4), while conventional criticism, by contrast, uses 'random descriptive jargon' (p. 3) and is merely 'amateur commentary' using only quasi-grammatical terms. Also, his 1980s writing repeated very similar arguments to those he had used in the 1960s against Bateson. Thus, opponents, he says in 1986, speak as if linguistics were a single entity, whereas actually there are many different techniques in use within it, some appropriate for literary study and some not. This is exactly the same point as he had made in the 1960s: 'there is no one linguistics ... bland undefined accounts of "linguistics" lead nowhere' (*Essays in Criticism*, 1967, p. 325). Likewise, not all stylistics in the 1960s made uncompromisingly exclusive claims for the discipline, so the more liberal attitude said to be distinctive of the new stylistics is not something which appears only in the 1980s. Thus, Fowler, again, in the Bateson dispute, stressed that just being a linguist isn't a qualification for dealing adequately with poetry. On the contrary 'although literature is language, and therefore open to ordinary formal linguistic investigation ... it has, like other formally distinctive texts, essentially distinctive contexts which the linguist no less than the critic must study' (*Essays in Criticism*, 1967, p. 325).

Hence, the grounds for setting up a sequence in which stylistics gives way to new stylistics are slender. Combative 'old' stylistics attitudes are common today and are explicit in much recent writing in the field. For instance, Nigel Fabb and Alan Durant, describing the difference between stylistics and literary criticism in the mid-1980s say that in the latter critical comment is 'often made without any accompanying systematic, or even explicit, scrutiny of its own methods or assumptions' (*The Linguistics of Writing: Arguments between language and literature*, Manchester University Press, 1987, p. 228). Thus, while it is true to say that stylistics today tends to be more open than before to input from those working in other areas of intellectual enquiry, it would be exaggerating to imply the kind of clean break with the hard line past implied by the term 'new stylistics'. The current mood of co-operation is represented by the 'Interface' series from Routledge, (series editor Ronald Carter), which aims to 'build bridges between the traditionally divided disciplines of language studies and literary studies'. It should be added that doubtless the old hard line attitudes against stylistics still exist too, but in recent years structuralism and post-structuralism, rather than stylistics, have usually been seen as the major threat to traditional values in criticism, with the consequence that most liberal humanist polemical writing has been directed at these targets.

How does stylistics differ from standard close reading?

Stylistic analysis attempts to provide a commentary which is objective and scientific, based on concrete quantifiable data, and applied in a systematic way. In contrast, as we have seen, conventional 'close reading' is often seen by the stylistician (to a greater or lesser extent) as impressionistic, intuitive, and randomised. All the same, the differences between the two approaches might well seem superficial to a casual observer, so it is worth trying to specify them. The specific differences between conventional close reading and stylistics include the following:

1. Close reading emphasises *differences* between literary language and that of the general speech community; it tends to isolate the literary text and see it as a purely aesthetic art object, or 'verbal icon', whose language operates according to rules of its own. Stylistics, by contrast, emphasises *connections* between literary language and everyday language. This difference of view about literary language is actually a continuation of a very old dispute. For instance, the critical break between Wordsworth and Coleridge lay in the fact that Wordsworth

believed that poetic language when most effective was at its plainest and most prose-like, that is, when it is as close as possible to the language actually used by 'men'. In contrast, Coleridge believed that poetic language depended for its effect on the poet's heightening or intensifying it (through patterning, compression, repetition, and so on) and thus making it more specialised and taking it further away from the patterns of everyday speech.

2. Stylistics uses specialised technical terms and concepts which derive from the science of linguistics, terms like 'transitivity', 'under-lexicalisation', 'collocation', and 'cohesion' (all of which are explained in the final section of this chapter). Terms like these are part of the technical vocabulary of a particular field of intellectual enquiry and they do not have any currency outside this field. Unless you were 'talking shop' with fellow students you could not introduce these terms into casual conversation without explaining what they meant and (more importantly) what they were for. In contrast, close reading (typically) uses lay-person's terms and concepts which may have a slightly 'bookish' air, but are nevertheless part of ordinary everyday language; terms, for instance, like 'verbal nuance', 'irony', 'ambiguity', 'paradox', and 'ambivalence'. If you started to explain the meaning of these terms in the same casual conversation, you would probably seem rather patronising, even though the use of these terms in criticism might be considered slightly specialised, and each of them has its own resonance and associations within the discipline. The point is, though, that these terms are clearly not 'technical' in the way that 'under-lexicalisation' is.

3. Stylistics makes greater claims to scientific objectivity than does close reading, stressing that its methods and procedures can be learned and applied by all. Hence, its aim is partly the 'demystification' of both literature and criticism. Thus, in relation to literature it aims to show, as we saw above, the continuity between literary language and other forms of written communication. In the case of criticism, it aims to provide a set of procedures which are openly accessible to all, in contrast to the tendency within close reading to stress the

need for the critic to develop 'tact' and 'sensitivity' towards the literary text and avoid spelling out a method or procedure to be followed. Hence, for instance, the notorious reluctance of F. R. Leavis to describe or set out in detail his critical methods. Likewise, readers often express the feeling that the language of literature achieves its effects in ways which may prove inherently inaccessible to analysis, so that at the core of literature is a kind of mysterious impenetrable essence. If, as many believe, the sentiments expressed in a poem are uniquely embodied in the form of words chosen by the poet, then it must follow that there are strict limits to what can be added by critical enquiry.

The ambitions of stylistics

1. *Stylisticians try to provide 'hard' data to support existing 'intuitions' about a literary work.* Stylistics is not always just about the interpreting of individual literary works, but when it is engaged in straight textual interpretation it often tries to back up the (as they would see them) impressionistic hunches of common readers with hard linguistic data. Thus, we might, in reading a Hemingway short story, register an impression something like 'Hemingway has a plain style which is very distinctive'. Stylisticians would try to be much more specific: their question might be 'what do we mean, exactly, by "plain"?' Well, perhaps we need no linguistic training to realise that Hemingway generally avoids descriptive words like adverbs and adjectives: where another writer might say something like 'Smith ran purposefully through the heavy rain' Hemingway would omit the adverb 'purposefully' and the adjective 'heavy'. He would want these things to emerge implicitly, which would actually, in his view, given them greater impact. So the sentence would be, simply, 'Smith ran through the rain'. The stylistician might calculate Hemingway's usage in a given tale, in a statement like 'seventy-three per cent of the nouns and verbs used by Hemingway in … are without adjectival or adverbial qualification'. There might be a comparision with work by other writers generally perceived

as having a less plain style, perhaps resulting in the claim that these writers have only thirty per cent of nouns and verbs unqualified. Of course, the calculating would be applied to a section of the work only, perhaps to a tale by each of the writers concerned which would be intuitively felt to be typical of each. The result is not to give us new information, exactly, about Hemingway, since every reader realises very quickly that his sparse, plain style is one of his most distinctive qualities. But it will have told us a good deal about precisely how, in linguistic terms, the plainness is achieved and maintained.

2. *Stylisticians suggest new interpretations of literary works based on linguistic evidence.* Stylistics brings a special expertise to bear on the linguistic features of a text, and therefore sees a dimension of the material which the ordinary reader would be unaware of. This dimension may well contain material which could alter our interpretation of the work. For instance, Colin MacCabe argues in an essay on stylistics that Falstaff in Shakespeare's history plays has an element of sexual ambiguity. He frequently refers, for example, to his large stomach, and how it makes bravery very difficult, but the word he uses is not 'stomach' but 'womb' ('My womb, my womb, my womb undoes me'). At the time the play was written, says MacCabe, the word 'womb' was in a state of semantic transition. That is to say, its meaning was gradually changing from an older sense to a newer one: in its old sense it was a general word for 'stomach' and was used interchangebly of both men and women. But it was also then acquiring its more specialised modern meaning, where it is gender-specific and designates a particular part of female anatomy. Since both senses of the word were possible while it was in the transition stage from one sense to the other, Falstaff's use of the word suggests a corresponding sexual ambivalence in himself. Only the reader in possession of this specialised knowledge about semantic change would realise this: other readers would at first be puzzled by the word, would then perhaps look it up in a glossary, and would finally conclude that the word is simply being used in an obsolete sense, and hence had no bearing upon questions of characterisation or interpretation.

There are, I think, problems in accepting MacCabe's account of this example: he assumes that words which are in process of semantic change have traces of both meanings present in every usage, but it seems more likely that in these cases a word can have either meaning, but not *both*. For example, the word 'disinterested' today is in process of semantic change, but every given usage signifies either 'impartial' or else 'not interested', and never a combination of these meanings. A more general problem is to decide the status of evidence which is below the threshold of perception of all readers except professional linguists. How, for instance, did such meanings get into the text? Deliberately planted by the author? Presumably not. And in what sense are they 'there' at all if normally imperceptible except to a group of readers whose existence, except in the case of present-day texts, could not have been predicted? All the same, the general point is clear: linguists use their specialised knowledge not just to support existing readings but to establish new ones.

3. *Stylisticians attempt to establish general points about how literary meanings are made.* The point here is that, like all the other new approaches to literature, stylistics is interested not just in the individual literary work, but also in much more general questions about how literature works. For instance, linguists argue that a literary effect is created simultaneously in terms of both form and content. In Hardy's *Tess of the D'Urbervilles*, Tess's subjection to the social and physical superiority of Alec is expressed both in terms of what is said, and in terms of the grammatical structure of the 'seduction' (or 'rape' scene), for his having power is reinforced subliminally by Alec (or some attribute of him) frequently being the subject of sentences, while Tess's lack of power is reinforced by her frequently being the grammatical object: thus sentences have patterns like: *he* [subject] *touched her* [object]; *his fingers* [subject] *sank into her* [object], and so on. This kind of argument, if accepted, has implications about how literary effects are created and how they operate. The implication is that the powerful literary effect is 'overdetermined', that is, it comes from different factors combining, so that content is subtly rein-

forced by grammatical structure, overall 'discourse structure', word choice, imagery, and so on. Literary meaning, this suggests, goes down to the very roots of language and is reflected at the level of grammar and sentence structure. Hence, no aspect of language is neutral; the patterns of grammar and syntax, morphemes, and phonemes are all implicated in literary meaning. Again, I think there are difficulties with this as a general argument: for instance, it seems to make authors into intuitive genius figures who instinctively 'know' the content of modern linguistics. All the same, the main point is clear: stylistics tries to establish things which are generally true about the way literature works.

STOP and THINK

The linguistic terminology used in stylistics may seem daunting if you have never been taught any formal grammar, but it is probably unwise to try to learn formal grammar as a prelude to sampling stylistics. A better way is to make use of a few basic reference tools and have these by you for consultation as you read some of the items listed at the end of this section. I would suggest you use *A Dictionary of Stylistics*, Katie Wales (Longman, 1989) and a good up to date compendium of English grammar. I have found the kind intended for advanced learners of English more useful than others. A good example is Michael Swann's *Practical English Usage*, Oxford University Press, 1980.

A problem to focus on as you begin your involvement with this topic is the one highlighted by Stanley Fish in his essay 'What is Stylistics and Why are they Saying such Terrible Things About It?' Fish says that there is always a gap between the linguistic features identified in the text and the interpretation of them offered by the stylistician. We might call this problem the hermeneutic gap ('hermeneutic' means concerned with the act of interpretation).

For instance, it may be said that an utterance uses a large number of passive verbs – those patterned 'I have been informed that ...': this is the linguistic feature. These passives, we may then be told, indicate a degree of evasiveness in the text: this is the interpretation.

The difficulty is knowing how we can be sure that there is a link between the use of the passive and evasiveness. Can we be sure that the user of the passive is usually being evasive in some way, for instance, trying to conceal the identity of the informant, and, so to speak, to conceal that concealment? (Was I being evasive when I used passives in the previous paragraph?) If the passive is only sometimes evasive, what are the circumstances which make it so?

In your reading of the following examples, then, and of some of the items listed at the end of the section, try to identify the moment when the critic passes from describing linguistic data to interpreting it – the moment when the 'hermeneutic gap' opens up – and consider how convincingly, or otherwise, it is bridged.

What stylistic critics do

1. They describe technical aspects of the language of a text – such as grammatical structures – and then use this data in interpretation.
2. The purpose of doing this is sometimes simply to provide objective linguistic data to support existing readings or intuitions about a literary work.
3. At other times the purpose is to establish a new reading, which may be based only, or mainly, on this linguistic data, and may challenge or counter existing readings.
4. These technical accounts of how meanings are made in literature are part of an overall project which involves showing that literature has no ineffable, mystical core which is beyond analysis: rather, it is part of a common 'universe of discourse' and uses the same techniques and resources as other kinds of language use.
5. To this end, stylistics does not confine itself to the analysis of literature and often juxtaposes literary and other kinds of dis-

course, for instance, comparing the linguistic devices used in poetry with those of advertising.

6. Stylistics moves beyond 'sentence grammar' to 'text grammar', considering how the text works as a whole to achieve (or not) its purposes (for instance, to amuse, to create suspense, or to persuade) and examining the linguistic features which contribute to these ends.

Stylistics: examples

Rather than considering a single example in detail, I will refer more briefly to three, each of which uses some technical aspect of language in critical interpretation. The first makes use of the linguistic terms 'transitivity' and 'under-lexicalisation'. What do these mean? The former refers to the different sentence patterns in which verbs ('doing words') can occur. Traditionally a verb is said to be transitive when the action it designates has a stated 'goal' or 'recipient' or 'object'. Thus, in the sentence 'She shut the door' the action of shutting is 'received' or 'suffered' by the door. Hence the verb 'shut' is said to be 'transitive', which roughly means 'passing through', in the sense that the action 'passes through' to the door. 'Door' is said to be the object of this verb in the sentence just cited. By contrast, in the sentence 'She vanished' the verb is said to be 'intransitive', since the action does not 'pass through' to any stated object – it just happens, and is, so to speak, self-sufficient. These two examples, then, represent different transitivity patterns, and while the grammatical categories 'transitive' and 'intransitive' are derived from traditional grammar, as originally devised to describe the structures of the Latin language, the abstract notion of 'transitivity', designating the range of patterns possible for verbs, derives from the work of the linguist M. A. K. Halliday in the 1960s and 1970s. Halliday made use of the concept in analysing fiction, and Roger Fowler follows him in this.

'Under-lexicalisation', finally, is a term invented by Fowler: it refers to cases where there is a 'lack of an adequate set of words to express specific concepts' (K. Wales). Thus, we might not know the word for a particular implement and instead call it a

'thingy' or a 'wotsit'; or we might forget the word for a particular object (the word 'handle', say) and use a vague descriptive
substitute instead (such as 'the holding thing'). These would be
examples of slightly different types of under-lexicalisation.

Let's now look at how a critic uses these terms in discussing
the opening of William Faulkner's novel *The Sound and the Fury*
(in the essay by Roger Fowler from the collection *Essays on style
and language*, 1966 already referred to). The opening is narrated
from the point of view of Benjy who is a thirty-three-year-old
man with the mind of a young child. Benjy is watching a game of
golf:

> Through the fence, between the curling flower spaces, I could see
> them hitting. They were coming towards where the flag was and I
> went along the fence. Luster was hunting in the grass by the flower
> tree. They took the flag out, and they were hitting. Then they put
> the flag back and they went to the table, and he hit and the other
> hit.

Fowler writes:

> There is a consistent oddity in transitivity: there are almost no tran-
> sitive verbs with objects, a preponderence of intransitives ('coming',
> 'went', 'hunting', etc.) and one transitive ('hit') used repeatedly
> without an object, ungrammatically.

This constitutes the linguisitic data. Fowler now takes the step
from description to interpretation: this 'oddity of transitivity'
(such as using the word 'hit' without saying what was hit) implies
that 'Benjy has little sense of actions and their effects on objects'.
This is, I think, a little over-specific, but clearly we notice, as we
read, that there is something strange about Benjy's language and
we register this as indicating that there is something strange about
his mind. The 'something strange' about the language concerns
the transitivity pattern. Implicitly, Fowler's point is that the
author's choosing this linguistic feature to disturb is significant,
for, of course, a disturbed state of mind could, in theory, be con-
veyed by disrupting *any* language feature at all. Secondly, Benjy's
under-lexicalisation is seen in the way he often uses descriptive
circumlocutions rather than the right words for things: thus, he

never uses the word 'golf' for what he is watching, and he calls a bush a 'flower tree'. This, again, is the data. Interpreting it involves the suggestion that doing this indicates the character's inability to perceive the world in socially acceptable ways, as most other people do. Thus, the stylistician explains the extent of the character's isolation by a stylistic analysis of aspects of the language associated with him.

Another example of the kind of linguistic data used by stylisticians is seen in Ronald Carter's analysis of W. H. Auden's poem 'Capital' in Carter & Burton, eds, *Literary Text and Language Study*, Edward Arnold, 1982. Carter makes use of the notion of 'collocation', a term which 'refers to the habitual or expected co-occurrence of words' (Wales). This is a reference to the fact that words frequently occur in groupings which have a degree of predictability, even when they fall short of being set phrases which invariably have the same pattern. (This aspect of language used to be exploited in the British TV game show 'Blankety-Blank'). To demonstrate what I mean, let me ask you to complete each of the following phrases with a single word (a different word in each case, and in each case putting in the word which first occurs to you):

A box of ... A black ... An uninvited ...

The note on p. 218 indicates the words I think you are likely to have used to fill these gaps. These phrases are not fixed clichés (like 'He went as white as a sheet'), but simply a product of the way each word in an utterance progressively narrows down the range of possibilities for the words which succeed it. Thus, if I say 'It's a fine ...' you can predict that the next word will be 'day' or 'afternoon', or some such. The sentence *could* be completed with the words 'way to calculate the height of a steeple', but it is very unlikely that any given occurrence of the opening 'It's a fine ...' would be completed in this way. Now, a common feature of poetry is to break habitual collocation patterns, so that words not usually seen together suddenly occur. Poets divorce words from their usual partners and provide unlikely new partnerships between words which we would never have imagined getting together. Thus Carter shows how Auden, at one point in the poem, avoids an expected collocation like saying that people are 'waiting patiently', and instead says of the idle rich in big cities that they are 'waiting *expensively* for miracles to happen' (my italics). Auden also mentions a part of the city in which political exiles live (and where they meet to plan their eventual return to power in their own countries) as a 'malicious village'. A more usual collocation for 'village' would combine it with approving adjectives to give phrases like 'friendly village' or 'picturesque village' or 'sleepy village'. Carter's overall point is that 'collocational breaks' of this kind signal parts of the poem which are 'thematically-charged' and will hence repay further investigation.

A final kind of linguistic data used by the stylistician concerns 'cohesion'. Cohesion is about 'lexical items' (words) which cross the boundaries between sentences, binding them into a single continuous utterance, even though they are *grammatically* separate sentences. Without cohesion a text has the awkward start-stop quality of a child's old-fashioned early reader, like this:

> This is Mandy. Mandy is my friend. Mandy and I go to the pictures together.

The stop–start quality can be removed and cohesion achieved by what linguistis call 'pronominalisation' (using pronouns), thus:

> This is Mandy. *She* is my friend. *We* go to the pictures together.

Notice that although these are still grammatically separate sentences they now flow as a single connected utterance, since the pronouns 'She' and 'We' refer back to people already named.
Modern writers have been interested in the effects of distorting patterns of cohesion, and an awareness of this concept helps to appreciate what is going on in something like the following, which is the start of a short story by the American writer Donald Barthelme:

> Edward looked at his red beard in the table-knife. Then Edward and Pia [not 'he and Pia] went to Sweden, to the farm. In the mailbox Pia found a cheque for Willie from the government of Sweden. It was for twenty three hundred crowns and had a rained-on look.

Pia [not 'she'] put the cheque in the pocket of her brown coat. Pia
[not 'She'] was pregnant. In London she had been sick everyday.

There are many other linguistic effects here apart from the dis-
tortions in the expected cohesion pattern which I have indicated.
Partly, the effect comes from the sense of incongruity which
arises when a grammatically continuous discourse frames content
which is logically, conceptually, and emotionally distorted and
fragmented. Also, the simple language and short sentences give
the tone of a child's reader, again, but the subject matter is very
incongruous with this tone, being particularly adult and traumatic. Through a particular way of using language, then, a certain literary effect is created, and in these circumstance we can
legitimately use linguistic techniques in our exploration.

Note

I have used these same examples several times with classes to
demonstrate the principle of collocation. The phrases have to be
completed without conferring and without prolonged delibera-
tion. Most people write 'A box of chocolates' or 'A box of
matches'. A few write 'A box of hankies' or 'A box of tricks'.
These four usually account for all the choices made by a group
of twenty. 'A black' is usually completed by 'cat' or 'box'. 'An
uninvited' is always completed by 'guest'. It is an absolute certainty that these phrases will never be completed in anything like
twenty different ways by twenty different people.

Selected reading

Birch, David, *Language, Literature, and Critical Practice: Ways of
    Analysing Text* (Routledge, 1989).
Carter, Ronald, ed. *Language, Discourse and Literature: An Introductory
    Reader in Discourse Stylistics* (Unwin Hyman, 1989).
Carter, Ronald, ed. *Language and Literature: An Introductory Reader in
    Stylistics* (Allen & Unwin, 1982).
    Chapter five is on Hemingway's 'Cat in the Rain'.
Carter, Ronald & Burton, Deirdre, eds, *Literary Text and Language*

Study, (Edward Arnold, 1982).

Chapter two, 'Responses to Language in Poetry'.

Chapman, Raymond, *Linguistics and Literature: An Introduction to Literary Stylistics* (Edward Arnold, 1974).

Basic and short.

Cluysenaar, Anne, *An Introduction to Literary Stylistics* (Batsford, 1976).
Thorough and basic.

Fabb, Nigel, *et al.*, eds, *The Linguistics of Writing: Arguments Between Language and Literature* (Manchester University Press, 1987).

Useful material. See especially the introduction, and the chapters by Marie Louise Pratt, Maurice Halle and Henry Widdowson.

Fish, Stanley, *Is There a Text in This Class?* (Harvard University Press, 1980).

See chapters two and ten, the two parts of the famous essay called 'What is Stylistics and Why are they Saying Such Terrible Things About it?'

Fowler, Roger, *Linguistic Criticism* (Oxford University Press, 1986).

A good general introduction.

Tambling, Jeremy, *What is Literary Language?* (Open University Press, 1988).

Has a useful appendix on 'Critical and Rhetorical Terms'.

Toolan, Michael, ed. *Language, Text and Context: Essays in Stylistics* (Routledge, 1992).

An interesting collection representative of recent trends in stylistics, particularly the strong emphasis on context. For an essay which quesitons the adequacy of this contextualising see Sara Mills's chapter 'Knowing your place: a Marxist feminist stylistic analysis'.

Widdowson, H. G. *Stylistics and the Teaching of Literature* (Longman, 1975).

A brief and simple guide.

Appendices

Appendix 1 Edgar Allan Poe, 'The oval portrait'

The chateau into which my valet had ventured to make forcible entrance, rather than permit me, in my desperately wounded condition, to pass a night in the open air, was one of those piles of commingled gloom and grandeur which have so long frowned among the Apennines, not less in fact than in the fancy of Mrs Radcliffe. To all appearance it had been temporarily and very lately abandoned. We established ourselves in one of the smallest and least sumptuously furnished apartments. It lay in a remote turret of the building. Its decorations were rich, yet tattered and antique. Its walls were hung with tapestry and bedecked with manifold and multiform armorial trophies, together with an unusually great number of very spirited modern paintings in frames of rich golden arabesque. In these paintings, which depended from the walls not only in their main surfaces, but in very many nooks which the bizarre architecture of the chateau rendered necessary – in these paintings my incipient delerium, perhaps, had caused me to take deep interest; so that I bade Pedro to close the heavy shutters of the room – since it was already night – to light the tongues of a tall candelabrum which stood by the head of my bed – and to throw open far and wide the fringed curtains of black velvet which enveloped the bed itself. I wished all this done that I might resign myself, if not to sleep, at least alternately to the contemplation of these pictures, and the perusal of a small volume which had been found upon the pillow, and which purported to criticise and describe them.

Long – long I read – and devoutly, devotedly I gazed. Rapidly and gloriously the hours flew by, and the deep midnight came. The position of the candelabrum displeased me, and outreaching my hand with difficulty, rather than disturb my slumbering valet, I placed it so as to throw its rays more fully upon the book.

But the action produced an effect altogether unanticipated. The rays of the numerous candles (for there were many) now fell within a niche of the room which had hitherto been thrown into deep shade by one of the bed-posts. I thus saw in vivid light a picture all unnoticed before. It was the portrait of a young girl just ripening into womanhood. I glanced at the painting hurriedly, and then closed my eyes. Why I did this was not at first apparent even to my own perception. But while my lids remained thus shut, I ran over in mind my reason for so shutting them. It was an impulsive movement to gain time for thought – to make sure that my vision had not deceived me – to calm and subdue my fancy for a more sober and more certain gaze. In a very few moments I again looked fixedly at the painting.

That I now saw aright I could not and would not doubt; for the first flashing of the candles upon that canvas had seemed to dissipate the dreamy stupor which was stealing over my senses, and to startle me at once into waking life.

The portrait, I have already said, was that of a young girl. It was a mere head and shoulders, done in what is technically termed a *vignette* manner; much in the style of the favorite heads of Sully. The arms, the bosom and even the ends of the radiant hair, melted imperceptibly into the vague yet deep shadow which formed the back-ground of the whole. The frame was oval, richly gilded and filagreed in *Moresque*. As a thing of art nothing could be more admirable than the painting itself. But it could have been neither the execution of the work, nor the immortal beauty of the countenance, which had so suddenly and so vehemently moved me. Least of all, could it have been that my fancy, shaken from its half slumber, had mistaken the head for that of a living person. I saw at once that the peculiarities of the design, of the *vignetting*, and of the frame, must have instantly dispelled such idea – must have prevented even its momentary entertainment. Thinking

earnestly upon these points, I remained, for an hour perhaps, half
sitting, half reclining, with my vision riveted upon the portrait.
At length, satisfied with the true secret of its effect, I fell back
within the bed. I had found the spell of the picture in an absolute
life-likeliness of expression, which at first startling, finally con-
founded, subdued and appalled me. With deep and reverent awe
I replaced the candelabrum in its former position. The cause of
my deep agitation being thus shut from view, I sought eagerly the
volume which discussed the paintings and their histories. Turning to the number which designated the oval portrait, I there read
the vague and quaint words which follow:

'She was a maiden of rarest beauty, and not more lovely than
full of glee. And evil was the hour when she saw, and loved, and
wedded the painter. He, passionate, studious, austere, and having
already a bride in his Art; she a maiden of rarest beauty, and not
more lovely than full of glee: all light and smiles, and frolicksome
as the young fawn: loving and cherishing all things: hating only
the Art which was her rival: dreading only the pallet and brushes
and other untoward instruments which deprived her of the countenance of her lover. It was thus a terrible thing for this lady to
hear the painter speak of his desire to pourtray even his young
bride. But she was humble and obedient, and sat meekly for many
weeks in the dark high turret-chamber where the light dripped
upon the pale canvas only from overhead. But he, the painter,
took glory in his work, which went on from hour to hour and
from day to day. And he was a passionate, and wild and moody
man, who became lost in reveries; so that he *would* not see that
the light which fell so ghastily in that lone turret withered the
health and the spirits of his bride, who pined visibly to all but
him. Yet she smiled on and still on, uncomplainingly, because she
saw that the painter, (who had high renown,) took a fervid and
burning pleasure in his task, and wrought day and night to depict
her who so loved him, yet who grew daily more dispirited and
weak. And in sooth some who beheld the portrait spoke of its
resemblance in low words, as of a mighty marvel, and a proof not
less of the power of the painter than of his deep love for her
whom he depicted so surpassingly well. But at length, as the labor
drew nearer to its conclusion, there were admitted none into the

turret; for the painter had grown wild with the ardor of his work, and turned his eyes from the canvas rarely, even to regard the countenance of his wife. And he *would* not see that the tints which he spread upon the canvas were drawn from the cheeks of her who sate beside him. And when many weeks had passed, and but little remained to do, save one brush upon the mouth and one tint upon the eye, the spirit of the lady again flickered up as the flame within the socket of the lamp. And then the brush was given, and then the tint was placed; and, for one moment, the painter stood entranced before the work which he had wrought; but in the next, while he yet gazed, he grew tremulous and very pallid, and aghast, and crying with a loud voice, "This is indeed Life itself!" turned suddenly to regard his beloved: – *She was dead!*

(Source: Edgar Allan Poe: *Selected Writings*, Penguin)

Appendix 2 Dylan Thomas, 'A refusal to mourn the death, by fire, of a child in London'

Never until the mankind making
Bird beast and flower
Fathering and all humbling darkness
Tells with silence the last light breaking
And the still hour
Is come of the sea tumbling in harness

And I must enter again the round
Zion of the water bead
And the synagogue of the ear of corn
Shall I let pray the shadow of a sound
Or sow my salt seed
In the least valley of sackcloth to mourn

The majesty and burning of the child's death.
I shall not murder
The mankind of her going with a grave truth
Nor blaspheme down the stations of the breath
With any further
Elegy of innocence and youth.

Deep with the first dead lies London's daughter,
Robed in the long friends,
The grains beyond age, the dark veins of her mother,
Secret by the unmourning water
Of the riding Thames.
After the first death, there is no other.

(Source: *Collected Poems 1934–52*, Dent)

Appendix 3 William Cowper, 'The castaway'

Obscurest night involv'd the sky,
  Th' Atlantic billows roar'd,
When such a destin'd wretch as I,
  Wash'd headlong from on board,
Of friends, of hope, of all bereft,
His floating home for ever left.

No braver chief could Albion boast
  Than he with whom he went,
Nor ever ship left Albion's coast,
  With warmer wishes sent.
He lov'd them both, but both in vain,
Nor him beheld, nor her again.

Not long beneath the whelming brine,
  Expert to swim, he lay;
Nor soon he felt his strength decline,
  Or courage die away;
But wag'd with death a lasting strife,
Supported by despair of life.

He shouted: nor his friends had fail'd
  To check the vessel's course,
But so the furious blast prevail'd,
  That, pitiless perforce,
They left their outcast mate behind,
And scudded still before the wind.

Some succour yet they could afford;

And, such as storms allow,
The cask, the coop, the floated cord,
   Delay'd not to bestow.
But he (they knew) nor ship, nor shore,
Whate'er they gave should visit more.

Nor, cruel as it seem'd, could he
   Their haste himself condemn,
Aware that flight, in such a sea,
   Alone could rescue them;
Yet bitter felt it still to die
Deserted, and his friends so nigh.

He long survives, who lives an hour
   In ocean, self-upheld;
And so long he, with unspent pow'r,
   His destiny repell'd;
And ever, as the minutes flew,
Entreated help, or cried – Adieu!

At length, his transient respite past,
   His comrades, who before
Had heard his voice in ev'ry blast,
   Could catch the sound no more.
For then, by toil subdued, he drank
The stifling wave, and then he sank.

No poet wept him: but the page
   Of narrative sincere,
That tells his name, his worth, his age,
   Is wet with Anson's tear.
And tears by bards or heroes shed
Alike immortalize the dead.

I therefore purpose not, or dream,
   Descanting on his fate,
To give the melancholy theme
   A more enduring date:
But misery still delights to trace
Its 'semblance in another's case.

No voice divine the storm allay'd,
   No light propitious shone;
When, snatch'd from all effectual aid,
   We perish'd, each alone:
But I beneath a rougher sea,
And whelm'd in deeper gulphs than he.

(Source: *The Penguin Book of English Romantic Verse*, ed. David
Wright, Penguin)

Where do we go from here? Further reading

General guides

Durant, Alan and Fabb, Nigel, *Literary Studies in Action* (Routledge, 1990).

Ambitious and innovative, but not always successful.

Eagleton, Terry, *Literary Theory: An Introduction* (Blackwell, 1983).

The first comprehensive guide to be published. Sometimes entertaining, sometimes difficult, and now in need of updating.

Lynn, Stephen, *Texts and Contexts: Writing about Literature with Critical Theory* (Harper Collins, 1994).

Very user-friendly and with a strong emphasis on theory as critical practice, but the emphasis on step by step help with writing seems excessive to me, since the writing tasks exemplified are so very specific.

Selden, Raman & Widdowson, Peter, *A Reader's Guide to Contemporary Literary Theory* (Harvester, 3rd edn, 1993).

Even-handed, detailed coverage: originally published soon after Eagleton's, and though it lacks his wit, it has the advantage of recent updating.

Webster, Roger, *Studying Literary Theory: An Introduction* (Arnold, 1990).

Very brief, but quite often clear where others are not.

Reference books

Coyle, Martin, *et al.*, eds, *Encyclopedia of Literature and Criticism* (Routledge, 1990).

A wealth of helpful material.

Cuddon, J. A. *A Dictionary of Literary Terms and Literary Theory* (Blackwell, 3rd edn, 1991).

Theory isn't its strongest point, but the long entries on major critical approaches are well-researched.

Hawthorn, Jeremy, *A Glossary of Contemporary Literary Theory* (Edward Arnold, 2nd edn, 1994).

Hawthorn, Jeremy, *A Concise Glossary of Contemporary Literary Theory* (Edward Arnold, 1992).

This is a shorter version of the above. I have found most of its entries very helpful.

Wales, Katie, *A Dictionary of Stylistics* (Longman, 1989).

Impressive in every way and always enlightening.

General readers

Barry, Peter, ed. *Issues in Contemporary Critical Theory* (Macmillan Casebook, 1987).

Some difficult material, but highly recommended.

Lodge, David, ed. *Modern Criticism and Theory: A Reader* (Longman, 1988).

An excellent source of material. Will give initial 'hands-on' experience of the writings of many of the major figures.

Newton, K. M., ed. *Theory into Practice* (Macmillan, 1992).

A strong collection of pieces on applied theory.

Newton, K. M., ed. *Twentieth Century Literary Theory: A Reader* (Macmillan, 1988).

Useful and wide-ranging.

Rice, Philip & Waugh, Patricia, eds, *Modern Literary Theory: A Reader* (Arnold, 2nd edn 1992).

Another excellent source.

Rylance, Rick, ed. *Debating Texts: A Reader in Twentieth Century Literary Theory and Method* (Open University and Oxford University Press, 1987).

Valuable and widely-used, with good editorial linking.

Selden, Raman, *The Theory of Criticism from Plato to the Present: A Reader* (Longman, 1988).

Comprehensive time-span, but the brevity of some of the extracts is irritating, and the groupings are sometimes eccentric.

Walder, Dennis, *Literature in the Modern World: Critical Essays and Documents* (Oxford University Press and Open University, 1990).

A very useful collection of important documents and statements, with excellent editorial linking.

Applying critical theory: twelve examples

Dollimore, Jonathan & Sinfield, Alan, eds, *Political Shakespeare: New Essays in Cultural Materialism* (Manchester University Press, 2nd edn 1994).

Much useful material. See, for example, chapter two 'Invisible bullets: Renaissance authority and its subversion, *Henry IV* and *Henry V*', Stephen Greenblatt. This is the classic 'New Historicist' essay, much reprinted. Also chapter five 'The patriarchal bard: feminist criticism and Shakespeare: *King Lear* and *Measure for Measure*' .

Easthope, Antony, ed. *Contemporary Poetry Meets Modern Theory* (Harvester, 1991).

Chapter five: 'Tony Harrison's languages' by Rick Rylance. Another example of a 'theoreticised' form of practical criticism. The approach is, roughly, 'culturalist' – it places the poetry within its contemporary setting using relevant documents, social data, etc. ('Culturalist' readings would be called 'new historicist' if the material were not contemporary.)

Gilbert, Sandra & Gubar, Susan, *The Madwoman in the Attic: The Woman Writer and the Nineteenth Century Literary Imagination* (Yale University Press, 1979).

Chapters on Austen, Brontës, George Eliot, etc.

Jacobus, Mary, *Reading Woman: Essays in Feminist Criticism* (Methuen, 1986).

Chapters on *Villette*, *Mill on the Floss*, & on Freud's case studies (see 'Dora and the Pregnant Madonna').

Kurzweil, Edith, *Literature and Psychoanalysis* (Columbia University Press, 1983).

Chapter fifteen is a psychoanalytic reading of Henry James's extraordinary tale 'The Jolly Corner'. Chapter twenty by William Empson 'Alice in Wonderland – The Child as Swain', from his book *Some Versions of Pastoral*.

Lodge, David, *After Bakhtin: Essays on Fiction and Criticism* (Routledge, 1990).

Chapter two: 'Mimesis and diegesis in modern fiction' examines different ways of presenting material in a novel, using Fay Weldon, George Eliot, James Joyce, etc., as examples (structuralism). Chapter five: 'Dialogue in the modern novel' examines different ways of presenting dialogue, using Evelyn Waugh as main example (linguistics).

Machin, Richard & Norris, Christopher, eds, *Post-structuralist Readings of English Poetry* (Cambridge University Press, 1987).

Chapters on Donne, Milton's 'Blindness' sonnet, Gray's 'Elegy', Coleridge's 'Ancient Mariner', and so on. Not always easy reading, but some good things here. Catherine Belsey's essay on Marvell's 'To his Coy Mistress' is actually a good example of the 'new historicist' approach to literature.

Muller, John P. & Richardson, William J., eds, *The Purloined Poe: Lacan, Derrida, and Psychoanalytic Reading* (Johns Hopkins University Press, 1988).

This collection of essays is about Poe's tale 'The Purloined Letter', which excited much attention in the late 1980s from critical theorists. But see also chapter six (pp. 101–32) extracted from Marie Bonaparte's 1930s book on Poe, which subjects him to a 'straight' psychoanalytic approach.

Murray, David, ed. *Literary Theory and Poetry: Extending the Canon* (Batsford, 1989).

Chapter three 'The imperfect librarian: text and discourse in *The Waste Land* and *Four Quartets*'. Chapter four 'Frames of reference: the reception of, and response to, three women poets' (Dickinson, Plath, Moore). These two chapters are good examples of 'theoreticised' practical criticism. They make use of techniques derived from feminism, deconstruction, and (in the latter case) psychoanalysis.

Selden, Raman *Practising Theory and Reading Literature: an Introduction* (Harvester, 1989).

Twenty-four short chapters give examples of all the main theories in practice – structuralism, post-structuralism, Marxism, feminism, and so on. Useful items but often excessively brief.

Stubbs, Patricia, *Women and Fiction: Feminism and the Novel, 1880–1920* (Harvester, 1979).

Essays on Hardy, Forster, Lawrence, Woolf, etc.

Tallack, Douglas, ed. *Literary Theory at Work: Three Texts* (Batsford, 1987).

Structuralism, Marxism, feminism, psychoanalysis, and deconstruction applied to three stories: Conrad's *Heart of Darkness*, Henry James's 'In the Cage', and D. H. Lawrence's 'St Mawr'.

Against theory

Ellis, John M., *Against Deconstruction* (Princeton University Press, 1989).

A well-argued book, temperate rather than belligerent in tone, and with a firm focus throughout on the effects of literary theory on the practice of reading literature.

Jackson, Leonard, *The Poverty of Structuralism: Literature and Structuralist Theory* (Longman, 1991).

Mainly on foundational errors in the underlying linguistics and philosophy of structuralism; has rather less on the consequences of structuralist theory for literary-critical practice.

Lerner, Laurence, ed. *Reconstructing Literature* (Blackwell, 1983).

See chapters one and five by Cedric Watts. A brusque attack on theory, but mainly about its philosophical shortcomings.

Paulin, Tom, *Ireland and the English Crisis* (Bloodaxe, 1984).

See pp. 148–54, 'English Now', which was originally a hostile review in the *London Review of Books* of *Re-Reading English*, ed. Peter Widdowson, an influential 'theory' book. The piece provoked a year of angry correspondence in the journal under the heading 'Critics at War'.

Tallis, Raymond, *Not Saussure: a Critique of Post-Saussurean Literary Theory* (Macmillan, 1988).

A vigorous critique of the use of Saussure's ideas by structuralists and post-structuralists.

Washington, Peter, *Fraud: Literary Theory and the End of English* (Fontana, 1989).

Mainly concerned with attacking the linking of radical critical theory and radical politics.

Index